Sunset
Edible Garden
Cookbook

Fresh, healthy cooking from the garden

Oxmoor House®

Sunset

Softcover: ISBN-10: 0-376-02797-5
            ISBN-13: 978-0-376-02797-9
Hardcover: ISBN-10: 0-376-02800-9
            ISBN-13: 978-0-376-02800-6
Library of Congress Control Number: 2011940460
First printing 2012
Printed in the United States of America

OXMOOR HOUSE
VP, Publishing Director: Jim Childs
Editorial Director: Susan Payne Dobbs
Creative Director: Felicity Keane
Brand Manager: Fonda Hitchcock

SUNSET PUBLISHING
President: Barb Newton
Creative Director: Mia Daminato
Photography Director: Yvonne Stender

CONTRIBUTORS TO THE *SUNSET EDIBLE GARDEN COOKBOOK*
Food Editor: Margo True
Editor: Pam Hoenig
Art Director: Tonya Sutfin
Production Manager: Linda M. Bouchard
Project Editor: Sarah H. Doss
Copy Editors: Lesley Bruynesteyn, Gloria Geller
Photo Coordinator: Danielle Johnson
Senior Imaging Specialist: Kimberley Navabpour
Proofreader: Denise Griffiths
Indexer: Ken DellaPenta

To order additional publications, call 1-800-765-6400

For more books to enrich your life, visit **oxmoorhouse.com**

Visit *Sunset* online at **sunset.com**

For the most comprehensive selection of *Sunset* books, visit **sunsetbooks.com**

To search, savor, and share thousands of recipes, visit **myrecipes.com**

SPECIAL THANKS
Associate Food Editor Elaine Johnson; Recipe Editor Amy Machnak; Test Kitchen Coordinator Stephanie Dean; former food staff writers Amy Traverso and Molly Watson; plus the *Sunset* recipe retesters—Angela Brassinga, Dorothy Decker, Sarah Epstein, Lenore Grant, Doni Jackson, Melissa Kaiser, Marlene Kawahata, Eve Lynch, Rebecca Parker, Bunnie Russell, Laura Shafsky, and Linda Tebben
We would also like to thank Kathleen Norris Brenzel, Julie Chai, Erika Ehmsen, Trina Enriquez, Mark Hawkins, Charla Lawhon, Laura Martin, Haley Minick, Marie Pence, Linda Lamb Peters, Alan Phinney, Lorraine Reno, Johanna Silver, Margaret Sloan, Sue B. Smith, Katie Tamony

PHOTOGRAPHY CREDITS
Iain Bagwell: 28, 39, 66, 90, 105, 122, 125, 162, 228, 237, 275, back cover bottom left; **James Baigrie:** 104, 146, 147; **Leigh Beisch:** 31, 36, 56, 75, 83, 87, 94, 100, 101, 107, 113, 172, 207, 208, 224, 266; **Mark Bolton/Garden Picture Library/Getty Images:** 259; **Annabelle Breakey:** 19, 30, 35, 42, 44, 45, 54, 57, 64, 73, 74, 76, 82, 85, 91, 97, 108, 110, 111, 116, 127, 135, 136, 137, 142, 149, 151, 158, 161, 171, 174, 177, 179, 182, 183, 186, 192, 194, 197, 204, 211, 213, 223, 225, 226, 227, 229, 233, 241, 245, 246, 247, 249, 257, 261, 263, 270, 277, back cover top right; **Rob D. Brodman:** 8 top left, 8 bottom left, 8 bottom right, 11 top right, 18, 140, 153, 157, 198, 201, back cover top left, back cover bottom right; **Rob Cardillo:** 51; **James Carrier:** 124, 187, 253, 273; **Jennifer Cheung:** 180; **Kathy Collins/Getty Images:** 80; **Alex Farnum:** 96, 260; **Sheri L. Giblin/FoodPix/Getty Images:** 232; **Dan Goldberg:** 22, 67, 77, 178, 214, 215; **Leo Gong:** 4–5, 32, 46, 48, 49, 69, 98, 121, 130, 139, 188, 189, 210, 222, 240; **Thayer Allyson Gowdy:** 248; **Lara Hata:** 217; **Jim Henkens:** 238; **Saxon Holt/PhotoBotanic:** 70; **Andrea Jones/Garden Exposures Photo Library:** 112, 168; **Yuhnee Kim:** 175, 206, 231; **Janet Loughrey:** 17; **Jennifer Martiné:** 114, 235; **Joshua McCullough/PhytoPhoto:** 128; **Kimberley Navabpour:** 102, 156, 242; **Ngoc Minh Ngo:** 29, 109, 115; **Panoramic Images/Getty Images:** 152; **David E. Perry:** 14; **Linda Lamb Peters:** 250; **Scott Peterson:** 155, 239; **Norm Plate:** 218; **Norman A. Plate:** 11 bottom left, 12–13, 61; **David Prince:** 21, 272; **Lisa Romerein:** 3, 63, 72, 84, 106, 190, 276; **Lisa Romerein/FoodPix/Getty Images:** 143; **Lisa Romerein/Riser/Getty Images:** 52, 132, 267; **Susan A. Roth:** 50; **Christine Schmidhofer:** 185; **Photo courtesy of Seed Savers Exchange:** 141; **Thomas J. Story:** Front cover, 1, 6, 11 top left, 16, 20, 24, 27, 40, 43, 47, 53, 60, 88, 89, 99, 103, 117, 119, 134, 145, 148, 154, 159, 163, 164, 167, 170, 193, 196, 200, 203, 205, 216, 251, 254, 255, 262, 268, 271, 274, 278 all, 279 all; **E. Spencer Toy:** 8 top right, 264, back cover middle; **Mark Turner:** 118, 220, 265; **Paul Viant/Digital Vision/Getty Images:** 258; **Bob Wigand:** 234, 243; **Mark Winwood/Photolibrary:** 11 bottom right

**Grilled apricot
puffs with honey
crème fraîche**
RECIPE P. 270

**Chicken and corn
summer chowder**
RECIPE P. 48

CONTENTS

INTRODUCTION

Cutting kernels off
homegrown corn for
Chicken and corn
summer chowder;
see recipe on page 48.

When I moved back to California after 11 years of living in tiny East Coast apartments, with a windowsill and potted herbs as my only garden, the first thing I planted was a tomato. It was a sturdy little seedling, one of many that our kind and prolific head gardener had set out on *Sunset's* give-away table. Its name was 'Taxi'; that was all I knew. I'd never grown anything beyond runty basil and oregano, and was a little worried that I'd fail, but I forged ahead and planted the seedling in a half wine barrel (the luxury of having space at last!). It exploded up and out into an enormous green plant loaded with the most meltingly delicious, sweet, tender yellow tomatoes I'd ever had, streaked with ribbons of pink—kind of like, well, a sunset. I couldn't believe I'd managed to grow them. I ate those tomatoes raw with salt and olive oil, made sauce, put them in everything, gave them to friends.

Those tomatoes were my gateway to the world of edible gardening—a huge, ever-expanding community of people who like to grow their own food, not just here in the West but all over the country. We're smitten by the flavors and textures of vegetables that are absolutely, perfectly ripe, eaten soon after we've picked them. We like being in charge of our food—who says we have to wait until a head of lettuce is "market-size"? We can snip the leaves when they're tiny and tender, or pull up carrots when they're still skinny and super sweet. We also like the nutritiousness of very fresh fruits and vegetables, which don't come fresher than from the backyard. And we like the experimentation that's possible when planting from seed. With seed catalogs full of unusual temptations, who can resist ordering a few 'Isis Candy' or 'Chianti Rose' tomatoes along with the beefsteaks?

HOW THIS COOKBOOK WORKS

When you have a garden filled with great ingredients, your cooking starts to revolve around whatever is ripest and best that day. So we've organized this cookbook around the crops themselves, starting with vegetables, pausing for herbs, and finishing with fruits. Each recipe is designed to celebrate the flavor and beauty of homegrown produce (and the work that went into raising it). That's why we've kept the cooking simple. For every vegetable or fruit, we list basic ways to cook it—steam, roast, sauté, and so on. With these techniques as your guide, you can season the food any way you like and create your own recipes. Or you can choose from the full-blown recipes that follow, many of which were inspired by the test garden here at *Sunset*.

One of my favorite parts of this book is the "Extra Reward" section in many of the chapters, which tells you how to use the less familiar parts of a plant—radish leaves, for instance (they're mild-tasting and nice in salads)—or how to use a fruit or vegetable at a certain stage in its life cycle (true "new" potatoes, harvested while the plant is still green, are moist and fragile, with skin as delicate as tissue paper). When you've put effort into growing something, why not use it to its fullest?

Every gardener knows what it's like when crops get ripe all at once. You've been waiting and waiting, and suddenly you are flooded with nectarines, or beans, or what seem like a thousand summer squash. We give you ways to keep up, in the section titled "Preserving the Harvest." These are helpful instructions for how to can, freeze, or dehydrate the overflow so that, long after the season is over, you'll have a stash in your pantry, available for good cooking.

We chose crops that make sense to grow at home for one or more reasons: They're easy to grow, or cheaper to grow than buy, or gratifyingly productive, or too fragile to endure packing and shipping. For each, we've picked our favorite varieties—ones that yield well and taste wonderful (check with your Cooperative Extension Office to see how they'll do in your area and when to plant and harvest). That said, our recipes will work just fine with store-bought, CSA (i.e., farm-share), or farmers' market produce. The point is to use the best and freshest vegetables, herbs, and fruits you can find.

Although we do give some gardening information in this book, including harvest tips and a basic introduction to edible gardening (see page 8), this is primarily a cookbook rather than a how-to on gardening. For more in-depth instruction for various plants and garden practices, see the *Sunset Western Garden Book of Edibles* or *The New Sunset Western Garden Book*.

Growing and cooking your own food, even if you only have time to take care of one tomato plant, is worth it for so many reasons. Obviously, there's the produce itself, and the convenience of having ingredients right outside your door. But there's also something valuable, especially in our hurried and tech-obsessed times, about an activity that's age-old, simple, and connected to nature. An edible garden—and cooking from it—can yield not just lunch or dinner, but pride and a sense of peace, too.

Margo True
Food Editor, *Sunset* magazine

1 Optimize sun exposure by planting short veggies in front and tall ones in back.

2 Provide rich soil like this crumbly loam.

3 Use bubblers in shallow furrows to irrigate rows of vegetable seedlings.

4 Sprinkle liquid fertilizer onto leaves and soil.

8 STEPS TO AN EDIBLE GARDEN

You can easily start growing your own personal supply of fresh vegetables, fruits, and herbs by following our checklist below.

① CHOOSE THE RIGHT SITE

Whether you grow your edibles in their own plot, in pots, or mixed among other plants in your existing landscape, make sure to give them a location that gets 6 to 8 hours of full sun per day for the best production and flavor. Before planting in a particular site, monitor it to make sure that, as the sun moves during the day, your crops won't be shaded by tall shrubs, trees, or buildings. Also choose a spot that's protected from heavy winds (though gentle breezes are fine) and, as much as possible, grow them on level ground to make planting and care easier.

② PROVIDE GOOD SOIL

Healthy gardens start with healthy soil, and most crops want to grow in ground that's rich, fertile, and well draining. Few plots have perfect soil—more often it's too sandy, which lets water and nutrients drain away quickly, or it's too heavy and claylike, which drains poorly and makes it hard for roots to spread. To figure out what kind of soil you have, give it the squeeze test: Thoroughly wet a patch of soil and let it dry out for a day. Then, pick up a handful and squeeze it firmly in your fist. Sandy soil will feel gritty and crumble in your hand; claylike soil will form a tight, slippery ball; and nice, loamy soil will be slightly crumbly but still hold a loose ball. Fortunately, no matter what type of soil you have, you can improve it by adding amendments such as compost, aged manure, and wood products.

If planting a new bed, slightly dampen the soil, then dig to a depth of about 10 inches, breaking up large dirt clods and removing stones. Spread 3 to 4 inches of compost or other organic material over the bed and add an organic fertilizer according to label instructions. Mix all of the amendments evenly into the soil, then level the bed with a rake. Water well and let the improved soil settle for at least a few days before planting. Where soil is extremely poor, plant in raised beds or containers.

③ WATER WELL

Whether you hand-water or install an automatic irrigation system, the frequency and amount of watering you'll need depends on your soil, the weather, and the age of your plants.

In general, edibles need moist, but not soggy, soil throughout their life span. For newly planted vegetable seedlings, this could mean watering two or three times a day depending on the weather—and vegetables that are flowering or beginning to set fruit, form heads, or develop edible roots need to be watered more often than older plants. As the plants grow and their roots reach deeper, you can water less often; mature nut and fruit trees and grapes require even less frequent irrigation because they have much deeper roots than annual vegetables.

Sandy soil drains quickly and requires the most frequent watering; loam needs less; and clay drains slowly and requires the least. And when it's hot outside, you should water more than when weather is cool.

④ FERTILIZE

Edible plants pull nutrients from the soil, water, and air. But while they are growing, they generally need a supplemental boost, especially if they're grown in containers. We recommend using organic fertilizers, particularly for edible gardens. They release their nutrients more slowly: Fertilizers are broken down by microorganisms in the soil, providing nutrients gradually as they decay. Chemical fertilizers, which dissolve in water, act faster than organic ones, but most do not last as long in the soil. Whatever you choose, be sure to follow package directions carefully.

⑤ CHOOSE WHAT TO PLANT

Growing your own edibles gives you access to literally thousands of fruit, vegetable, and herb varieties—which can be both thrilling and overwhelming. To get the most from your time and effort, it's a good idea to plant crops that you know you like and will eat, along with a few surprises just for fun, and only as much as you have space for.

When selecting crops, also think about how long you're willing to wait for your plants to start producing. There are generally three categories of edibles: perennials including fruit trees, hardy herbs like sage and oregano, and berries; warm-season annual crops like tomatoes, peppers, and squash; and cool-season annual crops such as lettuce, broccoli, and peas. Most annual crops are ready to harvest in just a few months. Perennials might produce a small crop the first year but often take two or more years to provide a substantial harvest.

⑥ GROW FROM SEEDS OR TRANSPLANTS

Once you've decided which crops to grow, you can either start them from seeds or use transplants from the nursery. With seeds, you can order exactly what you want online if your local nursery doesn't carry what you're looking for. Transplants are more expensive, but they have the advantage of being ready to plant right away.

If starting from seeds, be sure the ones you buy are fresh and are dated for the current year (though many remain viable for several years if stored in a cool, dry place). Start warm-season crops indoors in early spring to have plants ready to set out in the garden when the weather has warmed up, and start cool-season crops in time to transplant them into the garden in early spring or fall.

Many vegetables—like radishes, corn, peas, and beans—grow best if you plant the seeds directly where they are to grow in the garden, rather than starting them indoors and transplanting them later. Check the seed packet for sowing time for each crop.

Plant warm-season annual seedlings after all danger of frost has passed, when the soil is fairly dry and has warmed up. In mild-winter areas, plant cool-season annuals in late winter/early spring and late summer/early fall. Where winters are long and very cold, many cool-season crops can be grown in summer; check with your Cooperative Extension Office or local nursery for specific planting times. During the growing season, larger plants such as fruit trees and cane berries can be planted nearly anytime, except during the heat of summer.

⑦ MULCH

Mulching means placing organic or inorganic material over the soil surface around plants or on pathways to reduce evaporation, insulate soil, and prevent weeds from growing. Organic mulches—including compost, leaf mold, straw, shredded bark, wood chips, and grass clippings—are the most common and improve the soil by adding nutrients as they slowly decompose. Inorganic mulches, such as plastic sheeting, are especially useful for warming the soil and can speed up development of warm-season crops.

⑧ MANAGE PESTS, DISEASES, AND WEEDS

Preventing trouble is the most important step: You won't have to solve problems that don't get a chance to start in the first place. Keep your edibles healthy and stress-free by setting them out at the recommended planting time in amended soil, and giving them the care they need throughout the year. Whenever possible, select varieties resistant to specific pests or diseases, and check the plants in your garden frequently so you can deal with problems before they become severe.

For established gardens, hand-pulling or hoeing is your first line of defense against most weeds. If you're diligent for several consecutive years about removing annual weeds early in the season, before they set seed, their numbers will decline significantly. These methods also help control perennial weeds, as long as you catch the plants while they're young. Once perennials have matured, you usually have to dig out their roots to clear them. If you need to use an herbicide, choose a natural one like herbicidal soap, made from selected fatty acids. Undiluted white household vinegar (5 percent acetic acid) also kills weeds if applied during their first two weeks of life.

For more detailed information on any of the above guidelines, see *The New Sunset Western Garden Book* or the *Sunset Western Garden Book of Edibles*.

5 Organize crops to fit the site; squash, cauliflower, and corn fill raised beds.

6 Transplant seedlings when they've developed two sets of true leaves.

7 Spread bark mulch between rows to control weeds.

8 Drape bird netting over vulnerable crops.

Our favorite homegrown edibles

We winnowed down a long list of candidates to the plants on the following pages—all chosen because they taste wonderful freshly picked from a home garden. Most are relatively easy to grow, or gratifyingly productive, or both. In all cases, their vibrant flavors will transform your cooking.

'Blauwschokkers'
shelling peas

Vegetables

ARTICHOKES

WHY GROW THEM

Sunset is located in Menlo Park, California, which is near this country's Artichoke Central, and we look forward to harvesting them in our gardens in early summer (in more northerly areas, you may have to wait until late fall). If you have the climate for it, we urge you to try your hand at artichokes—they're a spectacular crop, and you'll reap a bounty of full-size and baby artichokes (see below).

EXTRA REWARD Baby artichokes! Though called babies, they are actually fully mature (albeit small and tender) artichokes that have grown low on the stalk, in the shade of the frondlike leaves of the artichoke plant. Unlike their larger siblings higher up the stalk, baby artichokes have no thistly chokes in their centers and are rendered entirely edible with just a little trimming.

WHEN TO HARVEST

Cut off artichokes with 1½ inches of the stem while they are still tight and plump.

HOW TO KEEP

Refrigerate, unwashed, in a plastic bag for up to 1 week.

PRESERVING THE HARVEST

FREEZE If your plants yield lots of artichokes all at once, you can easily freeze them. Trim them down to hearts (see page 23) and blanch in boiling water for 7 minutes. Drain, plunge in cold water to cool, drain again, and pack into resealable plastic freezer bags, leaving no headspace. Seal and freeze.

'Violetto'

Some of our favorite varieties

'Green Globe' This is the standard California artichoke.

'Imperial Star' A prolific producer of mild, thornless artichokes.

'Northern Star' A good choice if you live in a chilly winter climate.

'Purple Italian Globe' An heirloom variety that produces large, tender heads.

'Violetto' Produces deep violet–and–green thornless artichokes.

Basic Ways to Cook

BOIL Bring a large pot of salted water to a boil. Add trimmed artichokes (page 23), reduce heat, and simmer, covered, until leaves are tender when pierced with a sharp knife, about 40 minutes for full-size artichokes, 20 to 30 minutes for artichoke hearts, and 15 to 20 minutes for baby artichokes. Drain and enjoy hot, let cool to room temperature, or chill and serve cold (will keep up to 3 days refrigerated).

ROAST Fit trimmed artichoke halves (page 23) tightly together in a single layer in a pan just large enough to hold them. Pour in some olive oil, sprinkle with dried thyme, and roll to coat. Turn cut sides down. Seal pan with foil. Bake in a 375° oven until artichoke bottoms are tender when pierced, 40 to 50 minutes.

SAUTÉ Trim baby artichokes (see page 23). Bring a large pot of water to a boil and add 1 tbsp. salt. Add artichokes; simmer until tender, 10 to 20 minutes; and drain. Set a frying pan over medium-high heat. Add 1 oz. pancetta, chopped, and stir until fat is rendered. Add ¼ cup dry white wine and artichokes. Cook until wine is almost evaporated. Season with salt and pepper to taste.

GRILL Trim large or baby artichokes (see page 23), but cut off all or most of stems of large artichokes, since they tend to burn. Steam or boil artichokes until tender. Drain and let cool, then cut in half lengthwise and scrape out fuzzy choke at center. Brush halves with oil, sprinkle with salt, and grill over direct medium heat (about 350°), cut side down, until lightly browned, about 5 minutes; turn over and grill another 3 or 4 minutes.

Creamy artichoke dip

MAKES 1½ cups

TIME 15 minutes (excluding time to prep and cook artichoke hearts)

Get into the spirit of artichoke season by revisiting artichoke dip, that 1960s classic. We've opted for a simple dip that starts with cream cheese and artichoke hearts, then adds parmesan, parsley, lemon, and garlic for flavor. Serve with crackers, crostini, or crudités.

1 package (8 oz.) cream cheese
½ cup (about 2) artichoke hearts (page 23),
    boiled until tender (page 17), drained,
    and completely cooled
⅓ cup finely shredded parmesan cheese
1 tbsp. chopped flat-leaf parsley
2 tsp. fresh lemon juice
½ tsp. *each* salt and freshly ground black pepper
¼ tsp. finely shredded lemon zest
1 small garlic clove, finely chopped

Whirl all the ingredients together in a food processor, until mixture is blended and artichokes break into small pieces.

PER 2-TBSP. SERVING 40 CAL., 83% (33 CAL.) FROM FAT; 1.3 G PROTEIN; 3.7 G FAT (2 G SAT.); 0.7 G CARBO (0.2 G FIBER); 108 MG SODIUM; 11 MG CHOL.

GOOD FOR YOU

Artichokes are a good source of fiber, vitamin K (which plays a key role in helping blood coagulate), and folate (vital for pregnant women, since it can help reduce certain birth defects).

Roasted baby artichokes with spring salsa

SERVES 4 as a first course
TIME 2¼ hours

Artichokes star in this first course from Jeremy Fox, former executive chef of Ubuntu restaurant in Napa, but they share the plate with other produce from your garden or the farmers' market—like baby greens, fava beans, and fresh herbs. The toasted almonds and parmesan curls add layers of richness.

20 baby artichokes, stems trimmed to 1 in.
About ⅔ cup extra-virgin olive oil, divided
6 to 8 thyme sprigs
2 tsp. chopped rosemary
2 tbsp. finely shredded 'Meyer' or regular lemon zest, divided
½ tsp. kosher salt, plus more to taste
1 cup shelled fava beans
½ tsp. red chile flakes
1½ tsp. minced garlic
1½ tbsp. fresh 'Meyer' or regular lemon juice
¼ cup blanched almonds, toasted (see Flavor Note, right) and finely chopped
½ cup loosely packed dill fronds, chopped
¾ cup mild green olives such as Castelvetrano, pitted and torn in half
Chunk of parmesan cheese (at least 2 oz.), at room temperature
15 to 20 miner's lettuce or baby arugula leaves

1. Preheat oven to 300°. Trim artichokes (see page 23).
2. Pour ¼ cup oil into a small rimmed baking pan. Add artichokes, herbs, 4 tsp. lemon zest, and salt; turn to coat artichokes. Cover pan with foil and roast artichokes until tender when pierced with tip of a knife, 30 to 45 minutes.

3. While artichokes are roasting, bring a large pot of water to a boil. Add favas and cook 2 minutes. Drain and rinse with cold water. Slit tough skin on each bean with a paring knife or your fingernail and pop bean out of skin. Finely chop peeled beans, then set aside.
4. Uncover pan and set oven to broil. Broil artichokes, turning every minute or so, until browned all over, about 8 minutes. Transfer artichokes to a cutting board. Pour any oil from pan into a measuring cup, add enough extra oil to equal ½ cup, and pour into a large cast-iron or nonstick frying pan.
5. Heat artichoke oil over medium-high heat. Add fava beans and cook, stirring often, until favas are heated through, 3 to 4 minutes. Add chile flakes, garlic, and remaining 2 tsp. lemon zest and cook 1 minute. Pour into a bowl and gently toss with lemon juice, almonds, dill, and salt to taste. Add extra oil to loosen if you like.

6. Cut some artichokes in half and divide, with whole artichokes, among 4 plates (or arrange on a platter). Spoon salsa over and around artichokes and scatter olives here and there. Using a vegetable peeler, generously shave wide curls of parmesan over each plate. Top with miner's lettuce.

FLAVOR NOTE Toasting nuts gives them better flavor and extra crunch as well. To toast, spread them out in a baking pan and toast in a 350° oven until golden, 5 to 15 minutes, depending on the type of nut.

PER SERVING 697 CAL., 77% (535 CAL.) FROM FAT; 20 G PROTEIN; 61 G FAT (9.4 G SAT.); 30 G CARBO (15 G FIBER); 894 MG SODIUM; 9.6 MG CHOL.

Artichokes with garlic-thyme mayonnaise

SERVES 4

TIME 40 minutes

Here is a classic presentation for full-size artichokes.

1½ lemons (preferably 'Meyer')
2 large artichokes (each about 14 oz.), trimmed (page 23)
2 garlic cloves, minced
½ cup mayonnaise
2 tsp. chopped thyme
⅛ tsp. kosher salt
Pinch of freshly ground black pepper

1. Remove 10 to 12 thin curls of zest from whole lemon with a 5-hole zester (or use a vegetable peeler to remove 2 wide strips, then slice them into very thin strips); cut lemon in half. Fill a large pot halfway with water and squeeze juice from lemon into pot; toss in 2 squeezed halves.

2. Slice 1 artichoke in half lengthwise through stem. Use your thumb and a serrated grapefruit spoon to grasp any red-tinged center leaves; pull to remove. Scrape out and discard thistly choke. Slice pieces in half again and place quarters in pot with lemon water. Repeat with remaining artichoke.

3. Cover pot and bring to a boil over high heat. Remove lid and continue boiling until stems are tender and leaves pull off with little resistance, 15 to 20 minutes. Drain on paper towels and let cool.

4. Meanwhile, combine garlic, mayonnaise, thyme, and juice of remaining lemon half in food processor. Process 30 seconds, until smooth. Season with salt and pepper. Garnish with reserved lemon zest. Serve artichoke quarters with dipping sauce.

PER SERVING 157 CAL., 58% (91 CAL.) FROM FAT; 2.5 G PROTEIN; 10 G FAT (1.5 G SAT.); 17 G CARBO (6.5 G FIBER); 317 MG SODIUM; 7.6 MG CHOL.

Lemon-garlic grilled artichokes

SERVES 4 to 6
TIME 50 to 60 minutes

A short turn on the grill adds incalculable flavor to steamed artichokes. If you'd like to grill baby artichokes, there is no need to steam them first. Trim them, toss in the flavored oil, then onto the grill until they're crispy and tender all the way through.

6 artichokes
1 tbsp. plus ½ tsp. salt
Juice of 1 lemon plus 2 tbsp.
3 garlic cloves, minced
3 tbsp. olive oil
¼ tsp. freshly ground black pepper

1. Slice tops off artichokes, pull off small leaves, trim stems, and snip off thorny tips.
2. Bring 1 to 2 in. of water to a boil in a large pot. Add 1 tbsp. salt, juice of 1 lemon, and artichokes, bottom side down; cover and steam until artichoke bottoms pierce easily, 20 to 40 minutes.
3. While artichokes are steaming, combine garlic, oil, remaining 2 tbsp. lemon juice and ½ tsp. salt, and the pepper.
4. Prepare a charcoal or gas grill for direct medium heat (350° to 450°; you can hold your hand 5 in. above cooking grate only 5 to 7 seconds).
5. Drain artichokes. When cool enough to handle, cut each in half lengthwise and scrape out fuzzy choke at center. Brush artichokes with garlic mixture and set, cut side down, on grill. Grill, turning once, until lightly browned, 8 to 11 minutes.

PER SERVING 149 CAL., 40% (60 CAL.) FROM FAT; 6.9 G PROTEIN; 6.8 G FAT (0.9 G SAT.); 22 G CARBO (10 G FIBER); 643 MG SODIUM; 0 MG CHOL.

Chicken stew with artichoke hearts, olives, and lemon

SERVES 4

TIME About 45 minutes

Here is a perfect dish for when the weather blows a little cold and damp. Succulent chicken thighs are paired with artichokes and the flavors of Italian salsa verde—bright parsley, tart lemon, piquant capers, and green olives.

1 lb. boned, skinned chicken thighs

2 tbsp. flour

¾ tsp. each salt and freshly ground black pepper, plus more to taste

2 tbsp. olive oil

2 large garlic cloves, minced

1 tbsp. capers, drained and minced

Finely shredded zest and juice of 1 lemon

½ cup dry white wine

1¾ cups chicken broth

1 lb. 'Yukon Gold' potatoes, cut into ¾-in. cubes

8 artichoke hearts, boiled until tender (page 17), drained, and quartered if large (about 2 cups)

1 cup finely chopped flat-leaf parsley

1 cup pitted medium green olives

Lemon wedges

1. Cut each chicken thigh into 2 or 3 chunks. In a resealable plastic bag, combine flour, salt, and pepper. Add chicken, seal, and shake to coat.

2. Heat oil in a large pot over medium-high heat. Add chicken (discard excess flour) in a single layer and cook, turning once, until browned, 4 to 5 minutes total. Transfer to a plate.

3. Reduce heat to medium. Add garlic, capers, and lemon zest and stir just until fragrant, about 30 seconds. Add wine and simmer, scraping up browned bits from bottom of pan, until reduced by half, about 2 minutes. Add broth, potatoes, and chicken and return to a simmer. Lower heat slightly to maintain simmer, cover, and cook 10 minutes.

4. Add artichokes to pot and stir. Cover and cook until potatoes are tender when pierced, 8 to 10 minutes. Stir in parsley, lemon juice to taste, and olives. Season with additional salt and pepper to taste. Serve hot, with lemon wedges on the side.

TIMESAVER TIP Cube the potatoes or mince the garlic and capers while the chicken browns. Then, while the stew simmers, you can chop the parsley and juice the lemon.

PER SERVING 385 CAL., 37% (144 CAL.) FROM FAT; 29 G PROTEIN; 16 G FAT (2.6 G SAT.); 32 G CARBO (6.8 G FIBER); 1,252 MG SODIUM; 94 MG CHOL.

VARIATIONS

This stew easily adapts to other flavor combinations. Some of our favorites:

Make it red Add red chile flakes instead of the lemon zest (omit lemon juice), and substitute 1 can (14 oz.) petite diced tomatoes, with juices, for the white wine. Omit potatoes and use black olives instead of green.

Try fish Replace chicken with halibut chunks, omitting step 1 and skipping the browning in step 2 (simply sauté the garlic, capers, and lemon zest in the oil). Sprinkle the fish with salt and pepper, add to the stew with the artichokes, and cook until opaque in the center.

BASIC WAYS TO PREP

Trim full-size artichokes Trim ¾ in. off each artichoke stem and discard. Remove tough outer layer of remaining stem with a vegetable peeler. Cut 1 in. off tip of each artichoke and pull off cracked or especially thick leaves; discard. Snip spiky tips off remaining leaves.

Trim full-size artichokes to hearts Cut stem at base of artichoke, then snap off all the leaves, cut heart in half lengthwise, and scrape away the choke, leaving just the heart.

Trim baby artichokes Cut stem at base of artichoke. Peel back and snap off the leaves all around the base until you reach the tender layer of leaves that are yellow at the bottom and green at the top. You'll remove a lot of leaves. Cut off the top third of the remaining leaves (the pointy green part). With a paring knife, trim the remaining green, fibrous material from around the stem end of the artichoke.

BEANS

WHY GROW THEM

When it comes to certain types of snap (aka string or green) beans, unless you grow them yourself you might not get a chance to eat them. Supermarkets only occasionally carry haricots verts (aka filet beans), a pencil-slim French variety. Italian- or Romano-type flat beans are usually only sold at farmers' markets, but these broad, juicy, fleshy kinds (the Sophia Loren of the bean world) could easily become your favorite. And purple-podded beans, which hold their color when sliced raw for salads but turn dark green when cooked, make an exciting addition to your cooking too.

Shell beans like cannellini, kidney, edamame, and lima are also very much worth growing, because they're delicious fresh (but usually only available dried or frozen in stores).

EXTRA REWARD You get to harvest snap beans just the way you like them—tender and slender, or full size if you want them to have more heft or intend to braise them. The same goes for certain shell beans. When harvested while immature (about 3 inches long), fava and scarlet runner beans can be eaten still in the pod. And with fava beans, you also get the bonus of their greens; the broad, easy-to-pick leaves have an earthy sweet, faintly grassy flavor that can be enjoyed raw in salads or cooked.

WHEN TO HARVEST

(Snap beans) Gently pull ripe beans individually off clusters. **(Shell beans)** For eating fresh, harvest when the beans are fully formed and are bulging in the pod. For dried beans, see "Preserving the Harvest," below. **(Fava beans)** Pick when pods are young, for the best flavor. If eating the pods too, pick when no more than 3 inches long.

HOW TO KEEP

(Snap beans) Refrigerate, unwashed, in a plastic bag for up to 4 days. **(Shell beans)** For fresh, snap open the pods, remove the beans, and refrigerate in a plastic bag for 10 to 14 days. For dried, see below.

PRESERVING THE HARVEST

FREEZE (Snap beans) Cut beans into 2- to 4-inch lengths. Blanch in boiling water for 3 minutes; drain, plunge into cold water to cool, drain again, and pack in resealable plastic freezer bags, leaving ½-inch headspace. Seal and freeze. **(Shell beans)** Blanch the fresh shelled beans in boiling water, 2 minutes for small beans, 3 minutes for medium, and 4 minutes for large. Drain, cool, and pack as for snap beans. **DRY** For dried, use shell beans. Leave the pods on the plants until they are yellowed and brittle and the beans are rattling around inside. Remove the beans from the pods and store in an airtight container.

Basic Ways to Cook

BOIL (Snap beans) Boil whole or cut beans in 1 in. water, covered, until tender-crisp, 5 to 10 minutes for whole beans, 4 to 7 minutes for cut beans. **(Shell beans)** Boil 1 lb. fresh beans in 1½ in. water, covered, until tender to the bite, 15 to 25 minutes for full-size fava beans, 12 to 20 minutes for lima beans. **(Dried shell beans)** Soak beans overnight, covered by 2 in. water; drain, cover by 1 in. water, and simmer until tender (anywhere from 45 minutes to 1½ hours, depending on bean and how long it's been dried).

STEAM Arrange whole or cut snap beans on a rack and steam until tender-crisp, 10 to 15 minutes for whole beans, 8 to 12 minutes for cut beans.

STIR-FRY Cut snap beans into 1-in. pieces. In a large wok, stir-fry up to 5 cups in 1 tbsp. oil over high heat for 1 minute. Add 2 to 4 tbsp. liquid, cover, and cook until tender-crisp, 4 to 7 minutes more.

Some of our favorite varieties

FAVA BEANS

'Aquadulce' A good cold-tolerant variety (it can survive down to 15°F).

'Broad Windsor' Extremely tasty, this plant yields beans the size of a quarter.

SNAP (STRING) BEANS

'Emerite' Our choice for haricots verts.

'Kentucky Wonder' This stringless, flavorful, green pole bean is an old-fashioned favorite.

'Purple Queen' Purple when picked, these bush beans turn green when cooked.

'Ramdor' A lovely yellow variety.

SHELL BEANS

'Sayamusume' A high-yielding edamame variety that produces plump beans with sturdy, well-filled pods. It freezes well.

'Scarlet Emperor' A stunner in the garden, this type of scarlet runner bean produces bright red flowers that give way to velvety green pods. The beans are large, like big limas, and a shocking lipstick pink color that quickly darkens to purple once the beans are exposed to air.

Favas and ricotta on buttermilk crackers

SERVES 8
TIME 45 minutes

This simple recipe is a great show-case for the flavor of garden-fresh fava beans.

16 (2- by 4-in.) whole-wheat crackers, homemade (recipe follows) or store-bought
1 cup ricotta cheese
About ½ cup thinly sliced peppermint leaves
3 lbs. fava beans in the pod, shelled and peeled (see below)
2 tsp. sea salt, plus more to taste
About ¼ cup extra-virgin olive oil

Spread crackers with a thin layer of ricotta and top with mint and favas. Sprinkle with salt to taste and oil.

PER SERVING 496 CAL., 45% (226 CAL.) FROM FAT; 22 G PROTEIN; 26 G FAT (8.7 G SAT.); 57 G CARBO (4.4 G FIBER); 1,213 MG SODIUM; 32 MG CHOL.

HOW TO PEEL FAVA BEANS

Shell the beans from the fava pods. Bring a medium pot of water to a boil. Add beans to water and boil 1 to 2 minutes. Drain in a colander and rinse with cold water until cool enough to handle. Then, peel the rubbery outer skin from each bean: Tear it at the bean's round end (use a paring knife or your fingernail) and pop out the bean. Peeled fava beans are very perishable and will keep only a few hours, chilled airtight.

Buttermilk crackers

MAKES 16 crackers
TIME 40 minutes

2 cups whole-wheat flour, plus more for rolling
About 1 tbsp. sea salt
1½ tsp. crushed dried red serrano or arbol chiles (about 2)
¼ cup cold butter, cut into small pieces
⅔ cup buttermilk
1 tbsp. honey
About ¼ cup extra-virgin olive oil

1. Preheat oven to 375°. In a food processor, pulse flour, salt, and chiles to combine. Add butter and pulse until mixture looks like fine cornmeal. Pour in buttermilk and honey; pulse just until incorporated.
2. Turn dough out onto a lightly floured work surface and form into a ball. Dust a rolling pin with flour. Divide dough in half; set one half aside and cover with a damp kitchen towel to keep from drying out.
3. Pat remaining dough half into a rough rectangle, dust with flour, and roll out paper-thin. Trim off ragged edges (save scraps to reroll). Roll dough gently around rolling pin, then unroll it onto a baking sheet. Cut into 2- by 4-in. rectangles. Brush with oil and sprinkle with salt if you like. Poke all over with a fork. Repeat with remaining dough.
4. Bake 10 minutes. Switch position of sheets and bake until pale brown with some darker edges, about 3 minutes. Let cool on pans. Keep up to 1 week, airtight, at room temperature.

PER CRACKER 118 CAL., 50% (59 CAL.) FROM FAT; 2.6 G PROTEIN; 6.8 G FAT (2.4 G SAT.); 13.3 G CARBO (2 G FIBER); 292 MG SODIUM; 8 MG CHOL.

Sesame green bean salad

SERVES 6
TIME About 20 minutes

Reader Trisha Kruse of Eagle, Idaho, serves this with roast pork or grilled seafood, or adds hard-cooked eggs or tuna to make a main-course salad.

2 lbs. green beans, ends trimmed
¼ cup unseasoned rice vinegar
2 tbsp. toasted sesame oil
1 to 2 tbsp. soy sauce
1 tbsp. minced fresh ginger
2 tsp. toasted sesame seeds
1 tsp. minced garlic
1 tsp. honey
½ cup thinly sliced red onion, rinsed and drained
1½ cups fresh bean sprouts

1. Bring 3 qts. water to a boil in a large pot over high heat. Add beans and cook until tender-crisp, 3 to 5 minutes. Drain, immerse in ice water until cool, and drain again.
2. Mix vinegar in a serving bowl with sesame oil, soy sauce to taste, ginger, sesame seeds, garlic, and honey. Add green beans, onion, and bean sprouts and stir gently to coat.
3. Serve at room temperature, or chill airtight up to 3 hours and serve cold.

PER SERVING 107 CAL., 44% (47 CAL.) FROM FAT; 3.8 G PROTEIN; 5.2 G FAT (0.7 G SAT.); 14 G CARBO (3 G FIBER); 183 MG SODIUM; 0 MG CHOL.

Favas and ricotta on
buttermilk crackers

Fava greens, grapefruit,
and flower salad

Fava greens, grapefruit, and flower salad

SERVES 4 to 6
TIME 35 minutes

This is a delightful salad to make when your garden is up and running, fresh with new growth and flowering plants. Fava bean leaves have a somewhat grassy, earthy flavor; be sure to pick tender, young leaves.

2 pink grapefruit
2 tbsp. roasted walnut oil or olive oil
1 tbsp. minced shallot
½ tsp. kosher salt
¼ tsp. freshly ground black pepper
2 qts. loosely packed fava greens and tender sprigs
Edible flowers such as fava, borage, rosemary, mustard, sage, oregano, or individual chive petals (optional)

1. Finely shred zest of half a grapefruit, then cut off peel and membrane from both grapefruit. Cut fruit into thin rounds, saving juice.
2. Combine zest, juice, oil, shallot, salt, and pepper in a bowl and stir to blend. Toss fava greens and sprigs with dressing.
3. Spoon greens onto plates and tuck grapefruit into salads. If you like, scatter flowers on top.

PER SERVING 107 CAL., 42% (45 CAL.) FROM FAT; 2.8 G PROTEIN; 5.1 G FAT (0.5 G SAT.); 16 G CARBO (1.1 G FIBER); 165 MG SODIUM; 0 MG CHOL.

Green bean, hazelnut, and mint salad

SERVES 6
TIME About 30 minutes

With its citrusy dressing and rich, crunchy nuts, this is one of our favorite ways to serve green beans.

¾ cup hazelnuts
8 cups packed green beans (about ¾ lb.), ends trimmed
2 tbsp. chopped mint
1 tbsp. finely shredded lemon zest
2 tbsp. fresh lemon juice
½ tsp. salt
¼ cup hazelnut or extra-virgin olive oil

1. Preheat oven to 375°. Spread nuts out on a baking pan and bake until golden under skins (break one to test), 10 to 15 minutes. When nuts are cool enough to handle, rub in a kitchen towel to remove as many skins as possible. Chop coarsely and set aside.
2. Bring 3 qts. salted water to a boil in a 4- to 6-qt. pot over high heat. Add green beans and cook until tender-crisp, 5 to 10 minutes. Drain in a colander and plunge beans into a bowl of ice water to cool. Drain again and set aside.
3. Make dressing: Stir together mint, lemon zest and juice, and salt in a small bowl. Drizzle in oil, whisking constantly.
4. Toss beans in a large bowl with dressing and hazelnuts. Serve at room temperature.

TIMESAVER TIP This salad can be prepared up to 3 hours ahead.

PER SERVING 188 CAL., 86% (162 CAL.) FROM FAT; 2.8 G PROTEIN; 18 G FAT (1.3 G SAT.); 6.2 G CARBO (2.3 G FIBER); 197 MG SODIUM; 0 MG CHOL.

Braised whole-pod fava beans with dill

SERVES 6

TIME 45 minutes

Fava beans are a culinary highlight of spring, but double-shelling them takes time. Very young favas (3 inches long or less), though, can be eaten pod and all.

⅓ cup olive oil

1 sweet onion, halved and thinly sliced

1½ lbs. immature fava bean pods, ends trimmed
    and strings removed

¾ tsp. salt

1 tbsp. sugar

¼ cup plus 1 tbsp. chopped dill

Plain whole-milk or Greek-style yogurt

1. Put oil and onion in a large pot over medium-high heat. Cook until fragrant, about 1 minute. Add favas, salt, sugar, and ¼ cup water. Bring to a simmer. Cover and cook, stirring occasionally, 20 minutes.

2. Add ¼ cup dill, cover, and cook until fava pods are tender and starting to fall apart, about 10 minutes. Sprinkle with remaining 1 tbsp. dill and serve warm or at room temperature, with yogurt on the side.

PER SERVING (WITHOUT YOGURT) 222 CAL., 53% (117 CAL.) FROM FAT; 9.2 G PROTEIN; 13 G FAT (1.7 G SAT.); 24 G CARBO (FIBER N/A); 322 MG SODIUM; 0 MG CHOL.

Spicy, crunchy pickled green beans with lemon

MAKES 8 cups

TIME 45 minutes, plus overnight to chill

Kombu, a kind of kelp, gives this pickle a certain velvety umami character, especially when it's allowed to sit for a few days. Look for kombu in the Asian foods aisle of your grocery store. This pickle gets spicier with time.

1 lb. green beans, ends trimmed

2 cups unseasoned rice vinegar

¼ cup sugar

2 tbsp. kosher salt

6 small dried red chiles, such as Thai or arbol

1 tsp. pink peppercorns

3-in.-long piece kombu (dried kelp)

1 lemon, ends removed, halved lengthwise, cut
    into ⅓-in.-thick slices, and seeds removed

1. Bring a medium pot of water to a boil and blanch green beans until tender-crisp, 2 to 3 minutes. Drain and put in a large heatproof bowl.

2. Bring 2½ cups water to a boil in another medium pot with vinegar, sugar, salt, chiles, peppercorns, and kombu. As soon as liquid boils, pour over beans and add lemon. Let cool to room temperature.

3. Slit 3 chiles to let seeds spill into liquid. Chill, covered, overnight to let flavors develop. Serve cold. Keeps, chilled, up to 1 week.

PER ¼-CUP SERVING 5.4 CAL., 6% (0.3 CAL.) FROM FAT; 0.2 G PROTEIN; 0 G FAT; 1.3 G CARBO (0.4 G FIBER); 73 MG SODIUM; 0 MG CHOL.

ANOTHER WAY WITH WHOLE FAVAS

Jeremy Fox, former executive chef of Ubuntu restaurant in Napa, California, likes to roast baby fava bean pods. Put small fava pods (2 to 3 inches long) in a cast-iron skillet and roast in a 450° oven or on the stovetop over high heat until slightly charred. Toss with sea salt, a bit of olive oil, red chile flakes, 'Meyer' lemon juice, and minced garlic. Eat them pod and all.

Green bean and whole-grain penne salad

Green bean and whole-grain penne salad

SERVES 16
TIME 40 minutes

This salad, great for a picnic potluck, is all about contrasts in flavor and texture: chewy, nutty pasta mingled with crisp, sweet green beans and strewn with bits of crunchy bacon and creamy Roquefort. Use whole-wheat, mixed-grain, or brown-rice pasta.

1½ lbs. green beans, ends trimmed and cut into 1½-in. lengths

16 oz. whole-grain penne, rotini, rotelle, or fusilli pasta

½ cup mayonnaise

About ⅓ lb. Roquefort or other blue cheese

2 tbsp. red wine vinegar

3 tbsp. *each* finely chopped flat-leaf parsley and chives

5 slices thick-cut bacon, cooked until crisp and crumbled

½ tsp. freshly ground black pepper

Salt

1. Bring 2 large pots of salted water to a boil. Prepare a large bowl of ice water. In one pot, boil green beans 3 minutes; drain and plunge in ice water to stop cooking. In the other, cook pasta until tender to the bite, 9 to 12 minutes or according to package directions. Drain and rinse thoroughly under cold running water until completely cool.

2. Pulse mayonnaise, Roquefort, and vinegar in a food processor until well combined but still slightly chunky.

3. Toss together pasta, green beans, Roquefort dressing, parsley, chives, bacon, and pepper in a large bowl until pasta is well coated. Season to taste with salt.

TIMESAVER TIP Ingredients can be prepped and pasta cooked a day ahead (add 1 tbsp. extra-virgin olive oil to the cooked pasta) and chilled. Toss everything together just before serving. The dressing can be made ahead too; if it thickens, thin it with a little more vinegar or even milk.

PER 1-CUP SERVING 214 CAL., 42% (90 CAL.) FROM FAT; 7.9 G PROTEIN; 10 G FAT (3.3 G SAT.); 24 G CARBO (4.1 G FIBER); 363 MG SODIUM; 15 MG CHOL.

Fava bean and pearl couscous pilaf

SERVES 4
TIME About 1½ hours

This pilaf is terrific with grilled lamb and a butter lettuce salad.

1½ cups chicken broth

1 cup pearl (Israeli) couscous

½ tsp. dried oregano

¼ tsp. red chile flakes

½ tsp. finely shredded lemon zest

2 tsp. fresh lemon juice

2 tbsp. extra-virgin olive oil

About 2 lbs. fava beans, shelled and peeled (page 26)

Salt and freshly ground black pepper

1. Heat broth and ½ cup water to a boil in a medium saucepan. Add couscous, oregano, and chile flakes. Reduce heat and simmer, stirring occasionally, until couscous is tender and most of liquid has evaporated.

2. Remove from heat and stir in lemon zest and juice, oil, and fava beans; add salt and pepper to taste.

PER ½-CUP SERVING 424 CAL., 19% (79 CAL.) FROM FAT; 23.4 G PROTEIN; 9.1 G FAT (1.3 G SAT.); 73 G CARBO (2.3 G FIBER); 419 MG SODIUM; 1.9 MG CHOL.

Edamame salad

SERVES 8
TIME 20 minutes

This edamame salad, from reader Roxanne Chan of Albany, California, has a lovely complexity yet very few ingredients.

2 tbsp. toasted sesame oil
1 tbsp. unseasoned rice vinegar
2 tsp. soy sauce
½ tsp. Asian chili garlic sauce
1 lb. shelled edamame, cooked in salted boiling water until tender, drained, and rinsed with cool water to stop cooking
2 green onions, thinly sliced
¼ cup chopped mint
¼ cup sliced almonds

1. Whisk together oil, vinegar, soy sauce, and chili sauce in a small bowl. Set aside.
2. Combine edamame, green onions, mint, and almonds in a large bowl. Toss with dressing to coat.

PER SERVING 113 CAL., 60% (68 CAL.) FROM FAT; 6.6 G PROTEIN; 7.6 G FAT (0.6 G SAT.); 6.2 G CARBO (3.2 G FIBER); 93 MG SODIUM; 0 MG CHOL.

Chickpea cake with fava leaves and arugula salad

SERVES 6
TIME 1 hour, plus at least 1½ hours to chill

At Gather restaurant in Berkeley, executive chef and co-owner Sean Baker often embellishes this salad with other seasonal crops, like black trumpet mushrooms or nettles.

CHICKPEA CAKE
About 4 tbsp. olive oil, divided
1 cup chopped onion
1 qt. reduced-sodium vegetable broth
1⅔ cups chickpea (garbanzo) flour (see Quick Tips, right)
1 tsp. nutritional yeast (see Quick Tips, right)
1 tsp. chopped thyme
2 cups loosely packed fava leaves or baby spinach (see Quick Tips, right)
1 tsp. kosher salt

ARUGULA SALAD
1 qt. loosely packed baby arugula
½ cup *each* loosely packed fennel fronds and flat-leaf parsley
Fennel and Orange Dressing (recipe follows)

1. Make chickpea cake: Heat 1 tbsp. oil in a large, wide pot over medium heat. Cook onion, stirring often, until translucent, about 7 minutes. Add broth and heat until simmering. Sprinkle in chickpea flour and yeast, whisking until smooth.
2. Transfer mixture to a food processor. Purée until as smooth as baby food. Stir in thyme, fava leaves, and salt. Pour into a greased 9- by 13-in. baking dish. Lay a sheet of plastic wrap on top and use your hand to level mixture. Chill until cold, at least 1½ hours and up to 2 days.

3. Invert cake onto a cutting board. Cut into 12 squares, then cut each square again diagonally to make 24 triangles.
4. Heat 1 tbsp. oil in a large nonstick frying pan over medium-high heat. Working in batches, brown triangles, turning once, 8 minutes total; add oil as needed. Set 4 triangles on each of 6 plates.
5. Make salad: Toss arugula, fennel fronds, parsley, and half the dressing in a bowl. Spoon salad over chickpea triangles and serve remaining dressing on the side.

QUICK TIPS Find chickpea flour and nutritional yeast at natural-food stores or well-stocked grocery stores. If using spinach leaves instead of fava leaves, increase chickpea flour to 2 cups.

PER SERVING WITH 3 TBSP. DRESSING 395 CAL., 61% (242 CAL.) FROM FAT; 9.2 G PROTEIN; 28 G FAT (3.9 G SAT.); 30 G CARBO (6.2 G FIBER); 987 MG SODIUM; 0 MG CHOL.

Fennel and orange dressing

MAKES 1 cup
TIME 35 minutes

1 cup chopped fennel
1 cup chopped onion
7 tbsp. extra-virgin olive oil, divided
2 pinches saffron threads
1 pinch cayenne
1 pinch paprika
3 tbsp. Champagne vinegar
½ cup vegetable broth
1 tsp. finely shredded orange zest
1 tsp. chopped rosemary
½ tsp. kosher salt

1. Cook fennel and onion in 2 tbsp. oil in a large frying pan over medium-low heat until well caramelized, about 30 minutes.
2. Add saffron, cayenne, and paprika; cook until fragrant, 1 minute.
3. Remove from heat and add vinegar, broth, orange zest, rosemary, and salt. Let cool. Whisk in remaining oil.

PER TBSP. SERVING 60 CAL., 88% (53 CAL.) FROM FAT; 0.2 G PROTEIN; 6.2 G FAT (0.8 G SAT.); 1.7 G CARBO (0.4 G FIBER); 93 MG SODIUM; 0 MG CHOL.

Chickpea cake
with fava leaves
and arugula salad

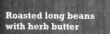

Roasted long beans
with herb butter

Roasted long beans with herb butter

SERVES 12
TIME 1 hour

Chinese long beans have wonderful deep flavor and are eye-catching besides.

2 garlic cloves, peeled
¾ cup butter, softened
1 tbsp. Dijon mustard
½ cup roughly chopped flat-leaf parsley
1 tbsp. fresh lemon juice
1 tsp. *each* kosher salt and freshly ground
    black pepper
3 lbs. yard-long beans (Chinese long beans)
    or regular green beans, ends trimmed
Coarse sea salt (optional)

1. Finely chop garlic in a food processor. Add butter, mustard, parsley, lemon juice, kosher salt, and pepper; whirl until well blended. Transfer to a bowl.
2. Meanwhile, boil a quarter of the beans at a time in a large pot of water until barely tender, about 3 minutes. Using tongs, immediately transfer beans to ice water and let cool, then transfer to a colander to drain.
3. Preheat broiler with a rack 5 to 6 in. from heat and another rack below it. Blot beans dry, then arrange lengthwise in 2 rimmed baking pans. Dot beans in each pan with about a quarter of butter mixture.
4. Set a pan on each of the racks; cook beans 1 minute. Toss to coat with butter and switch positions of pans. Cook until top beans are blistered and speckled brown, 4 to 9 minutes. Remove top pan from oven, then broil second pan the same way.
5. Transfer beans to a platter. Sprinkle with sea salt and serve with remaining butter if you like.

TIMESAVER TIP Prepare through step 2; chill butter and beans airtight up to 1 day.

PER SERVING 88 CAL., 60% (53 CAL.) FROM FAT; 2.2 G PROTEIN; 6 G FAT (3.7 G SAT.); 8.3 G CARBO (3.9 G FIBER); 144 MG SODIUM; 15 MG CHOL.

Summer beans with preserved lemon, almonds, and rosemary

SERVES 6
TIME About 35 minutes

"I like these beans at room temperature, sometimes with slices of tomato fresh from my garden," says Jesse Z. Cool, chef-owner of Flea St. Café in Menlo Park, California, and Cool Café in Menlo Park and Stanford. "But they're also great chilled as a summery salad."

¼ cup sliced almonds
1½ lbs. green, yellow, or purple beans,
    ends trimmed
3 or 4 wedges preserved lemon (see Flavor
    Note, right)
2 tbsp. finely chopped rosemary
2 tbsp. extra-virgin olive oil
1 or 2 garlic cloves, minced
Salt and freshly ground black pepper

1. In a 5- to 6-qt. pan over medium-low heat, toast almonds, stirring, until golden, 5 to 8 minutes. Remove from pan.
2. Add about 2 qts. water to pan and bring to a boil over high heat. Add beans to boiling water and cook just until tender-crisp, 3 to 6 minutes. Drain and rinse with cold water until cool.
3. Rinse preserved lemon thoroughly under running water; discard seeds and pulp. Finely chop lemon and put in a large bowl. Stir in rosemary, oil, and garlic to taste, then add beans, and salt and pepper to taste.
4. Mix in almonds just before serving.

FLAVOR NOTE You can buy preserved lemons in specialty-foods stores, or you can make your own (see Jesse Z. Cool's recipe on page 249; prepare them at least 2 weeks before using).

TIMESAVER TIP You can make the salad through step 3 up to 6 hours ahead; cover and chill.

PER SERVING 108 CAL., 65% (70 CAL.) FROM FAT; 3.1 G PROTEIN; 7.8 G FAT (1 G SAT.); 10 G CARBO (2.8 G FIBER); 2,204 MG SODIUM; 0 MG CHOL.

GOOD FOR YOU
Green beans are a good source of fiber and vitamin K. They also have a decent amount of vitamin C (however, since vitamin C isn't heat-stable, there isn't as much in cooked beans).

Linguine with walnuts, green beans, and feta

SERVES 4 to 6
TIME About 30 minutes

Roasting the beans deepens and sweetens their flavor. Combined with toasted walnuts and creamy, salty feta, they make a great vegetarian pasta dish.

1 cup walnut halves or pieces
12 oz. linguine
1 tbsp. olive oil
12 oz. slender green beans (¼ in. thick) such
    as haricots verts, ends trimmed
Salt and freshly ground black pepper
¼ cup roasted walnut oil or extra-virgin olive oil
2 tsp. finely shredded lemon zest
1 cup (5 oz.) crumbled feta cheese

1. Put walnuts in a rimmed baking pan and bake in a 350° oven until golden under skins (break one to check), 8 to 10 minutes. Pour from pan. Increase oven temperature to 500°.
2. Meanwhile, in a covered 5- to 6-qt. pot over high heat, bring about 3½ qts. water to a boil. Stir in linguine and boil, uncovered, until barely tender to bite, 8 to 10 minutes or according to package directions. Drain and return to pan.
3. Combine olive oil and green beans; spread level in baking pan. Sprinkle generously with salt and pepper. Roast until green beans just begin to brown, 4 to 6 minutes.
4. Combine walnut oil, lemon zest, and feta in a large serving bowl. Add pasta, walnuts, and green beans; mix gently. Season to taste with salt and pepper.

TIMESAVER TIP To make this dish come together quickly, start heating the oven and water before you prep the ingredients.

PER SERVING 520 CAL., 52% (270 CAL.) FROM FAT; 14 G PROTEIN; 30 G FAT (5.9 G SAT.); 51 G CARBO (3.4 G FIBER); 273 MG SODIUM; 21 MG CHOL.

Linguine with fava greens, shrimp, and green garlic

SERVES 4 to 6
TIME 1¼ hours

Not to worry—this huge amount of greens really does cook down. Fava flowers make a pretty garnish.

5 qts. loosely packed fava greens, rinsed and
    spun dry
6 tbsp. extra-virgin olive oil, divided
About ¾ tsp. *each* kosher salt and freshly ground
    black pepper, divided
½ cup minced green garlic (from about 4 heads,
    white and light green parts only; see Quick
    Tip, right)
1 tbsp. fennel seeds, crushed
Finely shredded zest of 1 lemon
1 cup Sauvignon Blanc
1 lb. medium shrimp (30 to 35 per lb.), shelled
    and deveined, with tails on
10 oz. linguine
Fava flowers (optional)

1. Heat a 12-in. frying pan over medium-high heat. Stir-fry one-third of the fava leaves at a time with 2 tsp. oil and a pinch each of salt and pepper until greens wilt, 2 minutes. Transfer to a bowl; tent with foil.
2. Reduce heat to medium-low. Add 3 tbsp. oil and stir in ½ tsp. *each* salt and pepper, the green garlic, fennel seeds, and lemon zest. Cook, stirring often, until garlic is softened, 5 minutes. Add wine and boil over high heat until reduced by half, 2 to 3 minutes. Reduce heat to medium.
3. Add shrimp in a single layer and cook, turning once, until cooked through, 2 to 3 minutes.
4. Cook linguine according to package directions. Drain, saving 1 cup water. Return pasta to pot and toss with shrimp mixture and 1 tbsp. oil. Add fava leaves and toss, pulling apart with forks. Mix in pasta water if linguine seems dry, plus more salt and pepper if you like. Spoon into a serving bowl and top with fava flowers if you like.

QUICK TIP If you don't have green garlic in your garden (see "Extra Reward," page 71) or can't find it at the farmers' market, use 2 tbsp. minced regular garlic plus 6 tbsp. green onions.

PER SERVING 445 CAL., 33% (147 CAL.) FROM FAT; 24 G PROTEIN; 17 G FAT (2.6 G SAT.); 52 G CARBO (2.3 G FIBER); 385 MG SODIUM; 112 MG CHOL.

Linguine with fava
greens, shrimp,
and green garlic

CORN

WHY GROW IT

Flavor, flavor, flavor. The minute you pick an ear of corn, its natural sugars begin an inexorable conversion into starch that refrigeration can only slow down somewhat. Growing your own will allow you to try the world's best recipe for corn on the cob: Bring a pot of water to a boil, go out to the garden, pick your corn, strip off the leaves (husk) and silk, drop into the boiling water, and cook 2 minutes; then scoop it out, and enjoy.

WHEN TO HARVEST

When the silks start to turn brown (about 3 weeks after they first appear), pull back the husk and try popping a kernel with your thumbnail. If the juice is milky, it's time to pick. (Clear juice means the corn isn't ripe yet; pasty means it's overripe.)

HOW TO KEEP

If you've got more corn than you can immediately cook, refrigerate the ears in their husks until you're ready to cook them; the husks keep the corn moist and fresh, and slow down the conversion of the sugars into starch. Or preserve it (below).

PRESERVING THE HARVEST

FREEZE For corn on the cob all winter long, remove the husks and silk and blanch corn in boiling water 3 minutes (for cobs 1¼ inches or less in diameter) to 5 minutes (for those over 1½ inches). Drain, plunge into cold water until completely cooled, drain again, and pack in resealable plastic freezer bags. Seal and freeze. For kernels, blanch whole ears 4 minutes, then plunge into cold water to cool. Drain, cut kernels from cobs, and pack in resealable plastic freezer bags. Seal and freeze.

DRY Using a dehydrator is the simplest and fastest way. Remove the husks and silk from the ears. Cut each ear into 2-inch lengths and set the pieces in a single layer on the dehydrator trays. Dehydrate until just dried, about 36 hours. Rub the dried kernels off the ears. Two ears will yield about ⅓ cup dried kernels. Store the dried kernels in airtight containers at room temperature for up to 9 months. You can add the dried kernels to rice or quinoa at the start of cooking, or to soups; you can also simply reconstitute the corn by giving it a 5- to 10-minute soak in boiling water.

Basic Ways to Cook

BOIL The easiest way to cook fresh corn is to bring a pot of unsalted water to a boil, drop in the husked ears, and boil 2 minutes. Or, for a gentle, slow-cook method, add corn, cover, and turn off the burner. The heat of the water will gently cook the kernels, and the corn will stay hot for at least an hour. Serve with butter, salt, and freshly ground black pepper.

ROAST Rub husked ears with butter. Wrap each in heavy-duty foil. Roast in a 375° oven until the kernels are tender when pierced, about 30 minutes.

GRILL Pull back (without detaching) the outermost layer of each husk. Remove the inner leaves and silk, then brush the kernels with olive oil or melted butter. Pull up the still-attached outer husk to cover each cob, tie it shut at the top with kitchen twine or a strip of husk, and grill the ears over a direct medium fire (350° to 450°; you can hold your hand 5 in. above cooking grate only 5 to 7 seconds) until tender, 10 to 15 minutes.

Some of our favorite varieties

'Bodacious' A sugar-enhanced variety with good corn flavor.

'Earlivee' and 'Fleet' These short-season varieties are excellent options for northern climates.

'Honey Select' This triple-sweet golden variety is so flavorful and tender, you can eat it uncooked, fresh off the stalk.

'Luscious' A bicolored (white and yellow) variety of Supersweet corn. Supersweet is a term for extra-sweet hybrid varieties that have a longer shelf life than regular sweet corn. They're sweeter than sugar-enhanced types.

'Miracle' A late-season corn that is crisp and sweet.

'Supersweet Jubilee' Tender and sweet with good corn flavor.

'Whiteout' A white variety of Supersweet corn.

Fresh corn cakes

MAKES 16 cakes

TIME 30 minutes

Dress up these cakes from reader Lynn Lloyd of Santa Cruz, California, with salsa and sour cream, and serve as an appetizer. They're also delicious as a side dish, simply smeared with butter.

1 cup fresh corn kernels (about 2 ears)
¼ cup chopped green onions
4 tbsp. vegetable oil, divided
2 large eggs, separated
¼ cup *each* flour and yellow cornmeal
½ tsp. salt
¼ tsp. freshly ground black pepper

1. Pulse corn and green onions in a blender or food processor until chopped but not smooth. Transfer to a large bowl and stir in 2 tbsp. oil and the egg yolks.

2. Combine flour, cornmeal, salt, and pepper in a small bowl. Add to corn mixture and mix thoroughly but gently.

3. Whisk or beat egg whites in a large clean bowl until soft peaks form. Fold into corn mixture.

4. Heat 1 tbsp. oil over medium-high heat in a large frying pan. Working in batches, drop large spoonfuls of corn mixture into pan (do not spread or flatten). Cook until edges begin to set and undersides are browned, about 2 minutes. Flip and cook until cakes are browned and cooked through. Cook remaining corn mixture the same way, adding remaining oil as necessary. Serve hot.

PER CAKE 63 CAL., 60% (38 CAL.) FROM FAT; 1.5 G PROTEIN; 4.2 G FAT (0.6 G SAT.); 5.2 G CARBO (0.4 G FIBER); 83 MG SODIUM; 26 MG CHOL.

Chilled corn soup

SERVES 6 as a first-course soup; makes 6 cups
TIME 45 to 60 minutes, plus 3 hours to chill

This summer soup is pure essence of corn. Blanching the basil, an herb that tends to blacken once it's cut, keeps it jewel green.

9 medium ears yellow corn, husks and
**   silk removed**
Salt
½ cup tightly packed basil
¼ cup extra-virgin olive oil

1. Bring a large pot of salted water to a boil. Add corn, cover, and cook for 2 to 3 minutes. (For a smoky flavor, you can roast or grill the ears instead of boiling them.) Drain corn. When cool enough to handle, slice kernels off the ears with a sharp paring knife.

2. In two batches, purée kernels in a blender with 4 cups water. Strain purée through a fine-mesh strainer into a large bowl, pressing to squeeze out the corn liquid, and throw away the kernel mash. Add salt to taste and chill soup until cold, at least 3 hours.

3. Meanwhile, boil basil for 2 to 3 seconds. Drain immediately, plunge in ice water, and drain again. Purée basil in a blender with ½ teaspoon salt and the oil.

4. Serve soup cold, drizzled with basil oil. (Any leftover basil oil will keep in an airtight container in the refrigerator for up to 3 days.)

PER 1-CUP SERVING 398 CAL., 49% (194 CAL.) FROM FAT; 9.6 G PROTEIN; 22 G FAT (3.6 G SAT.); 52 G CARBO (5.8 G FIBER); 42 MG SODIUM; 0 MG CHOL.

GOOD FOR YOU

In addition to being sweet and delicious, corn is a good source of fiber and contains smaller amounts of other vitamins and minerals.

Fresh corn salad with avocado and basil

SERVES 6
TIME 30 minutes

Kathy Kane of Menlo Park, California, combined the flavors of summer for this crowd-pleasing salad.

6 ears corn, husks and silk removed
2 cups halved cherry tomatoes
½ cup thinly sliced red onion
1 large avocado, pitted, peeled, and cut
    into ½-in. cubes
⅓ cup chopped basil
2 tbsp. Champagne vinegar
1 tsp. Dijon mustard
¼ cup extra-virgin olive oil
¼ tsp. *each* kosher salt and freshly ground
    black pepper

1. Cook corn in a large pot of boiling water until warmed through, 2 to 3 minutes. Drain and rinse with cold water until cool.
2. Meanwhile, combine tomatoes, onion, avocado, and basil in a large bowl. In a small bowl, combine remaining ingredients to make the vinaigrette, whisking until blended.
3. Cut corn kernels with a sharp paring knife from cobs and add to salad, then pour in vinaigrette and toss gently to combine.

PER SERVING 245 CAL., 62% (153 CAL.) FROM FAT; 4.5 G PROTEIN; 17 G FAT (2.5 G SAT.); 25 G CARBO (4.4 G FIBER); 92 MG SODIUM; 0 MG CHOL.

Honey-chipotle grilled corn

SERVES 8

TIME 20 minutes

Slathering the grilled corn with honey-chipotle butter gives it an extra hit of smokiness. Feel free to change up this recipe, from reader Trisha Kruse of Eagle, Idaho, by using the same grilling technique but with different flavored compound butters to suit your taste.

2 canned chipotle chiles in adobo sauce
½ cup butter, melted
⅓ cup mild-flavored honey, such as clover
1 garlic clove, minced
½ tsp. salt
8 ears corn in husks, with silks removed

1. Prepare a charcoal or gas grill for direct medium-high heat (about 450°; you can hold your hand 5 in. above cooking grate only 4 to 5 seconds). Combine chiles, butter, honey, garlic, and salt in a blender and whirl until smooth.

2. Put unhusked corn on grill and cook, turning occasionally, 15 minutes. Husks will blacken. Transfer to a work surface, remove husks, brush ears generously with some of butter mixture, and return ears to grill. Grill until lightly browned, about 5 minutes. Serve warm, with remaining butter.

PER EAR 232 CAL., 50% (117 CAL.) FROM FAT; 3.6 G PROTEIN; 13 G FAT (7.3 G SAT.); 31 G CARBO (2.9 G FIBER); 491 MG SODIUM; 31 MG CHOL.

HOW TO CUT OFF KERNELS

Hold a husked ear of corn upright in a deep, wide bowl. With a sharp paring knife, cut kernels off close to the cob, in a strip down one side. Rotate the cob to shear off all the kernels.

Santa Fe corn pudding

SERVES 6 to 8
TIME 1¼ hours

Most people have only had corn pudding made with frozen or canned corn. Prepared with fresh corn, it is a revelation. This Southwestern take from barbecue experts Bill Jamison and Cheryl Alters Jamison is studded with roasted chiles and crowned with a buttery crumb topping. Fresh or frozen roasted green chiles (such as 'Anaheim' or New Mexico varieties) will give the dish more flavor, but if these aren't available, you can substitute canned roasted green chiles.

4 cups fresh corn kernels (about 6 ears), divided
2 large eggs
1½ cups half-and-half
1 tsp. kosher salt
½ cup chopped roasted green chiles
1 cup crushed buttery salted crackers (such as Ritz Crackers or Carr's Croissant Crackers), divided
4 tbsp. butter, melted, divided
½ cup shredded Monterey jack cheese or pepper jack cheese

1. Preheat oven to 350°. Grease a 2-qt. baking dish with butter or oil.
2. Pulse 1¾ cups corn kernels in food processor until mixture is puréed but still a bit chunky, about 5 pulses. Set aside.
3. Whisk together eggs, half-and-half, and salt in a large bowl. Add whole and puréed corn kernels, green chiles, ¼ cup crackers, and 3 tbsp. melted butter. Stir to combine. Spoon mixture into prepared baking dish and scatter cheese over top.
4. Mix together remaining ¾ cup cracker crumbs and 1 tbsp. melted butter in a small bowl. Sprinkle over cheese.
5. Bake pudding until puffed and golden brown, 45 to 50 minutes. The edges should be a bit crusty and the center still a little jiggly. Serve hot.

PER SERVING 288 CAL., 59% (171 CAL.) FROM FAT; 8.7 G PROTEIN; 19 G FAT (10 G SAT.); 24 G CARBO (2.5 G FIBER); 427 MG SODIUM; 107 MG CHOL.

3 WAYS WITH FRESH CORN

In relish Cut raw kernels off the cob and mix with a little chopped red onion, chopped red bell pepper, toasted cumin seeds, unseasoned rice vinegar, sugar, red chile flakes, and salt. Great with grilled pork chops, steaks, chicken, and hot dogs.

Cut into wheels With a mallet or hammer, tap a heavy knife through husked ears of corn to cut them into wheels an inch or so wide. Cook them in boiling water just until hot, then drain and mix in a bowl with melted butter, minced garlic, chopped basil, salt, and pepper.

In salad Mix fresh raw or cooked corn kernels with bite-size pieces of butter lettuce, diced tomatoes, and chopped red onion. Dress with a vinaigrette of extra-virgin olive oil, white wine vinegar, Dijon mustard, salt, and pepper.

Chicken and corn summer chowder

SERVES 6

TIME 50 minutes

Hot soup for dinner in summer? When it's prepared with corn picked just minutes ago from the garden and finished with a fresh, bright topping of chopped avocado, tomato, and cilantro, of course!

2 slices bacon, chopped

1 onion, chopped

3 tbsp. flour

1 lb. 'Yukon Gold' potatoes, peeled and chopped

6 cups reduced-sodium chicken broth

4 cups shredded cooked chicken (from a 2½- to 3-lb. roasted chicken)

3 cups fresh corn kernels (about 4 ears)

¼ to ½ cup heavy whipping cream

2 ripe medium tomatoes, seeded and chopped

1 avocado, pitted, peeled, and chopped

1 cup loosely packed cilantro

2 limes, cut into wedges

Freshly ground black pepper

1. Cook bacon in a large, heavy pot over medium-high heat until fat renders and meat starts to brown. Add onion, reduce heat to medium, and cook until soft, about 3 minutes. Sprinkle with flour and cook, stirring, until flour smells cooked (you should get a whiff of baked pie crust) but hasn't started to brown, about 3 minutes.

2. Add potatoes and broth. Bring to a boil. Reduce heat to keep mixture simmering and cook until potatoes are barely tender, about 5 minutes. Add chicken and corn and bring to a boil. Reduce heat to low and stir in cream to taste. Heat through, about 2 minutes.

3. Serve in soup bowls, garnished with tomatoes, avocado, cilantro, a squirt or two of lime juice, and pepper to taste.

PER 2-CUP SERVING 504 CAL., 41% (207 CAL.) FROM FAT; 37 G PROTEIN; 23 G FAT (7.9 G SAT.); 40 G CARBO (4.8 G FIBER); 733 MG SODIUM; 109 MG CHOL.

Sweet corn ice cream

SERVES 8

TIME 40 minutes, plus chilling and freezing time

Sweet corn is a favorite ice cream flavor in Mexico, where the kernels are usually stirred in whole. We've grated them to extract their milky liquid, and used the kernels and liquid as part of the custard base.

2 ears corn, husks and silk removed
1 cup heavy whipping cream
1½ cups milk
½ cup sugar
4 large egg yolks
½ tsp. vanilla extract

1. Set a box grater in a large bowl. Using large holes, grate corn kernels (and their "milk") off cobs. Discard cobs.

2. Combine cream, milk, and corn in a medium saucepan over medium heat. Bring to a simmer. Meanwhile, in a medium bowl, whisk sugar and egg yolks until pale and thick. When cream mixture reaches a simmer, slowly ladle ½ cup of it into egg mixture, whisking constantly. Repeat with another ½-cup ladleful. Reduce heat to low, whisk warmed egg mixture into saucepan, and cook, whisking, until mixture thickens a bit, about 5 minutes.

3. Pour mixture into a medium bowl, stir in vanilla, cover with plastic wrap (letting the wrap sit directly on the mixture's surface so a skin doesn't form), and chill at least 2 hours and up to 1 day.

4. Freeze in an ice cream maker according to manufacturer's instructions. Serve immediately or transfer to an airtight plastic container and freeze up to overnight.

PER ½-CUP SERVING 242 CAL., 60% (144 CAL.) FROM FAT; 4.7 G PROTEIN; 16 G FAT (8.7 G SAT.); 23 G CARBO (1 G FIBER); 43 MG SODIUM; 153 MG CHOL.

CUCUMBERS

'Amira'

WHY GROW THEM

Store-bought cucumbers often look like they've been long off the vine (their smooth skin starting to wrinkle or soften in spots) and allowed to grow much too big, resulting in a greater seed-to-flesh ratio and a loss of flavor. And all have been given a wax job to protect their skin from dings in transit. Growing your own gives you access to super-fresh cucumbers, and means you can pick them at the right time in their development: when they're small, crisp, and full of flavor. Growing your own also lets you try lots of different varieties—long slicing cucumbers, which often have small white spikes on the skin; the smaller pickling cukes; and even the roundish, yellow, mild-flavored lemon cucumbers. There are also the so-called "burpless" varieties—their skin can be eaten without causing indigestion.

WHEN TO HARVEST

Pickling cucumbers should be harvested as soon as they have reached the proper size: 2 inches long for sweet pickles and 3 to 4 inches long for dill pickles. Slicing cukes can be allowed to grow 6 to 8 inches long (or more for extra-long varieties such as Armenian, which can grow up to 20 inches and still be fine). To keep cukes coming, harvest them 3 to 4 times a week.

'County Fair'

Some of our favorite varieties

'Amira' A Middle Eastern variety that's great for slicing.

Armenian Actually a melon, this long, curving, pale green fruit looks and tastes exactly like a cucumber—a very mild one, at that.

'County Fair' One of our favorite cucumbers for pickling.

'Diva' Produces cukes that are sweet and crunchy, with no spikes on the skin; this variety is very productive.

'Marketmore 76' A long, smooth slicing cucumber.

'Suyo Long' A long, slim, very mild Asian variety.

Basic Ways to Prepare

FLAVOR WATER Float slices of cucumber in a pitcher of water as a summer refresher; add lemon too, if you like.

QUICK-PICKLE Toss very thinly sliced cucumber with rice vinegar, salt, and pepper to taste.

SAUTÉ Peel, seed, and roughly chop a cucumber. Cook over medium-high heat in butter or olive oil until tender. Add chopped mint and season with salt and pepper.

AS A "CRACKER" Use thick slices of cucumber in place of toasts or crackers when serving dips or spreads such as hummus.

HOW TO KEEP

Refrigerate whole cucumbers in a plastic bag for up to 1 week.

PRESERVING THE HARVEST

Pickling cucumbers is a wonderful way to preserve your harvest. See our recipes on page 59. Cucumbers don't freeze well—they turn to mush—and aren't good dried, either.

Pimm's cup

MAKES 8 drinks
TIME 20 minutes

In England, Pimm's cup is a must at cricket matches. Often ginger ale is used along with or instead of the lemony soda, and sometimes a fortifying shot of gin goes in along with the Pimm's No. 1, a gin-based drink that is widely available in liquor stores in the United States. This version, from West Coast food stylist Valerie Aikman-Smith, is packed with cucumbers and citrus, making it extra-thirst-quenching and supremely summery. You can arrange the fruit, cucumber, and mint any way you like.

Ice
2 oranges, cut into rounds, then into half-moons
2 lemons, cut into rounds, then into half-moons
1 cucumber, sliced
2 cups Pimm's No. 1
4 cups Sprite or other lemon-lime soda
6 to 8 large mint sprigs, crushed gently,
    plus a few loose leaves

1. Fill 2 pitchers a quarter full with ice. To each, add a layer of orange slices, a few lemon slices, and a layer of cucumber slices. Repeat the layering. Pour in the Pimm's and Sprite, dividing equally between pitchers, and mix with a long-handled spoon. Poke mint sprigs and leaves down into drink.
2. Divide drink among 8 tall glasses, with a few slices of fruit and cucumber in each glass, along with some mint leaves.

PER DRINK 226 CAL., 0% FROM FAT; 1.3 G PROTEIN; 0.2 G FAT (0 G SAT.); 21 G CARBO (2.9 G FIBER); 16 MG SODIUM; 0 MG CHOL.

Cucumber Collins

MAKES 1 drink

TIME 5 minutes

Invite friends over for a Cucumber Collins—a delicate take on the classic Tom Collins. Maria Hunt, a San Diego author and the force behind *thebubblygirl.com*, created this recipe.

4 cucumber slices
3 fresh mint leaves
2 tbsp. Simple Syrup (page 204)
2 tbsp. fresh lime juice
3 tbsp. gin
Ice
¼ cup sparkling water
⅛ tsp. rose water*

Muddle cucumber slices, mint leaves, simple syrup, and lime juice in a cocktail shaker. Add gin and ice. Shake, pour over more ice, and top with fizzy water. Add rose water and stir.

Find with cocktail or baking supplies at well-stocked grocery stores, or at Middle Eastern markets.

PER ½-CUP SERVING 218 CAL., 0% (0.6 CAL.) FROM FAT; 0.3 G PROTEIN; 0.1 G FAT (0 G SAT.); 28 G CARBO (0.3 G FIBER); 14 MG SODIUM; 0 MG CHOL.

GOOD FOR YOU
Cucumbers are extremely low in calories (1 whole cup has just 20).

Turkish cucumber
and mint soup

Turkish cucumber and mint soup

SERVES 5
TIME 30 minutes

This cold soup is a delicious study in contrasts—the refreshing cucumber-yogurt base providing the backdrop for piquant garlic and lemon, bright mint and dill, and smoky Aleppo pepper, a chile grown in Syria and Turkey.

2 lbs. cucumbers, peeled, seeded, and cut
   into chunks
2 garlic cloves, minced
¼ cup fresh lemon juice
2 tbsp. extra-virgin olive oil
3 containers (7 to 8 oz. each) plain low-fat
   Greek-style yogurt
2 tsp. Aleppo pepper* or coarsely ground dried
   California chile, plus more to taste
1 tsp. kosher salt
½ tsp. freshly ground black pepper
½ cup chopped mint, plus small whole leaves
1 tbsp. chopped dill

1. Whirl cucumbers, garlic, lemon juice, oil, and 1 container yogurt in a blender until smooth. Pour into a stainless steel bowl and whisk in remaining yogurt, the Aleppo pepper, salt, and black pepper.
2. Nest bowl in ice water; stir often until cold, about 15 minutes.
3. Stir chopped mint and dill into soup just before serving. Sprinkle bowls with more Aleppo pepper if you like, and mint leaves.
Find Aleppo pepper in well-stocked grocery stores or buy online at penzeys.com

PER 1-CUP SERVING 151 CAL., 33% (50 CAL.) FROM FAT; 12 G PROTEIN; 5.8 G FAT (0.8 G SAT.); 14 G CARBO (1 G FIBER); 435 MG SODIUM; 0 MG CHOL.

Cucumber-potato salad

SERVES 8; makes 8 cups
TIME 30 minutes

For delicate, thin cucumber slices, use a mandoline—you'll find inexpensive, good-quality ones at Asian markets.

1½ lbs. small red thin-skinned potatoes
½ cup plain low-fat Greek-style yogurt
½ cup olive-oil mayonnaise or regular mayonnaise
½ cup roughly chopped dill
2 tbsp. red wine vinegar
1 tsp. kosher salt
½ tsp. freshly ground black pepper
1½ cups slivered red onion, rinsed and patted dry
1 cucumber, very thinly sliced

1. Bring 1 in. water to a boil in a medium pot. Set whole potatoes in a steamer basket and steam in pot, covered, until tender, 15 to 20 minutes. Cool in ice water, then pat dry.
2. Whisk yogurt, mayonnaise, dill, vinegar, salt, and pepper in a small bowl to combine.
3. Quarter potatoes and put in a large bowl. Add onion, cucumber, and half the dressing; gently stir to coat. Add more dressing if you like, or save to use as a dip.

TIMESAVER TIP You can prepare this up to 2 days in advance through step 2. Chill potatoes and dressing separately, and slice cucumber just before serving.

PER 1-CUP SERVING (USING HALF THE DRESSING) 154 CAL., 32% (49 CAL.) FROM FAT; 3.9 G PROTEIN; 5.5 G FAT (0.5 G SAT.); 21 G CARBO (2.1 G FIBER); 425 MG SODIUM; 5.8 MG CHOL.

HOW TO SEED A CUCUMBER
This is an easy way to make short work of seeding a cucumber. Cut the cuke in half lengthwise, then take a small, somewhat pointed spoon and drag it down the length of the cucumber, scooping out all the seeds in one motion. Repeat with the other half.

**Grilled salmon with
herbed cucumber salad**
RECIPE P. 58

Creamy cucumber-avocado salad dressing
RECIPE P. 58

Grilled salmon with herbed cucumber salad

SERVES 4

TIME 35 minutes

Quick little cucumber salads are wonderful paired with food off the grill—in this case, salmon, providing a cooling and crunchy contrast. Having a garden stash of cukes allows you to throw together an easy accompaniment like this one at a moment's notice. The recipe is from Maria Hines, chef-owner of Tilth and Golden Beetle restaurants in Seattle. (Photo on page 56.)

SAUCE

1 cup plain whole-milk yogurt

1 tbsp. chopped dill

1 tbsp. extra-virgin olive oil

2 tsp. fresh lemon juice

1/4 tsp. kosher salt

1/8 tsp. freshly ground black pepper

CUCUMBER SALAD

1/2 lb. cucumbers

2 tsp. *each* chopped chives and flat-leaf parsley

1 1/2 tsp. minced shallot

2 tsp. extra-virgin olive oil

3/4 tsp. fresh lemon juice

1/8 tsp. *each* kosher salt and freshly ground black pepper

SALMON AND SERVING

4 sockeye salmon fillets (each 5 to 6 oz., 1/2 to 1 in. thick), with skin

1 tbsp. olive oil

1/4 tsp. *each* kosher salt and freshly ground black pepper

Dill sprigs

1. Make sauce: Combine all ingredients in a bowl. Cover and chill until used.

2. Prepare a charcoal or gas grill for direct medium-high heat (about 450°; you can hold your hand 5 in. above cooking grate only 4 to 5 seconds).

3. Make salad: Cut cucumbers lengthwise into paper-thin strips, preferably with a mandoline. Put in a bowl with herbs and shallot; chill until used. In another bowl, mix oil, lemon juice, salt, and pepper; set dressing aside.

4. Prepare salmon: Rub all over with oil and sprinkle all over with salt and pepper. Fold a 12- by 20-in. sheet of heavy-duty foil in half crosswise. With a knife tip, poke dime-size holes through foil about 2 in. apart. Oil one side of foil.

5. Set foil with oiled side up on cooking grate. Set fillets slightly separated, skin side down, on foil. Grill, covered, until fish is barely cooked through, 7 to 12 minutes. With a wide spatula, slide fish from skin to a platter and tent with foil. If you want crisp skin, continue to cook skin on foil until crisp, 2 to 3 minutes more. Remove foil from grill, then gently peel off skin, using your fingers or a wide spatula (skin may break into pieces).

6. Set crisp skin, if using, on plates and set salmon on top. Discard any liquid from cucumber mixture, then quickly toss mixture with dressing and mound on fish. Garnish with dill sprigs. Serve immediately with yogurt sauce (salmon skin will soften as it stands).

PER SERVING 380 CAL., 56% (213 CAL.) FROM FAT; 34 G PROTEIN; 24 G FAT (4.8 G SAT.); 5.6 G CARBO (0.4 G FIBER); 409 MG SODIUM; 109 MG CHOL.

Creamy cucumber-avocado salad dressing

MAKES 2 cups

TIME 15 minutes

This rich and refreshing vegetable-based dressing is from Rose Ann Koffler of Salinas, California. It's wonderful tossed with baby greens and spring vegetables. (Photo on page 57.)

2 garlic cloves, minced

1/2 cucumber

1 avocado, pitted and peeled

1 cup baby spinach

1/2 cup loosely packed mint

2 spring onions (similar to green onions, with fatter bulbs) or regular green onions, ends trimmed

Juice of 1 lemon

2 tbsp. extra-virgin olive oil

1/2 tsp. white pepper

1 tsp. sea salt

Purée all ingredients with 3/4 cup water in a food processor until smooth. Refrigerate in airtight container until ready to use or up to 1 day.

PER 1/4-CUP SERVING 75 CAL., 80% (60 CAL.) FROM FAT; 0.8 G PROTEIN; 6.8 G FAT (0.9 G SAT.); 3.9 G CARBO (2 G FIBER); 288 MG SODIUM; 0 MG CHOL.

Dill pickle spears

MAKES 4 qts.

TIME 1 hour

For these pickles, you'll want to harvest your cucumbers when they are no more than 3 to 4 inches long—any larger and they will likely have formed hollows inside and won't pack as neatly into the jars. If you think you might be making these, consider growing your own dill as well and harvesting the seed heads. Just snip off and discard the stems. Otherwise, look for the seed heads at farmers' markets. This recipe is from reader Debbie Harpe, of Placentia, California.

¼ cup pickling spice

3½ cups distilled white vinegar

6 tbsp. sugar

¼ cup salt

5 lbs. (about 40) pickling cucumbers

8 dill seed heads (2 to 3 in. wide)

8 garlic cloves

12 small dried hot chiles (each 3 to 4 in. long; ¼ oz. total), such as arbol

1. Follow the directions in "Canning ABCs: Get Ready" (page 278), using 4 wide-mouthed quart-size jars, plus matching rings and lids.

2. Enclose pickling spice in a double layer of cheesecloth and tie tightly with string. In a 2- to 3-qt. pan over high heat, bring spice bag, 3½ cups water, vinegar, sugar, and salt to a boil, stirring often. Cover, reduce heat, and simmer, stirring occasionally, 15 minutes. Discard spice bag.

3. Meanwhile, discard any blossoms and stems from cucumbers. Quarter cucumbers lengthwise.

4. Place 2 dill seed heads, 2 garlic cloves, and 3 chiles in each jar. Pack cucumber quarters vertically into jars without forcing them, pushing them ½ in. below rim; cut off any tips of spears that stick above this level. Pour hot vinegar mixture over cucumbers, leaving ½-in. headspace (be sure liquid covers cucumbers). Release air bubbles and seal jars.

5. Process as directed in "Canning ABCs: Process Jars" (page 279), but keep water at 180° to 185° (not boiling, or pickles will get soft), checking with a thermometer, for 20 minutes (add 5 minutes for every 3,000 ft. in altitude above sea level). Cool, check seals, and store as directed (up to 1 year). For best flavor, let pickles stand at least 1 week before serving.

PER 2 SPEARS, DRAINED 10 CAL., 9.5% (0.9 CAL.) FROM FAT; 0.2 G PROTEIN; 0.1 G FAT (0 G SAT.); 2.5 G CARBO (0.3 G FIBER); 262 MG SODIUM; 0 MG CHOL.

Bread-and-butter pickles

MAKES 5 to 7 pts.

TIME 1½ hours, plus 12 hours to brine vegetables

Reader Stephanie Baldwin has fond memories of making these pickles as a child in New Zealand. She uses a mix of vegetables, incorporating 2 cups of each of the following: pickling cucumbers sliced ¼ inch thick, celery sliced ¼ inch thick, green beans cut into ½-inch lengths, chopped bell peppers, chopped cauliflower, and shredded cabbage.

3 qts. sliced or chopped vegetables (a mix or all pickling cucumbers; see above)

2¼ lbs. (about 4) onions, halved lengthwise and thinly sliced crosswise

½ cup salt

1 qt. distilled white vinegar

2½ cups sugar

1 tbsp. mustard seeds

2 tsp. celery seeds

2 tsp. turmeric

1. Combine vegetables, onions, salt, and 2½ qts. water in a large bowl (at least 6 qts.). Cover and chill at least 12 hours and up to 24 hours. Drain, rinse well, and drain again.

2. Follow the directions in "Canning ABCs: Get Ready" (page 278), using 6 pint-size jars (7 if making with cucumbers only), plus matching rings and lids.

3. Bring vinegar, sugar, mustard seeds, celery seeds, and turmeric to a boil in an 8- to 10-qt. pot over high heat, stirring often. Add vegetable mixture, cover, and return to a boil; reduce heat and simmer, stirring occasionally, until onions are limp, about 2 minutes.

4. Fill jars as directed in "Canning ABCs: Fill and Seal Jars" (page 278), leaving ½-in. headspace in each jar; be sure liquid covers vegetables (discard any leftover liquid). Bring water in canner to 180° to 185° (not boiling, or pickles will get soft) and process for 20 minutes (add 5 minutes for every 3,000 ft. in altitude above sea level). Cool, check seals, and store as directed (up to 1 year).

PER ¼ CUP, DRAINED 57 CAL., 1.6% (0.9 CAL.) FROM FAT; 0.6 G PROTEIN; 0.1 G FAT (0 G SAT.); 14 G CARBO (0.8 G FIBER); 293 MG SODIUM; 0 MG CHOL.

EGGPLANT

'Farmer's Long'

WHY GROW THEM

Few vegetable plants are handsomer than the eggplant. It resembles a little tree, with big, usually lobed leaves that are purple tinged; its drooping violet flowers are followed by the fruit—the eggplant, which are pretty near spectacular in their own right. Aside from letting you enjoy their natural beauty, backyard eggplant is also worth growing for the sheer joy of experimenting with the numerous varieties available, ranging from large oval Italian (globe) types to long slender Asian varieties to varieties with smaller fruit, including some that resemble eggs. And the colors range from purples so deep it looks black, to stunning lavenders, to green, orange, and white.

WHEN TO HARVEST

Pick fruit after they develop some color but before they lose their glossy shine. Once eggplant are allowed to get overripe, they acquire a strong taste as the seeds enlarge and get bitter.

HOW TO KEEP

Store in a paper bag in the refrigerator produce drawer for up to 2 weeks.

'Zebra'

Some of our favorite varieties

'Casper' A full-size eggplant that's bright white, as its name suggests.

'Fairy Tale' This Asian variety bears lavender and white-striped fruit on a dwarf plant. Pick when 4 inches long.

'Farmer's Long' A Japanese variety that produces long, slim eggplant colored a lovely hue of purple.

'Hansel' These can be picked as "babies" at 2 to 3 inches or when mature.

'White Egg' Yes, they look just like small white eggs.

'Zebra' An Italian variety, it bears striking white-streaked purple fruit.

Basic Ways to Cook

TO SALT OR NOT TO SALT? Although many varieties (and virtually all Asian types) are sweet and mellow, Italian eggplant can sometimes be bitter. To tame them, trim the skin and a thin layer of flesh underneath, then cut the eggplant into cubes or slices. Sprinkle with salt all over and let drain in a colander in the sink for 30 minutes. Pat dry before continuing to cook.

ROAST Cut eggplant into ½-in.-thick slices; brush all sides with oil. Arrange in a single layer in a shallow baking pan. Bake in a 450° oven until well browned and soft when pierced, 20 to 30 minutes. To make the eggplant taste extra-mellow—and definitely if you are purée-ing it for a dip or a filling—remove the seeds.

GRILL You can grill slices of eggplant, or grill the entire eggplant and use the flesh as the basis for a dip or other dish. *For slices:* Prepare a charcoal or gas grill for direct high heat (450° to 550°; you can hold your hand 5 in. above cooking grate only 2 to 4 seconds). Slice the eggplant ½ in. thick across or lengthwise, depending on how you plan to use it. Brush with olive oil, then grill on both sides until softened. *For the entire eggplant:* Heat grill to high with an area left clear or turned off for indirect heat. Pierce eggplant in several places with a knife. Grill eggplant over indirect heat, covered, until very tender, 20 to 30 minutes. Let stand until cool enough to touch; slit eggplant lengthwise and scrape flesh from skin.

SAUTÉ Eggplant can soak up oil like a sponge, so to eliminate the need for lots of oil, steam eggplant before sautéing it: Put eggplant cubes or slices in a wok or 12-in. frying pan with a little water (¼ cup per 1 lb. eggplant), then simmer, covered, until eggplant is tender when pierced, about 5 minutes. To sauté, uncover the pan, add 2 tsp. oil per lb. of eggplant, and turn often until browned, 8 to 10 minutes.

Sicilian bruschetta

SERVES 12, plus leftovers; makes 5 cups
TIME 50 minutes

Caponata, the classic sweet, tangy Sicilian eggplant-pepper relish, is addictive spooned over toasts with mild, creamy ricotta cheese.

1 loaf (1 lb.) crusty Italian bread such as ciabatta, cut into ⅓-in.-thick slices
About 6 tbsp. olive oil, divided
1 large eggplant, cut into ½-in. dice (about 4 cups)
2 tbsp. minced garlic
1 cup *each* chopped celery, red bell pepper, and green olives
¼ cup *each* red wine vinegar and tomato paste
½ cup *each* raisins and toasted pine nuts
2 tsp. *each* kosher salt and sugar
¼ cup *each* chopped basil, oregano, and flat-leaf parsley
1 cup ricotta cheese

1. Preheat oven to 350°. Lay bread on a baking sheet and drizzle with about 2 tbsp. oil. Bake until toasted and light golden brown, about 5 minutes. Set aside.
2. Heat 2 tbsp. oil in a large nonstick frying pan over medium-high heat. Cook eggplant, stirring often, until softened and starting to brown, about 8 minutes. Transfer to a bowl; set aside.
3. Cook garlic in remaining 2 tbsp. oil in same pan, stirring, until fragrant, about 1 minute. Add celery, bell pepper, and olives, stirring to combine, and cook until softened, 5 to 8 minutes. Stir in ¼ cup water, the vinegar, tomato paste, raisins, and pine nuts, and cook until heated through. Stir in reserved eggplant, salt, and sugar, then mix in herbs.
4. Spread each toast with ricotta, then top with caponata.

TIMESAVER TIP Prepare the caponata and toasts up to 2 days ahead. Chill the caponata and store toasts airtight at room temperature.

PER SERVING 275 CAL., 59% (162 CAL.) FROM FAT; 8.2 G PROTEIN; 18 G FAT (3.2 G SAT.); 29 G CARBO (2.8 G FIBER); 715 MG SODIUM; 10 MG CHOL.

Smoky eggplant raita

SERVES 4
TIME 45 minutes

Because of its rich meatiness, eggplant stands up well to strong flavors, including the smoky goodness of the grill. Use a charcoal grill for the deepest flavor.

1 lb. slender Italian or Asian eggplant
About ½ tsp. cumin seeds
1 tbsp. extra-virgin olive oil
¼ large red onion, thinly sliced
1 large garlic clove, minced
1 cup plain whole-milk yogurt
2 tbsp. chopped cilantro, plus more for garnish
¼ tsp. sugar
About ½ tsp. kosher salt
About ⅛ tsp. cayenne

1. Prepare a charcoal or gas grill for indirect high heat. *If using a charcoal grill:* Light 50 to 60 briquets and let burn until covered with ash, 20 to 30 minutes. Mound to one side. The area over the section cleared of coals is the indirect heat area. *If using a gas grill:* Turn all burners to high and close lid. When temperature inside reaches 450° to 550°, turn off one burner. The area over the turned-off burner is the indirect heat area.
2. Pierce eggplant in several places with a knife. Grill eggplant over indirect heat, covered, until very tender, 20 to 30 minutes. Let stand until cool enough to touch; meanwhile, continue with recipe.
3. Toast cumin seeds in a small, dry frying pan over medium heat on stovetop, until fragrant and beginning to darken, 2 to 3 minutes. Transfer to a mortar and pound fine with pestle.
4. Warm oil in pan over medium heat. Cook onion 3 minutes. Add garlic, then cook until both are softened, about 2 minutes more. Let cool slightly.
5. Slit eggplant lengthwise and scrape flesh from skin. Chop flesh coarsely; set aside.
6. Combine yogurt, onion mixture, cilantro, and sugar in a bowl. Add eggplant and stir gently. Season to taste with salt, cumin, and cayenne. Garnish with a little more cilantro.

TIMESAVER TIP You can prepare this dish through step 5 up to 1 hour ahead; hold at room temperature.

PER ½-CUP SERVING 97 CAL., 52% (50 CAL.) FROM FAT; 3.3 G PROTEIN; 5.8 G FAT (1.8 G SAT.); 9.7 G CARBO (3.3 G FIBER); 271 MG SODIUM; 8 MG CHOL.

Sicilian bruschetta

Grill-roasted vegetable pitas with grilled lamb

MAKES 8 to 10 mini pita sandwiches or 4 or 5 regular-size pita sandwiches
TIME 1½ hours, plus at least 3 hours to marinate

Roasting summer produce—eggplant, tomatoes, zucchini, and peppers—on a baking sheet on the grill yields silky, melt-in-your-mouth vegetables (and the baking sheet keeps the pieces from falling through the grate). We tuck them into pita pockets with or without chunks of skewer-grilled lamb.

9 tbsp. extra-virgin olive oil, divided
¼ cup soy sauce
2 tbsp. Worcestershire
½ cup red wine
3 tsp. kosher salt, divided
1½ tsp. freshly ground black pepper, divided
2 lbs. boneless lamb, cut into 1½-in. chunks
2 red bell peppers, seeds and ribs removed, cut into
    ¾-in.-wide wedges
2 red onions, cut into 1-in.-wide wedges
1 large eggplant, quartered lengthwise and cut into
    1-in.-thick slices
2 small zucchini, cut crosswise into ¼-in.-thick slices
3 Roma tomatoes, quartered lengthwise and seeded
3 garlic cloves, chopped
3 tbsp. balsamic vinegar
¼ cup coarsely chopped walnuts
½ cup crumbled feta cheese
8 to 10 mini pitas, halved

1. Whisk together 2 tbsp. oil, the soy sauce, Worcestershire, wine, 1 tsp. salt, and ½ tsp. pepper in a large bowl. Stir in lamb and refrigerate 3 hours or overnight.

2. Prepare a charcoal or gas grill for indirect medium-high heat (400° to 450°; you can hold your hand 5 in. above cooking grate only 6 or 7 seconds). *If using a charcoal grill:* Light 50 to 60 briquets and let burn until covered with ash, 20 to 30 minutes. Mound to one side. The area over the section cleared of coals is the indirect heat area. *If using a gas grill:* Turn all burners to high and close lid. When temperature inside reaches 400°, turn off one burner. The area over the turned-off burner is the indirect heat area.

3. Toss peppers, onions, eggplant, zucchini, and tomatoes in a large bowl with remaining 7 tbsp. olive oil, 2 tsp. salt, and 1 tsp. pepper, and the garlic. Transfer vegetables to a rimmed baking sheet (not nonstick).

4. Put baking sheet on indirect heat area and cook until vegetables are beginning to get very tender, 30 to 60 minutes, tossing vegetables every 15 minutes. Drizzle vegetables with vinegar, toss to coat, and cook 15 minutes more. Remove baking sheet from grill and let vegetables cool.

5. Prepare grill for lamb: *If using charcoal:* Add 5 briquets (if coals look significantly burned down) to bring heat back to medium-high. *If using gas:* Turn all burners to medium-high.

6. Toast walnuts in a medium frying pan over low heat on stovetop, tossing frequently, until light golden and fragrant, about 10 minutes. Transfer to a medium bowl and toss with feta and cooled vegetables.

7. Skewer lamb onto 4 metal skewers (10 to 12 in.) and grill 5 minutes per side for medium (if using charcoal, grill over direct heat). With a fork, push lamb off skewers and into a bowl.

8. Spoon vegetable mixture into halved pitas and top with lamb if you like.

TIMESAVER TIP The vegetables can be grilled a day ahead and refrigerated, covered. Allow to come to room temperature and toss with feta and walnuts before serving.

PER MINI PITA SANDWICH 467 CAL., 54% (252 CAL.) FROM FAT; 26 G PROTEIN; 28 G FAT (8.2 G SAT.); 29 G CARBO (3 G FIBER); 987 MG SODIUM; 77 MG CHOL.

GOOD FOR YOU
Eggplants are rich in a variety of antioxidants; plus they have a little bit of fiber.

Grilled eggplant naan wraps with tahini-yogurt dressing

SERVES 4

TIME 30 minutes

You may want to grill extra vegetables—they're fantastic the next day.

1 large eggplant, cut into ½-in.-thick rounds
2 ripe tomatoes, quartered
2 tbsp. olive oil
¼ cup tahini (sesame paste)
1 cup plain low-fat Greek-style yogurt
1 tbsp. minced garlic
3 tbsp. fresh lemon juice
1 tsp. kosher salt
4 pieces naan bread, warmed
6 cups baby spinach

1. Prepare a charcoal or gas grill for direct high heat (450° to 550°; you can hold your hand 5 in. above cooking grate only 2 to 4 seconds). Brush eggplant and tomatoes with oil, then grill until softened. Cut tomato quarters in half.
2. Whisk together tahini, yogurt, garlic, lemon juice, and salt.
3. Top each piece of naan bread with 1½ cups spinach, a few pieces of eggplant, 4 tomato pieces, and a spoonful of the yogurt mixture. Roll to eat.

PER WRAP 445 CAL., 41% (181 CAL.) FROM FAT; 17 G PROTEIN; 20 G FAT (3.9 G SAT.); 55 G CARBO (11 G FIBER); 899 MG SODIUM; 3.8 MG CHOL.

Grilled eggplant, tomatoes, and zucchini

SERVES 4
TIME 45 minutes

This basic method works for other vegetables too, including green onions and halved bell peppers. A bit of black pepper, fresh herbs, or parmesan cheese makes a tasty finishing touch.

2 tbsp. salt, plus more for sprinkling
2 medium eggplant, cut diagonally about ¾ in. thick
2 small zucchini, halved lengthwise
4 Roma tomatoes, halved lengthwise
About ⅓ cup olive oil

1. Dissolve salt in 3 qts. cold water in a large bowl. Add eggplant slices and weight with a plate or inverted bowl. Let sit 30 minutes.

2. Meanwhile, prepare a charcoal or gas grill for direct medium-high heat (about 450°; you can hold your hand 5 in. above cooking grate only 4 to 5 seconds).

3. Drain and dry eggplant and lay with zucchini and tomatoes on a platter. Brush one side of vegetables with olive oil and sprinkle with salt.

4. Brush grill with vegetable oil. Lay vegetables on grill, oiled side down. Close lid of gas grill and cook until grill marks form, about 5 minutes.

5. Brush dry side of vegetables with olive oil and sprinkle with salt. Turn over, close lid of gas grill, and cook until tender, 3 to 5 minutes. Serve vegetables hot or at room temperature.

PER SERVING 256 CAL., 67% (171 CAL.) FROM FAT; 4.4 G PROTEIN; 19 G FAT (2.5 G SAT.); 23 G CARBO (5.6 G FIBER); 748 MG SODIUM; 0 MG CHOL.

Peanut-stuffed eggplant with spiced yogurt

SERVES 4
TIME 50 minutes

Reader Kusum Patel of West Sacramento contributed this deliciously spicy vegetarian main course from her native north India. If 'White Egg' eggplant aren't available, use any slender Asian eggplant.

²/₃ cup finely chopped roasted, salted peanuts
8 tbsp. chopped cilantro, divided, plus more
    for garnish
3 tbsp. vegetable oil
2 tbsp. plus 1 tsp. minced fresh ginger
4 tsp. sugar
2 tsp. salt, plus more to taste
1 tbsp. *each* red chile flakes and ground coriander
1 tbsp. plus ½ tsp. cumin seeds
1¾ tsp. turmeric, divided
1¾ lbs. (8 to 12) 'White Egg' eggplant (each about
    2 in. wide, 3 in. long) or use 8 to 12 pieces slender
    Asian eggplant (each about 1½ to 2 in. wide,
    3 in. long)
1½ cups basmati rice
¾ cup plain yogurt

1. Combine peanuts in a bowl with 6 tbsp. cilantro, the oil, 2 tbsp. ginger, the sugar, salt, red chile flakes, coriander, 1 tbsp. cumin seeds, and 1½ tsp. turmeric.

2. Trim stems but not calyxes (which resemble green petals) from eggplant. From bottom end, quarter each eggplant lengthwise three-quarters of way to stem end. (If using slender eggplant, trim one end of each piece to sit flat, then quarter each piece lengthwise from untrimmed end three-quarters of way to trimmed end.) Gently open cuts in each eggplant and pack in peanut-cilantro filling. As filled, arrange eggplant upright in a 3- to 4-qt. saucepan; they must fit snugly.

3. Add ²/₃ cup water to pan. Cover, bring to a boil, then reduce heat and simmer until eggplant are tender when pierced, 15 to 20 minutes (if overcooked they may fall apart).

4. Meanwhile, bring 3 cups water to a boil in a 3- to 4-qt. pan over high heat. Add rice; reduce heat and simmer, covered, until liquid is absorbed, about 20 minutes.

5. While eggplant and rice cook, shake remaining ½ tsp. cumin seeds in a small pan over high heat until seeds darken, 1 to 2 minutes. Coarsely grind with a mortar and pestle or in a clean coffee grinder, then combine with yogurt, ½ cup water, and remaining 2 tbsp. cilantro, 1 tsp. ginger, and ¼ tsp. turmeric. Season to taste with salt.

6. Gently spoon eggplant into a dish, taking care to keep pieces together. If desired, skim and discard fat from pan juices, then pour juices around eggplant. Serve eggplant over rice with yogurt sauce. Garnish with additional cilantro if you like.

PER SERVING 466 CAL., 49% (229 CAL.) FROM FAT; 13 G PROTEIN; 26 G FAT (4 G SAT.); 77 G CARBO (9 G FIBER); 1,395 MG SODIUM; 6 MG CHOL.

Caramelized pork kebabs with Chinese eggplant

SERVES 4
TIME 40 minutes

These tender, sweet-spicy pork kebabs combine the flavors of China and Vietnam.

1 pork tenderloin (1¼ to 1½ lbs.)
2 tbsp. Thai or Vietnamese fish sauce (*nam pla*
    or *nuoc mam*)
3 tbsp. reduced-sodium soy sauce
2 tbsp. *each* oyster sauce and minced garlic
3 tbsp. sugar
1 tbsp. Sriracha chili sauce
3 slender Chinese or Japanese eggplant (½ lb. each)

1. Trim pork of fat and silverskin and cut crosswise into ¼-in.-thick slices. Arrange slices between layers of plastic wrap and, with a meat mallet or rolling pin, pound paper-thin.

2. Prepare a charcoal or gas grill for direct high heat (450° to 550°; you can hold your hand 5 in. above cooking grate only 2 to 4 seconds). In a bowl, mix fish sauce, soy sauce, oyster sauce, garlic, sugar, and chili sauce. (If you like, double the marinade and save half to use as a sauce.) Add pork and toss to coat. Let stand 10 minutes. Weave strips of meat onto eight 10-in. metal or soaked wooden skewers.

3. Halve each eggplant crosswise, then lengthwise; on flesh side, score each piece a few times with a sharp knife. Add eggplant to pork marinade and turn to coat on all sides.

4. Put skewers on center of grill and surround with pieces of eggplant, skin side down. Cover and cook 2 minutes. Turn meat over, cover, and cook 2 minutes more. Remove meat from grill. Cook eggplant, covered, turning often, 4 to 6 minutes, or until very soft but not burned.

PER SERVING 301 CAL., 21% (63 CAL.) FROM FAT; 37 G PROTEIN; 7 G FAT (2.5 G SAT.); 22 G CARBO (3.6 G FIBER); 1,363 MG SODIUM; 104 MG CHOL.

Caramelized pork
kebabs with
Chinese eggplant

GARLIC

WHY GROW IT

Because not all garlic varieties are created equal in size or bite, and it's fun to experiment. *Softneck garlic* is primarily what you find in most supermarkets, its bulb consisting of an outer layer of medium-size cloves and inner layers of smaller cloves. *Hardneck garlic* bulbs have large cloves on the outside and none in the center and are preferred by most chefs for their superior flavor. *Giant or elephant garlic* is closely related to the leek and yields fist-size bulbs with a mild garlic flavor. And if you grow your own garlic, you'll have fresh, juicy cloves—a revelation if all you've known is long-stored store-bought garlic.

EXTRA REWARD Actually, you get two, one being *green garlic*. This is the immature garlic plant, pulled up by its roots while the leaves are still green and the cloves undeveloped. You might not want to sacrifice plants to do this, but if you've overplanted and need to thin your crop, know that you can eat your thinnings. Just trim the roots away and use them as you might very pungent green onions. Slightly older green garlic will have formed pliable skins around each succulent little clove, which you may want to pull off (they're slightly tough). Your other bit of gardening lagniappe is *garlic scapes*. These are the flower stalks that form on hardneck varieties of garlic and should be trimmed to encourage growth of the cloves. Again, don't throw these trimmings away—think of them as garlic chives, just more substantial. They make a nice addition to stir-fries.

WHEN TO HARVEST

Around July, when the garlic plant's green leaves begin to turn yellow, stop irrigating for about 2 weeks, then carefully lift the bulbs out of the ground with a garden fork. Pulling by hand may crack the bulbs and decrease their shelf life.

How to Roast Garlic

Cut tops off garlic heads (enough to expose cloves). Brush cut side of each garlic head with extra-virgin olive oil, then sprinkle with salt and pepper to taste. Place each head on a sheet of foil; enclose. Bake 40 minutes in a 400° oven. Remove, open foil, and drizzle each garlic head with ½ tsp. extra-virgin olive oil. Return open packets to oven and bake for 20 minutes. Remove garlic from oven and squeeze garlic cloves from skins (or pop cloves out with a knife). If using right away, you can mash the garlic with a fork. For longer storage, place peeled cloves on a baking sheet and freeze. Transfer to small resealable plastic freezer bags, freezing ½ cup of cloves per bag. Will keep up to 3 months.

HOW TO KEEP

Store cured heads (see "Preserving the Harvest," below) of garlic in mesh or paper bags in a cool (around 50°), airy place out of direct sunlight for up to 6 months.

PRESERVING THE HARVEST

To cure garlic (which you must do before storing it), hang the bulbs by their stalks in bundles in a dry, well-ventilated area until the skins are papery, about 3 weeks. Brush away the dirt, cut off most of the roots, and clip the tops to 1 inch (unless you want to braid them).

Some of our favorite varieties

SOFTNECK

'California Early' Mild flavor and stores well.

'California Late' A little more pungent in flavor than the Early.

'Silver Rose' Cloves have a rosy hue.

'Silverskin' A good choice for braiding.

HARDNECK

'German Extra Hardy' Very strong flavor.

'Korean Red' Has purple-striped paper covering; cloves are very strong flavored and have a rosy blush.

'Music' Pungent flavor with large cloves.

'Spanish Roja' This variety is known for its purple-blushed skin. The large, crisp, juicy cloves peel easily and the flavor is pungent, though not bitingly so; the cloves turn buttery soft when cooked.

Garlic, parmesan, and Cajun fries

SERVES 8

TIME 25 minutes

These shortcut fries pack a powerful flavor punch.

1 package (28 oz.) frozen shoestring french fries
½ cup finely shredded parmesan cheese
2 tbsp. minced garlic
½ tsp. Cajun seasoning
Kosher salt

1. Bake fries according to package directions.
2. Transfer hot fries to a large bowl. Add parmesan, garlic, and Cajun seasoning, tossing to coat well. Season to taste with salt.

PER SERVING 203 CAL., 31% (63 CAL.) FROM FAT; 5.3 G PROTEIN; 7 G FAT (2.2 G SAT.); 30 G CARBO (2.6 G FIBER); 198 MG SODIUM; 4.8 MG CHOL.

GOOD FOR YOU
Garlic is a good source of allicin, a phytochemical that early research suggests may, in high doses, help protect against certain types of cancer. If you eat it raw, it's a source of vitamin B_6 too (the vitamin is destroyed by heat).

Three-cheese garlic bread

SERVES 12

TIME 20 minutes

With a double dose of garlic (both fresh and granulated) and three different kinds of cheese, this super-charged garlic bread is guaranteed to become a family favorite.

2 garlic cloves, peeled
½ cup butter, softened
1 tsp. granulated garlic
¼ tsp. cayenne
1 loaf (1 lb.) French bread
½ cup freshly grated parmesan cheese
1 cup *each* shredded sharp cheddar and
     jack cheese

1. Preheat broiler with one rack on bottom of oven and one rack about 4½ in. from heating element.

2. Whirl garlic in a food processor until finely chopped. Add butter, granulated garlic, and cayenne and whirl until well blended. Cut French bread in half lengthwise and spread with garlic butter. Set, cut side up, on a baking sheet and broil on bottom rack until butter is sizzling, about 2 minutes.

3. Toss together parmesan, cheddar, and jack cheeses in a medium bowl. Remove bread from oven and sprinkle with cheeses. Broil bread on top oven rack until cheese has melted and is just beginning to turn golden, about 1½ minutes.

4. Transfer bread to a cutting board and cut into 1½-in.-wide slices.

PER SERVING 261 CAL., 55% (144 CAL.) FROM FAT; 9.5 G PROTEIN; 16 G FAT (9.3 G SAT.); 20 G CARBO (1 G FIBER); 480 MG SODIUM; 43 MG CHOL.

Roasted garlic toasts
with olio nuovo

from garlic heads (or pop cloves out with a knife) into a bowl. Mash garlic with a fork.
4. Bake ciabatta slices on a baking sheet until well toasted, 6 to 8 minutes, turning over once.
5. Spread roasted garlic on toasts. Drizzle with olio nuovo and sprinkle with salt and pepper.

PER TOAST 124 CAL., 36% (45 CAL.) FROM FAT; 3 G PROTEIN; 5 G FAT (1 G SAT.); 17 G CARBO (0.7 G FIBER); 138 MG SODIUM; 1 MG CHOL.

Garlic-stuffed mushrooms

SERVES 4 to 6
TIME 1½ hours

The vast amount of garlic used in this recipe is tempered by being slowly cooked in cream, resulting in a rich, mild garlic stuffing.

2 heads garlic, cloves separated and peeled
1 cup heavy whipping cream
1 tsp. salt
1 cup panko (Japanese-style bread crumbs)
    or fine dried bread crumbs
24 large button or cremini mushrooms,
    stems removed
2 tsp. olive oil
¼ tsp. freshly ground black pepper

1. Slowly cook garlic and cream in a small saucepan over low heat until garlic is soft enough to mash with a spoon, about 45 minutes. (Cream will be reduced and thick.) Remove from heat and mash garlic into cream with a fork, making a rough purée. Stir in salt and panko and mix thoroughly.
2. Preheat oven to 450°. Lay mushroom caps, top side down, on an oiled baking sheet. Brush edges with oil and fill centers with garlic cream.
3. Bake until beginning to brown, about 15 minutes. Let sit 5 to 10 minutes. Lift mushrooms from any released liquid and arrange on plates or a platter. Sprinkle with pepper.

PER SERVING 231 CAL., 66% (153 CAL.) FROM FAT; 4.9 G PROTEIN; 17 G FAT (9.4 G SAT.); 17 G CARBO (1.8 G FIBER); 438 MG SODIUM; 54 MG CHOL.

Roasted garlic toasts with olio nuovo

MAKES 14 toasts
TIME 1 hour, 20 minutes

Italian for "new oil," olio nuovo is an extra-virgin olive oil less than three months old. Intensely green, with a pungent, vibrant taste, it stands up well to roasted garlic's strong flavor. However, olio nuovo quickly loses its bite, so use it as soon as possible after purchase. (Most California-produced brands of olio nuovo appear in late fall, soon after the harvest, and often sell out quickly.)

2 heads garlic
2 tsp. olive oil, divided
Kosher salt and freshly ground black pepper
1 loaf ciabatta, sliced ¼ in. thick (you will
    need 14 slices)
About ¼ cup olio nuovo or extra-virgin
    olive oil

1. Preheat oven to 400°. Cut tops off garlic heads (enough to expose cloves) and discard. Brush cut side of each garlic head with ½ tsp. extra-virgin olive oil, then sprinkle with salt and pepper to taste. Place each garlic head on a sheet of foil; enclose in foil. Bake 40 minutes.
2. Remove foil packets from oven, untwist tops, and drizzle each garlic head with another ½ tsp. extra-virgin olive oil. Return open garlic packets to oven and bake for 20 minutes.
3. Remove garlic from oven and increase oven temperature to 450°. Squeeze garlic cloves

Garlic-stuffed
mushrooms

Sonia's special steaks
RECIPE P. 79

**Vietnamese-style spicy
crab with garlic noodles**
RECIPE P. 79

Braised spring vegetables with green garlic

SERVES 4
TIME 1 hour

A glorious use for fresh green garlic. Slowly cooking it in olive oil, along with the other vegetables, brings out the fullest and sweetest flavors. If you don't have fava beans, you can leave them out and double the amount of peas.

2 lbs. fava beans in the pod, shelled (about 2 cups)
Juice of 1 lemon
4 large artichokes
1 head fennel, fronds attached
5 green garlic stems
5 green onions
¼ cup olive oil
½ tsp. salt, plus more to taste
1 lb. English peas in the pod, shelled (about 1 cup)
2 tbsp. extra-virgin olive oil

1. Bring a large pot of water to a boil. Add favas and cook 2 minutes. Drain and rinse with cold water. Tear tough skin on top of each bean and pop bean out of skin. Set beans aside.

2. Fill a large bowl with water and add lemon juice. Working with 1 artichoke at a time, trim and discard stem end and 2 in. of prickly top. Pull off and discard all tough outer leaves until only tender, very light green and yellow leaves remain (you may need to trim top further to fully remove leaves). Trim any tough green peel from stem. Be aggressive; you want the entire trimmed artichoke to be edible. Quarter artichoke lengthwise and scrape out the fuzzy choke (any choke left behind will add a lot of bitterness). Put trimmed artichoke in lemon water. Repeat with remaining artichokes.

3. Trim fennel head of dark and medium green tops. Chop feathery fronds and reserve 2 tbsp. of them. Discard remaining tops. Halve head lengthwise and cut into ¼-in.-thick wedges. Set aside.

4. Trim root ends and dry or tough dark green leaves from green garlic and green onions. Cut into 2-in. pieces (if green garlic has a small bulb on end, halve it lengthwise). Set aside.

5. Heat the ¼ cup olive oil in a large pot over medium-high heat. Add fennel wedges and drained artichokes. Sprinkle with salt and stir until sizzling. Add green garlic, green onions, and 1 cup water; cover, reduce heat to medium, and cook, stirring occasionally, until artichokes are tender, about 20 minutes.

6. Add peas and fava beans, cover, and cook 2 minutes. Stir in fennel fronds and remove from heat. Add salt to taste.

7. Divide evenly among 4 shallow bowls and drizzle with the extra-virgin olive oil.

PER 1-CUP SERVING 420 CAL., 47% (198 CAL.) FROM FAT; 15 G PROTEIN; 22 G FAT (3.1 G SAT.); 49 G CARBO (19 G FIBER); 515 MG SODIUM; 0 MG CHOL.

Garlic fried jasmine rice

SERVES 4
TIME 45 minutes, plus at least 2 hours to chill

In the Philippines, garlic fried rice is a staple for breakfast, but Tim Luym used to serve it for dinner too, at his former restaurant Poleng Lounge in San Francisco. He loves the chewier texture and higher nutritional content of brown jasmine rice compared with white.

1½ cups brown jasmine rice
1½ tbsp. plus 1 tsp. canola oil
1 tbsp. minced garlic
Kosher salt and freshly ground black pepper

1. Rinse rice thoroughly in a fine strainer under running water, then pour into a medium saucepan with 1¾ cups water. Bring to a boil over high heat. Reduce heat and simmer, covered, until water is absorbed, 15 to 18 minutes. Remove pan from heat and let stand, covered, 10 minutes.

2. Pour rice into a rimmed baking pan. Let cool, then chill, uncovered, until firm and dry, at least 2 hours.

3. Heat 1½ tbsp. oil in a 12-in. frying pan over medium-high heat. Add rice and heat, stirring gently, until hot, 1 to 2 minutes. With a wooden spoon, clear a space in center of pan; pour in remaining 1 tsp. oil and stir garlic into oil. Let garlic sizzle for about 30 seconds, then stir into rice to combine. Season to taste with salt and pepper.

TIMESAVER TIP Cook rice through step 2 up to 1 day before using; chill, covered.

PER SERVING 306 CAL., 21% (64 CAL.) FROM FAT; 5.7 G PROTEIN; 7.1 G FAT (0.8 G SAT.); 54 G CARBO (2.5 G FIBER); 5.3 MG SODIUM; 0 MG CHOL.

HOW TO PEEL A GARLIC CLOVE

Sometimes the garlic peel just doesn't want to come loose. A foolproof way to get it off is to smash the clove with the side of a chef's knife, then peel off the paper.

Sonia's special steaks

SERVES 4

TIME 30 minutes

These steaks, from reader Sonia Ottusch of Malibu, California, are a garlic lover's dream. Be watchful when cooking the garlic; just a few seconds too long and your garlic can go from golden brown to burnt, which would be a tragedy, as there is so much of it. (Photo on page 76.)

10 large garlic cloves, chopped
2 tbsp. olive oil
¼ cup *each* balsamic vinegar and soy sauce
2 beef rib-eye steaks (each about 1 in. thick
  and 20 oz., cut in half crosswise)
Kosher salt and freshly ground black pepper

1. Cook garlic in oil in a medium frying pan over low heat, stirring often, until golden, about 3 minutes. Drain garlic on paper towels; save oil for other uses.
2. Preheat oven to broil. Combine vinegar and soy sauce. Lay steaks flat and, using a paring knife, cut a 2-in.-wide pocket in the side of each steak. Spoon a quarter of the garlic into each pocket. Generously sprinkle steaks with salt and pepper.
3. Place steaks on broiler pan and spoon 1 tbsp. vinegar mixture over each. Cook steaks 4 in. from heat, turning once, 5 to 7 minutes total for medium-rare (cut to test). Serve with remaining vinegar sauce.

PER SERVING 409 CAL., 66% (270 CAL.) FROM FAT; 28 G PROTEIN; 30 G FAT (10 G SAT.); 5.3 G CARBO (0.2 G FIBER); 1,098 MG SODIUM; 87 MG CHOL.

Vietnamese-style spicy crab with garlic noodles

SERVES 4 to 6

TIME 1½ hours

Don't plan on kissing anyone after eating this garlic-laden creation. Frying the crab first is optional, but it adds superb flavor and makes the crabmeat more tender. The results will be even more transcendent if you start with raw crab: Get it freshly prepared from a fishmonger, use it immediately, and fry it a minute or two longer than cooked crab. (Photo on page 77.)

1 cup flour
1½ tsp. plus 1 tbsp. salt
1½ tsp. freshly ground black pepper
½ tsp. cayenne
2 Dungeness crabs, cooked, cleaned, quartered,
  and cracked
Vegetable oil for frying, plus 3 tbsp.
10 garlic cloves, chopped
½ lb. spaghettini (thin spaghetti)
3 tbsp. butter, at room temperature
6 small dried red chiles
2 tbsp. finely grated fresh ginger
4 green onions, chopped
4 serrano chiles, seeds and ribs removed,
  chopped
⅓ cup sake or other unseasoned rice wine
1 cup loosely packed basil, chopped
½ cup loosely packed mint, chopped
½ cup loosely packed cilantro

1. Combine flour, 1 tsp. salt, 1 tsp. pepper, and the cayenne in a large bowl. Pat crab pieces dry with paper towels and toss (in batches) with flour mixture. Remove crab and shake off excess flour. Set aside.
2. Heat 3 in. oil to 375° in a wok or large pot. Lay out paper towels for draining crab and garlic. Fry crab in batches (do not crowd wok) until golden, about 5 minutes per batch. Drain on paper towels.
3. Add garlic to oil and fry until golden brown, 2 to 3 minutes. Remove with a slotted spoon or small fine-mesh strainer and drain on paper towels. Set garlic aside; cool and discard oil.
4. Bring a large pot of water to a boil. Add 1 tbsp. salt and the spaghettini. Cook until tender to the bite, 5 to 10 minutes. Drain, transfer to a serving bowl, and toss with butter and half the fried garlic. Cover and put in a warm place.
5. Heat a wok or pot (large enough to hold all the crab) over high heat. Add remaining 3 tbsp. oil, the dried chiles, and ginger. Cook, stirring constantly, until fragrant, about 30 seconds. Add green onions, serrano chiles, and remaining ½ tsp. salt. Cook, stirring, until onions wilt, about 1 minute. Add sake and cook, stirring, until it is reduced by about half. Stir in crab, cover, and cook until crab is heated through, about 3 minutes.
6. Remove lid and cook, stirring, until any liquid evaporates. Stir in basil, mint, cilantro, and remaining ½ tsp. pepper. Cook, stirring, until herbs have wilted. Stir in remaining fried garlic. Transfer crab to a warm platter and serve hot with garlic noodles.

TIMESAVER TIP For a quicker version of this dish, skip steps 1 and 2 (frying the crab). Put 1 cup of the oil in a small saucepan over high heat and start recipe with step 3.

PER SERVING 610 CAL., 43% (261 CAL.) FROM FAT; 27 G PROTEIN; 29 G FAT (7.1 G SAT.); 56 G CARBO (4.2 G FIBER); 1,292 MG SODIUM; 105 MG CHOL.

ASIAN GREENS

Bok choy (*pak choi*)

WHY GROW THEM

Depending on where you live, you might not have ready access to these healthful and tasty greens. This category is a catchall for a number of different types of green leafy vegetables important to Asian cooking, and having them in your garden allows you to acquaint yourself and experiment with them in the kitchen.

EXTRA REWARD You get to harvest when you choose. Many Asian greens can be enjoyed as baby greens as well as mature leaves.

WHEN TO HARVEST

Harvest bok choy when loose headed and 10 to 12 inches tall. Harvest the central stalk and side shoots of Chinese broccoli when the stalk is 8 to 10 inches tall or flower buds are just beginning to form. You can start harvesting Chinese leaf mustard greens when the plants are just 2 inches tall and continue until the leaves turn tough or bitter. 'Tatsoi' and mizuna, both relatively tender, can be eaten cooked or—especially separated into leaves—in salad.

HOW TO KEEP

Bok choy (baby and mature) can be refrigerated, unwashed, in a plastic bag for up to 2 days. For other Asian greens, remove and discard damaged, yellowed, or wilted leaves. Rinse well under cold running water, shake off excess water, and pat dry. Wrap in paper towels and refrigerate in a plastic bag. Use most greens as soon as possible; mustard greens will keep up to 4 days.

Basic Ways to Cook

PAN-STEAM This method preserves the shape of small greens, whole or halved lengthwise. Remove and discard damaged, yellow, or tough leaves from 1 lb. fleshy Asian greens, 4 to 8 in. long, such as baby bok choy or small Chinese leaf mustard greens. If the head or stalk is thicker than 2 in. at the base, cut lengthwise into halves or quarters to make about 1 in. thick. Immerse in water and swish to dislodge grit; drain. Set a 5- to 6-qt. pan over high heat. When hot, add $1/2$ cup water and greens; cover and cook until barely tender to the bite, 3 to 5 minutes. Drain greens and pour into a serving bowl. If desired, drizzle with 2 tbsp. oyster sauce or soy sauce and 2 to 3 tsp. toasted sesame oil; sprinkle with 1 tbsp. toasted sesame seeds.

STIR-FRY To stir-fry individual leaves, such as 'Tatsoi' or mizuna, skip to last part of method. For sturdier, fleshier greens, remove and discard any damaged, yellow, or tough leaves from 1 lb. Asian greens, 4 to 8 in. long, such as mature bok choy or Chinese leaf mustard greens. Trim and discard tough stem ends. For tough stalks, remove any thick side stems attached to the center stalk; discard the center stalk and use stems. Rinse well. *For bok choy:* Cut leaves and stalks diagonally or crosswise into $1/4$-in.-thick slices; separate leaves from stalks. *For Chinese leaf mustard greens:* Trim stalk ends, especially if fibrous (a white, woody center is an indication). If the skin on the stalks is tough, peel and discard. Cut greens into 3-in. lengths, separating leaves and thin stems from thicker stems or stalks. If any pieces are thicker than $1/2$ in., cut to that thickness. Set a 14- to 16-in. wok or 12-in. frying pan over high heat. When hot, add 1 tbsp. *each* vegetable oil and garlic; stir until garlic begins to brown, about 15 seconds. Stir in thicker stem or stalk pieces and 3 tbsp. water. Cover and cook until stems are tender-crisp, 2 to 3 minutes. Uncover, add leaves and thin stems, and stir until leaves are barely wilted, 1 to 2 minutes. Add salt to taste and pour into a serving bowl.

Some of our favorite varieties

Baby bok choy Small, curvaceous, jade green heads (4 to 10 inches) with mellow flavor. Try 'Mei Qing Choi', a medium-size variety—tender, crisp, sweet, and mild, with a hint of mustard.

Bok choy (*pak choi*) Dark green leaves and smooth ivory stalks with a crisp, juicy texture and a mild, slightly cabbagelike flavor. 'Tatsoi' is a close relative but more compact with thinner stalks.

Chinese broccoli (*gai laan*) Similar in flavor and texture to regular broccoli, but with a slight mustardlike taste.

Chinese leaf mustard greens (*gai choy*) Several forms, with a mild-to-pungent mustard bite and jade green leaves and stems—some broad, smooth, and succulent with ruffled leaves; others thin with smoother leaves.

Mizuna With its decoratively serrated dark green leaves, it's a looker in the garden. Its mildly peppery flavor is great in stir-fries and salads. Shrinks rather a lot when cooked, like spinach.

Mustard greens and fontina filo pie

SERVES 9

TIME 2 hours

A twist on spinach pie, this flaky pastry makes for a tasty starter at any party.

2 lbs. Chinese mustard greens, thick ribs removed and leaves chopped (see Timesaver Tip, below)
1 tbsp. extra-virgin olive oil
½ tsp. *each* kosher salt and freshly ground black pepper
About ¼ cup unsalted butter, melted
6 sheets filo dough, thawed and cut into 7½-in. squares (to make 12)
8 oz. fontina cheese (preferably Italian), shredded

1. Cook greens in batches in a large pot of boiling water until tender, 1 to 2 minutes, and transfer batches to a bowl of ice water.
2. Preheat oven to 375°. Drain greens and squeeze as dry as possible. In a bowl, stir greens with oil, salt, and pepper.
3. Butter an 8-in. square baking pan and lay 1 filo square in bottom. Brush lightly with butter and top with 5 more squares, buttering each. Top with greens, then cheese. Repeat filo layering and buttering with remaining sheets, then cut through all the layers into 9 pieces. Bake until golden and crisp, about 55 minutes.

TIMESAVER TIP You can use 3 bags (10 oz. each) of chopped mustard greens instead; they'll be slightly chewier, though, since the ribs are included.

PER SERVING 219 CAL., 63% (138 CAL.) FROM FAT; 10 G PROTEIN; 15 G FAT (8.5 G SAT.); 12 G CARBO (3.4 G FIBER); 394 MG SODIUM; 43 MG CHOL.

GOOD FOR YOU
Most greens are high in vitamin K. Bok choy is also a good source of vitamins A and C and folate.

Asian greens and tofu soup

SERVES 6
TIME 1 hour

This nourishing soup gets most of its flavor from freshly made dashi, an easy, quick Japanese broth made from seaweed and flaked bonito fish—it's savory without tasting fishy. We like to use a combination of Asian greens, but spinach is fine too. Find kombu (dried seaweed) and bonito flakes at Asian markets and well-stocked grocery stores.

2 pieces kombu (dried seaweed; 4 in. each)
½ cup *each* dried bonito flakes and white or
    yellow miso
4 cups mixed Asian greens such as 'Tatsoi' and
    Chinese broccoli, coarsely chopped
3 cups bok choy leaves, coarsely chopped
2 bunches green onions, trimmed and thinly sliced
2 tsp. finely grated fresh ginger
1 package (12.3 oz.) extra-firm silken tofu,
    patted dry and cut into ½-in. cubes
Sriracha chili sauce (optional)
Toasted sesame oil (optional)

1. Make dashi: In a medium pan, soak kombu in 8 cups cold water for 20 minutes. Bring to a boil and add bonito. Remove from heat, let sit 5 minutes, then strain through a fine-mesh strainer into a large saucepan.
2. Whisk 2 cups hot dashi with miso in a bowl until smooth; stir back into pan of dashi.
3. Bring liquid to a gentle simmer (do not boil) and stir in greens, bok choy, green onions, and ginger. Once greens have wilted, stir in tofu and let simmer 5 minutes, then divide among bowls. Serve with chili sauce and/or sesame oil if you like.

PER SERVING 115 CAL., 24% (28 CAL.) FROM FAT; 10 G PROTEIN; 3.1 G FAT (0.4 G SAT.); 14 G CARBO (4.2 G FIBER); SODIUM N/A; 0 MG CHOL.

Spicy garlic grilled baby bok choy

SERVES 4

TIME 25 minutes

Having your own fresh source for baby bok choy is reason enough for growing a garden. Grilling the halved heads is a particularly tasty way of serving them.

2 tbsp. *each* reduced-sodium soy sauce,
   Asian chili garlic sauce, and canola oil
3 tbsp. unseasoned rice vinegar
1 tbsp. sugar
2 tsp. finely chopped garlic
4 heads baby bok choy (about 1 lb. total),
   halved lengthwise
¼ cup chopped roasted cashews

1. Prepare a charcoal or gas grill for direct medium heat (350° to 450°; you can hold your hand 5 in. above cooking grate only 5 to 7 seconds).

2. Make dressing: Combine soy sauce, chili garlic sauce, oil, vinegar, sugar, and garlic in a small bowl.

3. Set bok choy halves in a rimmed baking dish and brush with two-thirds of the soy-garlic mixture. Wrap bok choy tops with foil. Set bok choy directly on grill, cut side down, and cook, turning once, until slightly softened and streaked brown, 5 to 6 minutes.

4. Remove foil from leaves and set bok choy on a platter. Brush with remaining soy-garlic mixture and sprinkle with cashews.

PER SERVING 145 CAL., 68% (99 CAL.) FROM FAT; 3.6 G PROTEIN; 11 G FAT (1.3 G SAT.); 9.7 G CARBO (1.6 G FIBER); 498 MG SODIUM; 0 MG CHOL.

Fusilli with mustard greens and currants

SERVES 6
TIME 30 minutes

We've taken the classic Italian pasta combination of spinach, sweet dried currants, and garlic and kicked it up with robust mustard greens.

¾ lb. whole-wheat fusilli
⅓ cup pine nuts
2 tbsp. olive oil
4 garlic cloves, sliced
¼ tsp. red chile flakes
⅓ cup dried currants
¾ lb. Chinese mustard greens, thick ribs removed
   and leaves chopped
½ tsp. kosher salt
Freshly shredded parmesan cheese

1. Cook pasta in boiling water according to package instructions.
2. Meanwhile, toast pine nuts in a large, dry frying pan over medium heat; set aside. Add oil to pan, then add garlic and chile flakes. Cook, stirring, until fragrant, 1 minute. Add currants, the greens with rinsing water clinging to them, and salt. Cover; cook until greens are tender, about 5 minutes. Stir in drained pasta and pine nuts. Serve with parmesan.

PER SERVING 320 CAL., 26% (83 CAL.) FROM FAT; 12 G PROTEIN; 9.2 G FAT (1.3 G SAT.); 53 G CARBO (9.5 G FIBER); 116 MG SODIUM; 0 MG CHOL.

Chinese-style beef, sweet potato, and bok choy stew

SERVES 4

TIME 35 minutes

Chinese five-spice powder infuses this colorful stew with a warm, anise-y note.

4 large garlic cloves

1 piece fresh ginger (1 in. square), peeled, cut into chunks

1¼ lbs. beef rib-eye steaks (about 1½ steaks)

½ tsp. kosher salt

1 tbsp. vegetable oil

2 tsp. Chinese five-spice powder

3 cups reduced-sodium beef broth

2 tbsp. soy sauce

1 (12 oz.) deep orange–fleshed sweet potato (often labeled "yams")

12 oz. baby bok choy

2 green onions

1. Whirl garlic and ginger in a food processor until minced. Trim fat from steaks and cut across the grain into ¼-in.-thick slices, discarding pockets of fat. Sprinkle meat with half the garlic mixture and all of the salt.

2. Heat oil in a 5- to 6-qt. pot over high heat. Brown half the beef lightly all over, stirring occasionally, 3 to 6 minutes. With a slotted spoon, transfer meat to a plate. Repeat with remaining beef.

3. Reduce heat to medium. Add remaining garlic mixture to pan and cook until softened, about 30 seconds. Stir in five-spice powder, then broth and soy sauce. Peel sweet potato, halve lengthwise, and cut into ⅓-in.-thick slices. Add to broth. Cover and bring to a boil over high heat, then reduce heat and simmer 2 minutes.

4. Meanwhile, trim ends from bok choy, rinse, separate leaves, and cut into wide diagonal slices. Stir bok choy into stew and simmer just until wilted, about 2 minutes. Stir in beef and cook until hot, 1 to 2 minutes. Trim, then cut green onions into 3-in. slivers.

5. Ladle stew into bowls and garnish with onions.

PER SERVING 508 CAL., 62% (315 CAL.) FROM FAT; 30 G PROTEIN; 35 G FAT (13 G SAT.); 17 G CARBO (3 G FIBER); 1,285 MG SODIUM; 96 MG CHOL.

Pinot-braised duck with spicy greens

SERVES 4

TIME 2¼ hours

Michael Wild, cofounder and chef-owner of BayWolf restaurant in Oakland, loves duck with Pinot Noir, and here he pairs them right in the pot. Michael always recommends getting two bottles of wine for this dish: a reasonably priced Pinot Noir to cook with and the best one you can find—or a good red Burgundy—to drink with it (for drinking, he likes Pinot from Au Bon Climat, in Santa Barbara County, or Ponzi Vineyards, in Oregon's Willamette Valley). For a lighter sauce, we've substituted chicken broth for the rich duck stock he uses.

4 duck legs (about 8 oz. each)

Salt and freshly ground black pepper

1 tsp. herbes de Provence

About 1 bottle (750 ml.) Pinot Noir

2 tbsp. olive oil, divided

¼ cup minced shallots

4 cups reduced-sodium chicken broth

1 fresh thyme sprig

1 dried bay leaf

1 tbsp. butter

1 onion (about 8 oz.), chopped

1½ lbs. Chinese mustard greens, thick ribs removed and leaves sliced crosswise

2 garlic cloves, minced

1 flat anchovy (optional), minced

About ¼ tsp. cayenne

About 1 tbsp. fresh lemon juice

1. Preheat oven to 375°. Lay duck legs, skin side up, in a roasting pan that just holds them comfortably. Sprinkle with salt, pepper, and the herbes de Provence. Roast 1 hour.

2. Spoon fat from pan and save for other uses or discard. Pour wine over duck; it should be deep enough so meat is immersed but not so deep as to cover skin (skin should be exposed). Continue roasting until skin is golden red, about 30 minutes longer.

3. Meanwhile, pour 1 tbsp. oil into a 1½- to 2-qt. pan over medium-high heat; add shallots and cook, stirring often, until they begin to brown, about 2 minutes. Add broth, thyme, and bay leaf; boil, stirring occasionally, until reduced to about 1½ cups, about 45 minutes. When duck is done, add 1 cup braising liquid to broth mixture and boil, stirring often, until mixture has reduced by one-quarter, about 15 minutes. Pour through a fine-mesh strainer into a small pitcher or bowl.

4. While broth is reducing, prepare mustard greens: In a 12- to 14-in. frying pan over medium-high heat, melt butter with remaining 1 tbsp. oil. Add onion and cook, stirring often, until tinged with brown, about 7 minutes. Add half the greens, stir until wilted, then add remaining greens. Add garlic and anchovy if using and cook until fragrant, about 1 minute more. Remove from heat and season to taste with cayenne, lemon juice, and salt and pepper.

5. Mound greens on plates and set duck legs on top. Serve pan juices alongside.

PER SERVING 370 CAL., 47% (175 CAL.) FROM FAT; 33 G PROTEIN; 20 G FAT (5.4 G SAT.); 16 G CARBO (1.1 G FIBER); 537 MG SODIUM; 106 MG CHOL.

Chinese-style beef,
sweet potato,
and bok choy stew

STURDY GREENS

'Nero di Toscana' kale

WHY GROW THEM

Swiss chard, collards, broccoli rabe (rapini), kale, and other sturdy greens (sometimes called winter greens) are nutrient and antioxidant powerhouses. They're easy to grow and some, like Swiss chard and kale, are positively beautiful additions to the garden. They're incredibly versatile in the kitchen, possessing a wonderful range of flavors and textures: Swiss chard, which, depending on the variety, runs from mild and slightly smoky (green) to earthy (red), and is relatively tender; collards, with their robust, slightly bittersweet taste; and the many flavors of kale—nutty (ornamental kale), robust and herbaceous (green kale), full-bodied and grassy ('Lacinato' or dinosaur kale), or very strong and slightly bitter (purple kale). All are wonderful boiled or braised, and some (like kale) make vibrant, hearty salads.

EXTRA REWARD You get to decide when to harvest, meaning you can wait till the leaves get full size or pick the still-tender young leaves (great for salads).

WHEN TO HARVEST

A great way to harvest these greens is to pick the outer, oldest leaves. This allows the plant to keep growing and producing while you enjoy your harvest bit by bit. Wait until your plant is happily established with leaves maturing and new leaves growing out from the middle. Snap off outer leaves at their base, where they join the stem.

HOW TO KEEP

Discard any damaged, wilted, or yellowed leaves. **(Swiss chard)** Refrigerate, unwashed, in a plastic bag for up to 3 days. **(Other sturdy greens)** Rinse well under cold running water, shake off excess, and pat dry. Wrap in paper towels and refrigerate in a plastic bag. Use as soon as possible (within 4 or 5 days); sturdy greens will toughen as they age.

Basic Ways to Cook

BOIL **(Greens)** Coarsely chop or shred the greens. Boil, covered, in 1 in. water until tender to the bite, 5 to 15 minutes, depending on the green. **(Swiss chard)** From 1½ to 2 lbs. chard, cut the stems crosswise into ¼-in.-thick slices. In a wide frying pan, boil stems, covered, in ¼ in. water for 2 minutes. Add leaves and cook just until stems and leaves are tender-crisp, 1 to 2 minutes more.

STEAM **(Swiss chard)** Arrange sliced chard stems on a rack. Steam for 3 minutes. Add shredded or whole leaves and steam until tender-crisp, 2 to 4 minutes more.

PRESERVING THE HARVEST

FREEZE If you've got a bountiful harvest of greens, think about freezing some in premeasured amounts to add to soups and other preparations during the winter months. Cut the heavy stems off young leaves and wash well. Blanch collards in boiling water 3 minutes and all other greens 2 minutes. Drain, plunge into cold water to cool, drain again, and pack in resealable plastic freezer bags, leaving ½-inch headspace. Seal and freeze.

'Bright Lights' Swiss chard

Some of our favorite varieties

'Bright Lights' This Swiss chard has leaves ranging in color from green to burgundy, and stalks in various shades of yellow, orange, pink, purple, and red.

'Champion' An especially robust variety of collard greens.

'Fordhook Giant' A heavy-yielding variety of Swiss chard, with dark green leaves and white stalks.

'Nero di Toscana' A Tuscan heirloom kale with strappy, dark green leaves that form statuesque, upright plants. Also sold as 'Lacinato' or dinosaur kale. Very flavorful.

'Winterbor' A super-ruffled variety of kale; grows vigorously and stands up to cold temperatures. Its leaves turn sweeter after frost.

Orange, radicchio, and oregano salad
RECIPE P. 92

Vegetable minestrone
RECIPE P. 93

Orange, radicchio, and oregano salad

SERVES 6
TIME 25 minutes

The dressing for this salad relies on a smart low-fat cooking technique: Reduce the juice to concentrate its sweetness and create a thick texture, so you don't have to add much oil. (Photo on page 90.)

½ cup fresh orange juice
1 tbsp. extra-virgin olive oil
1 tsp. red wine vinegar
¾ tsp. kosher salt
1 tbsp. chopped oregano plus 2 tbsp. leaves
3 navel oranges
1 head radicchio, torn into pieces
½ cup thinly slivered red onion

1. Cook juice in a small saucepan over high heat until reduced to 2 tbsp., about 5 minutes; let cool. In a small bowl, whisk together juice, oil, vinegar, salt, and chopped oregano.
2. Cut ends, peel, and outer white membrane from oranges; slice into rounds. In a bowl, gently toss oranges, radicchio, onion, and oregano leaves with dressing to coat.

PER SERVING 71 CAL., 31% (22 CAL.) FROM FAT; 1 G PROTEIN; 2.6 G FAT (0.4 G SAT.); 13 G CARBO (1.8 G FIBER); 242 MG SODIUM; 0 MG CHOL.

Broccoli rabe and ham in ginger broth

SERVES 4 to 6
TIME 30 minutes

Spicy greens meet tender ham in this restorative soup.

About 5 cups chicken broth
6 slices fresh ginger
2 large garlic cloves, crushed
1 red chile, cut into rings
8 to 12 oz. broccoli rabe, Chinese mustard greens, or regular mustard greens, ends trimmed and cut into 2-in. lengths
1 cup thin, wide strips cooked ham

1. Simmer broth with ginger, garlic, and 2 to 4 chile rings in a large saucepan over medium heat for 8 to 10 minutes.
2. Add greens and ham and enough extra broth to cover greens. Bring to a boil, covered, and cook until greens are barely tender, 2 to 3 minutes.
3. Ladle soup into bowls and top each serving with more red chile rings if you like.

PER SERVING 85 CAL., 34% (29 CAL.) FROM FAT; 9.7 G PROTEIN; 3.2 G FAT (0.9 G SAT.); 6 G CARBO (0.3 G FIBER); 1,639 MG SODIUM; 23 MG CHOL.

Escarole and white bean soup

SERVES 4; makes 8 cups
TIME About 30 minutes

Wavy green escarole adds vivid color and complex flavor—without bitterness—to a simple, brothy white bean soup.

8 oz. escarole
1 tbsp. olive oil
1 onion (8 oz.), chopped
2 garlic cloves, minced
⅓ cup chopped prosciutto or Westphalian ham
5 cups reduced-sodium chicken broth
1 can (15 oz.) cannellini (white) beans, rinsed and drained
Salt and freshly ground black pepper
Grated parmesan cheese

1. Cut base off escarole; rinse and drain leaves. Cut leaves crosswise into ¼-in.-wide ribbons.
2. Set a 4- to 5-qt. pan over medium-high heat. When hot, add oil, onion, garlic, and prosciutto; stir often until onion is soft, 3 to 5 minutes.
3. Add broth and beans, cover, and bring to a boil over high heat. Stir in escarole and cook just until wilted, about 1 minute. Add salt and pepper to taste.
4. Ladle into bowls and serve with grated parmesan on the side.

PER SERVING 196 CAL., 25% (49 CAL.) FROM FAT; 19 G PROTEIN; 5.4 G FAT (1 G SAT.); 19 G CARBO (6.2 G FIBER); 360 MG SODIUM; 7.6 MG CHOL.

GOOD FOR YOU
Kale, collards, and Swiss chard are excellent sources of vitamins A (indispensable for vision), C, and K.

Vegetable minestrone

SERVES 10

TIME 1 hour

The variety of the vegetables and legumes, and the Italian trick of cooking a bit of parmesan rind in the soup for added flavor and richness create a palate-pleasing minestrone miles beyond the bland bean-and-pasta version. The soup is flexible too; add your favorite vegetables or use whatever is bountiful in your garden. (Photo on page 91.)

1 bunch Swiss chard

4 medium tomatoes

2 cans (15 oz. each) cannellini (white) beans, rinsed and drained, divided

2 tbsp. olive oil

4 garlic cloves, minced

2 medium carrots, cut into ¼-in. dice

2 medium zucchini, quartered lengthwise and cut into ¼-in. pieces

½ tsp. salt

½ cup dry white wine

2 cups shredded savoy or green cabbage

1 can (14.5 oz.) chickpeas (garbanzos), rinsed and drained

3- to 4-in. parmesan cheese rind

4 cups reduced-sodium chicken broth

About ½ cup freshly shredded parmesan cheese

1. Bring a large pot of water to a boil. Meanwhile, cut stems from Swiss chard leaves by making a V-shaped cut into each leaf around the stem. Finely chop stems, cut leaves into ribbons, and set both aside separately.

2. Boil tomatoes for 30 seconds. Lift out with a slotted spoon and rinse under very cold water. Remove skin with a paring knife or vegetable peeler. Cut tomatoes into quarters, remove seeds, and chop. Set aside.

3. Purée half the cannellini beans with ½ cup water in a blender until smooth. Set bean purée aside.

4. Cook oil and garlic in a large pot over medium-high heat until fragrant, about 2 minutes. Add carrots, zucchini, reserved chopped chard stems, and salt. Cook, stirring, until stems are tender, about 5 minutes. Add wine and cabbage. Cook, stirring, until cabbage wilts, 2 to 3 minutes.

5. Add reserved chard leaves, the whole cannellini beans, chopped tomatoes, bean purée, chickpeas, parmesan rind, and broth. Bring to a boil, then reduce heat to maintain a steady simmer. Cook until all vegetables are tender and flavors blend, about 15 minutes. Remove parmesan rind. Serve soup hot, topped with shredded parmesan.

TIMESAVER TIP This recipe makes a lot, but the minestrone freezes well, up to 3 months, ready to be defrosted for lunch or dinner.

PER SERVING 182 CAL., 28% (50 CAL.) FROM FAT; 11 G PROTEIN; 5.6 G FAT (1.4 G SAT.); 22 G CARBO (6.4 G FIBER); 694 MG SODIUM; 3.9 MG CHOL.

Sautéed broccoli rabe with garlic and chiles (*rape fritte*)

SERVES 8

TIME 50 minutes

Italian cooking teacher Rosetta Costantino of Oakland, California, re-creates her native Calabria in her steeply sloped vegetable garden. Using produce from her garden, she often makes this dish for Christmas Eve.

3 lbs. broccoli rabe

⅓ cup extra-virgin olive oil

8 garlic cloves, halved lengthwise if large

2 small dried red chiles, such as peperoncini, Thai, or Chinese, torn in half

½ tsp. kosher salt, plus more to taste

1. Trim broccoli rabe, removing tough parts of stems and any stems with a hollow core. Split stems (or quarter them if large). Rinse well.

2. Bring a large pot of water to a boil. Add broccoli rabe in batches if necessary (it wilts quickly) and cook until tender, 2 to 5 minutes. Set aside about ¼ cup cooking liquid, then drain broccoli rabe in a colander. Let sit until cool enough to handle, about 15 minutes, then squeeze gently to remove excess moisture.

3. Heat oil in a 12-in. skillet over medium heat. Add garlic and chiles and sauté until garlic is golden, about 1 minute. Add broccoli rabe and salt and toss to coat with oil. Increase heat to high and cook until broccoli rabe is heated through and flavorful, about 5 minutes (if it looks dry, moisten with some of the reserved cooking liquid). Season with salt to taste. Serve hot or at room temperature.

FLAVOR NOTE Blanching the broccoli rabe before sautéing removes some of its natural bitterness.

PER SERVING 109 CAL., 77% (84 CAL.) FROM FAT; 3.5 G PROTEIN; 9.3 G FAT (1.3 G SAT.); 6.1 G CARBO (0.1 G FIBER); 146 MG SODIUM; 0 MG CHOL.

Chard-stem
gratin

Chard-stem gratin

SERVES 4
TIME 45 minutes

Stems from Swiss chard are often mistakenly thought of as too tough or fibrous to eat. Actually, all they need is a bit of extra cooking to make them tender and sweet. Here is one of our favorite ways to use a lot of "leftover" stems. While this recipe calls for stems from two bunches of chard, it is adaptable to however many you have—just adjust the amount of cheese and bread crumbs proportionately.

1 tbsp. salt
Stems from about 2 bunches Swiss chard, trimmed of discolored ends
1 garlic clove, halved
1 tbsp. butter, softened, plus more for dish
½ cup panko (Japanese-style bread crumbs) or soft white bread crumbs (about 1 slice whirled in a blender or food processor)
½ cup freshly grated parmesan cheese

1. Preheat oven to 375°. Bring a large pot of water to boil. Add salt and chard stems. Boil until stems are tender to the bite, 10 to 15 minutes. Drain and set aside.
2. Rub a shallow medium baking dish with cut sides of garlic clove halves. Butter dish, then put in chard stems. In a sealable plastic bag, mix bread crumbs, parmesan, and 1 tbsp. butter. Sprinkle mixture on stems. Bake until top is browned and crisp, about 15 minutes. Serve hot or warm.

PER SERVING 113 CAL., 50% (56 CAL.) FROM FAT; 5.9 G PROTEIN; 6.2 G FAT (3.7 G SAT.); 8.7 G CARBO (1.6 G FIBER); 893 MG SODIUM; 16 MG CHOL.

Braised winter greens with bacon

SERVES 8
TIME About 1¾ hours

Old-fashioned long-cooked winter greens are pure comfort; sneak in some top-quality bacon and zippy mustard seeds, and they're worthy of a dinner party. This recipe is from cookbook author and co-owner of Robert Sinskey Vineyards, Maria Helm Sinskey.

8 slices (about 10 oz.) applewood-smoked bacon, chopped
4 tbsp. extra-virgin olive oil, divided
6 large garlic cloves, peeled
6 lbs. mixed winter greens, such as Swiss chard, mustard greens, and/or kale
About 2 cups reduced-sodium chicken broth
2 tbsp. *each* yellow mustard seeds and red wine vinegar
Kosher salt and freshly ground black pepper

1. Cook bacon in a large pot over medium heat, stirring often, until fat is rendered and bacon begins to brown, 10 minutes. With a slotted spoon, transfer bacon to paper towels to drain. Add 2 tbsp. oil and the garlic to pot; cook, stirring often, until garlic is golden, 3 to 5 minutes.
2. Meanwhile, rinse greens and trim off ends. Cut out tough center ribs and slice them crosswise into 1-in. lengths; quarter the leaves. Add ribs to pot and cook, stirring often, until they begin to soften, 6 to 7 minutes. In batches, add leaves to pot, stirring until all are wilted. Add 1¾ cups broth, the mustard seeds, and cooked bacon; cover and simmer until greens are tender to the bite, 45 minutes to 1 hour, checking occasionally to make sure liquid hasn't completely evaporated; add more broth if it has.
3. Drain greens (reserve liquid for other uses) and mound in a bowl. Stir in vinegar and salt and pepper to taste, then drizzle with remaining 2 tbsp. oil.

PER SERVING 338 CAL., 77% (261 CAL.) FROM FAT; 10 G PROTEIN; 29 G FAT (8.7 G SAT.); 14 G CARBO (5.5 G FIBER); 1,028 MG SODIUM; 24 MG CHOL.

Gorgonzola and radicchio risotto

SERVES 8
TIME 50 minutes

Let your radicchio stay in the ground during mildly frosty weather—it will get sweeter.

10 to 12 cups reduced-sodium chicken broth
3 tbsp. olive oil, divided
2 tbsp. plus 1 tsp. butter
1 medium onion, chopped (about 1½ cups)
2½ cups risotto rice such as Arborio
¾ cup dry white wine
¾ tsp. salt, divided, plus more to taste
1 small head radicchio
⅓ lb. gorgonzola dolce or other mild, creamy
    blue cheese, broken into pieces
½ tsp. freshly ground black pepper
¼ cup chopped flat-leaf parsley

1. Bring broth to a simmer in a medium pot. Keep at a simmer, covered, over low heat.
2. Heat 2 tbsp. oil and 2 tbsp. butter over medium heat in a heavy-bottomed 8-qt. pot. Add onion and cook, stirring occasionally, until translucent and beginning to turn golden, about 10 minutes. Add rice and cook, stirring constantly, until just edges of the grains look translucent, about 3 minutes.
3. Add wine and ½ tsp. salt and cook, stirring, until wine is completely absorbed by rice. Add about ½ cup hot broth to rice and cook, stirring constantly, until broth is completely absorbed by rice; reduce heat to medium-low if mixture starts to boil. Continue adding broth ½ cup at a time, stirring until each addition is absorbed before adding the next, until rice is just tender to the bite, 15 to 30 minutes (you will have broth left over). Keep rice at a constant simmer.
4. While rice is cooking, cut radicchio into shreds. Heat remaining 1 tbsp. oil in a large skillet over medium heat and add radicchio and ¼ tsp. salt. Cook, stirring occasionally, until wilted and tender, 2 to 4 minutes.

5. Remove rice from heat and stir in cheese, wilted radicchio, pepper, parsley, remaining 1 tsp. butter, and salt to taste. For a looser risotto, stir in 1 to 2 cups remaining broth.

PER 1-CUP SERVING 366 CAL., 37% (135 CAL.) FROM FAT; 12 G PROTEIN; 15 G FAT (6.7 G SAT.); 47 G CARBO (4.6 G FIBER); 1,229 MG SODIUM; 26 MG CHOL.

Swiss chard and sausage frittata

SERVES 8

TIME 30 minutes

This recipe, from reader Louise Carnes of San Anselmo, California, makes a good brunch or light dinner, accompanied by a salad.

2 tbsp. olive oil

2 Italian turkey sausages (8 oz. total), casings removed

½ cup *each* sliced red bell pepper, sliced mushrooms, and chopped onion

1 bunch Swiss chard, chopped

8 large eggs

½ cup shredded cheddar cheese

¼ tsp. kosher salt

1. Preheat broiler with a rack set 4 in. from heat. Heat oil in a large, ovenproof frying pan over high heat. Cook sausage, stirring often, until browned, 3 minutes. Add bell pepper, mushrooms, and onion and cook until vegetables are soft, 3 minutes. Stir in Swiss chard, reduce heat to medium, and cook, stirring occasionally, until wilted, 10 minutes.

2. Meanwhile, whisk eggs in a large bowl until starting to foam. Stir in cheese and salt. Pour mixture into pan with vegetables; cook on stove until the bottom sets, about 3 minutes.

3. Transfer pan to oven and broil until frittata is firm and browned, 3 minutes. Cut into 8 wedges and serve.

PER SERVING 195 CAL., 64% (124 CAL.) FROM FAT; 14 G PROTEIN; 14 G FAT (3.5 G SAT.); 4.4 G CARBO (1.2 G FIBER); 478 MG SODIUM; 236 MG CHOL.

Pappardelle with chicken and winter greens

SERVES 6

TIME 1 hour

Radicchio and chard are a good combination, but you can use any sturdy greens.

1 bunch (1 lb.) green Swiss chard
½ medium head radicchio
1 medium lemon
2 tbsp. olive oil
3 large garlic cloves, thinly sliced
½ cup reduced-sodium chicken broth
⅓ cup *each* dry sherry and whipping cream
1 cup shredded asiago cheese, divided
3 cups shredded skinned cooked chicken
    (from a 2½- to 3-lb. rotisserie chicken)
Salt and freshly ground black pepper
8 oz. dried pappardelle pasta

1. Bring a large pot of well-salted water to a boil over high heat. Meanwhile, trim stems and ribs from chard (save for another use, such as soup). Cut leaves crosswise into ⅓-in.-wide ribbons. Peel any rubbery outer leaves from radicchio and cut out tough core; discard both. Slice remaining leaves crosswise into ⅓-in.-wide ribbons. Zest lemon and set aside zest. Juice lemon and set aside 3 tbsp. juice.

2. Heat oil in a 12-in. frying pan over medium heat. Add garlic and cook until just translucent, about 2 minutes. Increase heat to medium-high. Add broth, sherry, chard, radicchio, and lemon zest. Turn to coat and cook until chard is just tender to the bite, 2 to 3 minutes. Add cream and half the cheese; stir to combine. Stir in chicken and cook until warmed through. Stir in lemon juice and season with salt and pepper.

3. Meanwhile, cook pappardelle in boiling water according to package directions. When pasta is cooked, drain and add to frying pan; use tongs to combine. Transfer pasta to a serving bowl, sprinkle with remaining cheese, and serve.

FLAVOR NOTE If you like your chard tender rather than tender-crisp, cook it longer in step 2 (take a piece from the pan and taste it).

PER 1½-CUP SERVING 448 CAL., 40% (180 CAL.) FROM FAT; 27 G PROTEIN; 20 G FAT (9.1 G SAT.); 35 G CARBO (2.4 G FIBER); 846 MG SODIUM; 94 MG CHOL.

Swiss chard pesto pasta

SERVES 4

TIME 15 minutes

Using fresh chard leaves in place of the usual basil is a great way to enjoy the classic sauce year-round. You could also try spooning the pesto over squares of pan-browned polenta instead of pasta. This recipe is from reader Wendy Skidmore of Los Altos, California.

2 large garlic cloves, peeled
2 cups loosely packed chopped Swiss chard leaves
½ cup chopped walnuts
¼ cup freshly grated parmesan cheese, plus parmesan shaved with a vegetable peeler
¼ cup *each* loosely packed flat-leaf parsley and olive oil
½ tsp. salt
¼ tsp. freshly ground black pepper
6 oz. whole-wheat angel hair pasta

1. Pulse garlic in a food processor to chop. Add chard, walnuts, grated parmesan, and parsley; whirl until finely chopped. Scrape down bowl. Add oil, salt, and pepper and process just until smooth.
2. Cook pasta in boiling water according to package directions. Drain, then toss with the pesto until well coated. Serve topped with shavings of parmesan.

PER SERVING 416 CAL., 56% (234 CAL.) FROM FAT; 12 G PROTEIN; 26 G FAT (3.8 G SAT.); 36 G CARBO (5.6 G FIBER); 503 MG SODIUM; 5 MG CHOL.

Steamed halibut packages

SERVES 6

TIME 1 hour

You'll need two bunches of chard to get enough large leaves to wrap the fish, and a two-tiered bamboo steamer to steam it. It's essential that the lemons be sliced paper-thin—a mandoline or very sharp knife works well. And because the halibut is the star of this recipe, make sure that you use the freshest fish available.

1 tbsp. salt, plus more to taste
2 bunches Swiss chard, stems removed and discarded
1 cup chopped flat-leaf parsley
2 tbsp. chopped thyme
8 tbsp. (1 stick) butter, divided
6 halibut fillets (each 6 to 8 oz. and about 1 in. thick)
Freshly ground black pepper
2 lemons, sliced paper-thin
2 tbsp. minced shallot
¼ cup fresh lemon juice

1. Bring a large pot of water to boil and add salt. Fill a large bowl with ice water and set aside. Select 12 largest chard leaves (save remaining chard for another use) and cook in boiling water 1 minute. With tongs or a slotted spoon, transfer chard to ice water.
2. Drain chard and spread leaves out on clean, dry kitchen towels.
3. Arrange one large leaf on work surface horizontally and arrange a second leaf on top of and perpendicular to the first. Sprinkle some of the parsley and thyme down center of leaves, then top with ½ tbsp. butter. Generously season halibut with salt and pepper and set 1 fillet on butter and herbs. Arrange 4 lemon slices over top of fillet. Fold chard leaves around fish to enclose. Place packet, seam side down, in a steamer basket large enough to hold

all 6 packets (or use a two-tiered bamboo steamer). Repeat with remaining fillets.

4. Fill a large, high-sided frying pan or a wok with enough water to come ¾ in. up sides, and bring water to a boil. Add steamer basket and cover. Steam fish until just cooked through, 6 to 8 minutes. Very carefully cut into one packet to check fish for doneness.

5. While fish is steaming, make beurre blanc: Put shallot and lemon juice in a small nonreactive saucepan over medium heat. Cook until liquid is reduced to 1 tbsp. Remove from heat and whisk in remaining 5 tbsp. butter, 1 tbsp. at a time, until emulsified. Season to taste with salt and pepper.

6. Serve fish packets topped with beurre blanc.

PER SERVING 396 CAL., 45% (180 CAL.) FROM FAT; 45 G PROTEIN; 20 G FAT (10 G SAT.); 11 G CARBO (4.5 G FIBER); 1,728 MG SODIUM; 105 MG CHOL.

Flank steak braciole

SERVES 4

TIME 1½ hours

Braciole is a traditional Italian braised beef dish usually stuffed with meat and cheeses. Ours is stuffed with greens. If you have any filling left over, serve it as a side dish or save for another night, to toss with pasta.

3 tbsp. olive oil

1 small onion, diced (about 1 cup)

2 garlic cloves, minced

½ tsp. anchovy paste

1 medium bunch kale, ribs removed and coarsely chopped (to yield about 4 cups)

3 cups chicken broth, divided

¼ cup grated romano or aged asiago cheese

¼ cup *each* dried currants and toasted pine nuts

¼ tsp. *each* salt and freshly ground black pepper, plus more to taste

1 flank steak (about 1½ lbs.)

2 tbsp. vegetable oil

1 cup dry red wine

1. Heat olive oil in a large frying pan over medium-high heat. Add onion and cook until lightly browned, about 3 minutes; add garlic and anchovy paste and cook 2 minutes more. Add kale and sauté until beginning to wilt. Stir in 1 cup broth and cook until most of the liquid has evaporated and greens are completely wilted, about 10 minutes.

2. Remove pan from heat and stir in cheese, currants, pine nuts, salt, and pepper.

3. Lay flank steak on a large piece of plastic wrap and top with a second piece of plastic wrap. Using a meat mallet or bottom of a heavy skillet, pound beef to an even thickness of ⅜ in. Discard top sheet of plastic wrap. Spread filling on beef in a ½-in.-thick layer, leaving a ½-in. border on all sides.

4. Roll beef around filling, beginning with a long edge and using plastic wrap as a guide, and place it on counter, seam side down. Tie beef with butcher's twine at 1-in. intervals, then tie one string around roll lengthwise so ends are tucked in and the filling is contained. Sprinkle beef generously with salt and pepper to taste.

5. Heat vegetable oil in a large high-sided frying pan over medium-high heat. Add beef and cook, turning, until well browned all over, about 8 minutes. Pour in wine and remaining 2 cups broth, cover, lower heat until liquid in pot is gently simmering, and cook 13 minutes.

6. Transfer beef from pot to a cutting board, cut off butcher's twine, and cover with foil. Bring braising liquid to a boil over high heat and boil until reduced to ½ cup, about 15 minutes. Slice beef into ½-in. slices and serve with gravy.

PER SERVING 619 CAL., 60% (369 CAL.) FROM FAT; 43 G PROTEIN; 41 G FAT (12 G SAT.); 21 G CARBO (3 G FIBER); 822 MG SODIUM; 94 MG CHOL.

TENDER GREENS

'Sea of Red' cutting lettuce, background; spicy mesclun mix, foreground

WHY GROW THEM

Because you can have fresh, flavorful greens ready when you are. You can choose from a veritable candy store of different types and varieties ranging in flavor from peppery, slightly bitter arugula to sweet, nutty mâche (also known as lamb's lettuce), and in texture from mature spinach (which will stand up to sautéing and braising) to tender young butter lettuces.

EXTRA REWARD Grow your own mesclun (baby lettuces) and microgreens. For mesclun, you can either buy a special seed mix (almost every seed company offers its own special blend) or grow your own mix of sweet and spicy greens. Snip the leaves off when they are 3 to 4 inches long. For microgreens, harvest when the plant forms its first set of true leaves, which follow the initial seed leaves (cotyledons).

WHEN TO HARVEST

This depends on the type of green. For heading lettuces and endive, you can pick leaves anytime from the seedling size on. Harvest the entire plant after heads form. For mâche and spinach, you can snip off outer leaves as the plants mature, or wait to harvest the whole clump. For arugula, cut tender young leaves; older, larger ones usually taste too sharp. Nip off and eat the flower buds or flowers as they appear.

HOW TO KEEP

Discard any wilted, damaged, or yellowed leaves. Rinse with cold water, shake off excess, and dry well. Layer between paper towels, roll up gently, and refrigerate your salad roll in a plastic bag—romaine up to 5 days, other greens up to 2 days.

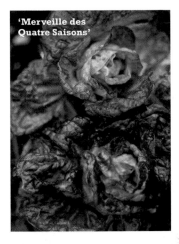

'Merveille des Quatre Saisons'

Some of our favorite varieties

'Black-seeded Simpson' A fast-growing, old-fashioned loose-leaf lettuce variety; has a pale green hue.

'Brunia' A French variety of red oak-leaf lettuce and one of the prettiest, with slender, deeply notched leaves tinged a reddish bronze.

'Forellenschluss' A loose-leaf romaine from Austria, its name is German for "speckled trout," an apt description for its red-speckled light green leaves.

'Green Curled' A variety of curly endive; very hardy.

'Little Gem' A smaller, fatter variety of romaine, with its characteristic crisp texture and flavor. Perfect for braising or grilling.

'Merveille des Quatre Saisons' (Marvel of Four Seasons) A French heirloom variety of red butterhead lettuce, with loosely cupped green leaves that are tinged with shades of ruby, rose-pink, and bronze.

'Sea of Red' Its long, narrow, tender leaves are a brilliant deep red. Makes a showstopping salad.

Basic Ways to Cook

GRILL Cut heads in half lengthwise, brush all over with olive oil, and lay on a grill preheated to medium-high (450°; you can hold your hand 5 in. above cooking grate only 4 to 5 seconds). Cook, turning once, until lettuces are softened and streaked brown, 6 to 10 minutes depending on the variety. Also works with heads of radicchio cut in half lengthwise.

STEAM Steam about 1½ lbs. spinach, covered, in the water that clings to leaves after rinsing, until wilted and bright green, 2 to 4 minutes.

STIR-FRY Use leaves whole or coarsely chopped. Stir-fry up to 5 cups lightly packed leaves, using 1 tbsp. oil, for 30 seconds. Cover and cook until leaves are wilted, 2 to 3 minutes more.

Spinach

Greek spinach dip

MAKES 2½ cups
TIME 20 minutes

This savory spinach dip takes its flavor cues from spanakopita. Serve it with warm pita bread or crisp crudités.

1 tbsp. minced garlic
¼ cup chopped shallots
4 green onions, chopped
2 tbsp. olive oil
12 oz. spinach, washed well and heavy stems trimmed
½ tsp. *each* salt and finely shredded lemon zest
2 tsp. fresh lemon juice
1 cup plain Greek-style yogurt
½ cup finely crumbled feta cheese
2 tbsp. chopped dill
Freshly ground black pepper

1. Cook garlic, shallots, and green onions in oil in a large frying pan over high heat until fragrant. Add spinach; cook until wilted.
2. Scoop spinach into a food processor using a slotted spoon; pulse until roughly puréed. Add salt, lemon zest and juice, yogurt, feta, and dill. Pulse once to mix. Add pepper to taste.

PER ¼-CUP SERVING 86 CAL., 69% (59 CAL.) FROM FAT; 3.7 G PROTEIN; 6.5 G FAT (3.2 G SAT.); 3.6 G CARBO (1 G FIBER); 227 MG SODIUM; 10 MG CHOL.

Creamy lettuce soup

SERVES 4; makes 7 cups
TIME 45 minutes

The French classic, rediscovered. It's a wonderful springtime soup.

1½ lbs. green lettuce, such as 1½ large heads romaine or 2 heads butter lettuce
2 large leeks (white and light green parts only), split lengthwise, rinsed well, and sliced
2 tbsp. butter
¼ tsp. freshly grated nutmeg, plus more for sprinkling
Finely grated zest of 1 lemon
¾ tsp. kosher salt
¼ tsp. freshly ground black pepper
1 qt. reduced-sodium chicken broth
½ cup half-and-half

1. Cut ribs from lettuce and chop. Chop leaves. Set both aside separately.
2. Cook leeks and lettuce ribs in butter in a 5- to 6-qt. pot over medium heat with nutmeg, lemon zest, salt, and pepper, stirring occasionally, until tender, about 10 minutes.
3. Stir in lettuce leaves and broth, cover, and bring to a boil over high heat. Reduce heat and simmer until lettuce is tender, 1 to 2 minutes.
4. Whirl soup in batches in a blender until very smooth, pouring as blended into a large bowl. Return soup to pot and stir in half-and-half. Heat, stirring, over medium heat until steaming (don't let it come to a boil), about 2 minutes.
5. Ladle soup into bowls or cups and sprinkle more nutmeg on top.

PER 1½-CUP SERVING 174 CAL., 48% (84 CAL.) FROM FAT; 9.7 G PROTEIN; 9.4 G FAT (5.9 G SAT.); 14 G CARBO (3 G FIBER); 832 MG SODIUM; 26 MG CHOL.

Arugula parmesan salad

SERVES 8

TIME 15 minutes

The addition of just a touch of balsamic vinegar enhances arugula's distinctive peppery flavor in this deliciously simple salad from cookbook author Martha Rose Shulman.

1 tbsp. plus 2 tsp. red wine vinegar

1 tsp. balsamic vinegar

1 small garlic clove, minced

6 tbsp. extra-virgin olive oil

Salt and freshly ground black pepper

10 to 12 oz. arugula

1 tbsp. chopped herbs such as chervil, tarragon, flat-leaf parsley, and chives

3 oz. parmesan cheese, shaved with a vegetable peeler

1. Whisk together both vinegars, the garlic, and oil in a bowl. Add salt and pepper to taste.

2. Put arugula in a large bowl and toss with herbs and dressing. Add parmesan, toss one more time, and serve.

PER SERVING 142 CAL., 82% (117 CAL.) FROM FAT; 4.8 G PROTEIN; 13 G FAT (3.3 G SAT.); 2 G CARBO (0.6 G FIBER); 181 MG SODIUM; 7.2 MG CHOL.

GOOD FOR YOU
Lettuces are high in vitamins A, C, and K—major contributors to good health. All the more reason to eat salad daily!

Eat-your-garden salad

SERVES 6

TIME 20 minutes

Tender greens—a mix of mild and spicy—freshly picked from your garden, plus flowers, take salad to a whole new level.

2½ tbsp. grapeseed, safflower, or canola oil

1 tbsp. unseasoned rice vinegar

½ tsp. kosher salt

¼ tsp. freshly ground black pepper

1 tsp. minced tarragon

1 Persian cucumber or ⅓ English cucumber

About 50 sugar snap peas

¼ cup loosely packed chervil sprigs (optional)

3 oz. mâche clusters (about 3 loosely packed cups)

4 oz. mesclun (about 6 loosely packed cups)

4 medium radishes, sliced in half lengthwise

Your choice of: bachelor's buttons (whole and petals), calendula and carnation petals, whole Johnny-jump-ups, nasturtium petals, pansy petals, and stock flowerets (15 to 20 whole flowers total)

1. Whisk together oil, vinegar, salt, pepper, and tarragon in a bowl.

2. Thinly slice cucumber. Split 30 of the fatter pea pods and remove the peas; set aside. Gently rinse chervil, mâche, and mesclun and gently spin twice in a salad spinner to thoroughly dry leaves.

3. Put greens in a large bowl and toss gently but thoroughly with 3 tbsp. dressing (leaves should be barely coated), adding more dressing if necessary.

4. Divide greens among plates. To each salad, add a few slices of cucumber, some sugar snap peas (both whole pods and just the peas), and some radishes. Drizzle with any remaining dressing if you like, and top with whole flowers and flower petals.

PER SERVING 67 CAL., 77% (51 CAL.) FROM FAT; 1 G PROTEIN; 5.7 G FAT (0.5 G SAT.); 3.2 G CARBO (0.5 G FIBER); 101 MG SODIUM; 0 MG CHOL.

Green goddess chicken wraps

SERVES 4

TIME 40 minutes

Stuffed with tender young spinach leaves and fresh herbs snipped right out of the garden, this brightly flavored wrap is a fine thing to eat for lunch in spring.

1 garlic clove, peeled
2 tbsp. *each* roughly chopped flat-leaf parsley, chives, and tarragon
1 tbsp. fresh lemon juice
2 tsp. capers
1 canned anchovy fillet
1 tbsp. white wine vinegar
1/2 cup *each* mayonnaise and sour cream
1/4 tsp. kosher salt
2 cups shredded skinned rotisserie chicken
4 whole-wheat burrito-size tortillas (11 1/2 to 12 in. wide)
1 yellow bell pepper, seeds and ribs removed, cut into strips
4 oz. mushrooms, thinly sliced
4 thin slices muenster cheese, cut in half
4 oz. baby spinach

1. Whirl garlic in a food processor until finely chopped. Add herbs, lemon juice, capers, anchovy, vinegar, mayonnaise, sour cream, and salt and whirl until well blended.
2. Toss chicken in a medium bowl with about 3/4 cup dressing until evenly coated.
3. Lay tortillas flat on a work surface. Arrange equal portions of chicken down the center of each. Evenly top chicken with bell pepper, mushrooms, cheese, and spinach, then drizzle 1 tbsp. more dressing over each wrap's filling (save remaining dressing for another use). Fold tortillas over short sides of filling, then roll up, starting from long side of filling.

PER WRAP 606 CAL., 55% (335 CAL.) FROM FAT; 34 G PROTEIN; 37 G FAT (11 G SAT.); 32 G CARBO (4.6 G FIBER); 714 MG SODIUM; 108 MG CHOL.

Grilled lettuces with manchego

SERVES 4

TIME About 20 minutes

'Little Gem', a type of miniature romaine lettuce, is great for grilling because its leaves are long and closely stacked rather than loose and floppy.

3 canned anchovy fillets, drained and finely chopped
2 1/2 tbsp. extra-virgin olive oil
1 tbsp. fresh lemon juice
Salt and freshly ground black pepper
2 'Little Gem' lettuces or 4 hearts of romaine
2 oz. manchego cheese, shaved into thin curls with a vegetable peeler
1 lemon, cut into wedges

1. Prepare a charcoal or gas grill for direct medium-high heat (about 450°; you can hold your hand 5 in. above cooking grate only 4 to 5 seconds).
2. With the flat side of a knife, mash anchovies to a paste. In a small bowl, whisk together oil, lemon juice, anchovy paste, and salt and pepper to taste.
3. Cut lettuces in half lengthwise, keeping leaves attached to cores. Brush all over with 1 1/2 to 2 tbsp. anchovy dressing.
4. Lay lettuces on grill; close lid on gas grill. Cook, turning once, until lettuces are softened and streaked brown, about 8 minutes.
5. Place lettuces cut side up on a platter. Drizzle remaining dressing over lettuces and top with manchego curls. Serve with lemon wedges.

PER SERVING 149 CAL., 79% (117 CAL.) FROM FAT; 6.2 G PROTEIN; 13 G FAT (4.8 G SAT.); 5.2 G CARBO (2.7 G FIBER); 206 MG SODIUM; 17 MG CHOL.

Grilled open-face ham, brie, and arugula sandwiches

MAKES 20 small sandwiches; serves 10 to 20 as an appetizer or 10 for lunch
TIME 20 minutes

Spicy arugula is the foil for rich, creamy brie in these grilled cheese sandwiches from reader Karen Biggs of Lake Forest Park, Washington. Serve them as an appetizer at your next backyard party.

¼ cup olive oil, plus more for grilling bread
Finely shredded zest and juice of 1 lemon
1 garlic clove, minced
1 tsp. sugar
Salt and freshly ground black pepper
20 slices (½ to ¾ in. thick) ciabatta (1 loaf)
1 lb. brie cheese, cut into ¼- by 2-in. slices
¾ lb. thinly sliced ham
8 oz. arugula

1. Put oil, lemon zest and juice, garlic, sugar, and salt and pepper to taste in a blender. Pulse to combine. Set lemon dressing aside.
2. Prepare a charcoal or gas grill for direct medium heat (350° to 450°; you can hold your hand 5 in. above cooking grate only 5 to 7 seconds). Brush bread on both sides with oil and sprinkle with salt and pepper. Grill 2 minutes. Turn bread over, top with cheese, close lid, and grill until cheese melts, 1 to 2 minutes. Transfer bread to a platter.
3. Top cheese evenly with ham. In a large bowl, toss arugula with reserved lemon dressing and arrange a handful on each sandwich. Drizzle any remaining dressing over sandwiches.

PER 2-SANDWICH SERVING 245 CAL., 59% (144 CAL.) FROM FAT; 12 G PROTEIN; 16 G FAT (4.9 G SAT.); 22 G CARBO (1.2 G FIBER); 580 MG SODIUM; 32 MG CHOL.

Devil's mess

SERVES 6
TIME 40 minutes

This is a big scramble of eggs, hot pork sausage, spinach, and chiles in which all the flavors remain distinct. It's from Big Sky Café in San Luis Obispo, California.

1 tbsp. olive oil
1 medium onion, chopped
8 oz. mushrooms, sliced
1/2 tsp. *each* kosher salt and freshly ground
    black pepper
1 cup chopped andouille sausage (about 6 oz.)
10 large eggs
1 tbsp. minced garlic (about 3 cloves)
1/4 tsp. red chile flakes, or to taste
6 oz. spinach (about 2 qts.), washed well,
    thoroughly dried, and heavy stems trimmed
Hot sauce (optional)

1. Heat oil in a large nonstick frying pan over medium heat. Add onion, mushrooms, salt, and pepper and stir often until onion is light golden, about 10 minutes.
2. Increase heat to medium-high, add sausage, and stir often until sausage has browned slightly and released some fat, about 5 minutes.
3. Meanwhile, whisk together eggs and 3 tbsp. water in a medium bowl.
4. Reduce heat to medium and add garlic and chile flakes. Stir until garlic is fragrant, about 1 minute. Add spinach to pan and toss with tongs until it has wilted, about 2 minutes. Transfer sausage-vegetable mixture to a bowl and wipe pan clean.
5. Add eggs to pan and scramble just until set, 4 to 5 minutes, then gently stir in sausage-vegetable mixture. Serve with hot sauce if you like.

PER SERVING 244 CAL., 63% (153 CAL.) FROM FAT; 17 G PROTEIN; 17 G FAT (4.9 G SAT.); 7 G CARBO (1.8 G FIBER); 463 MG SODIUM; 370 MG CHOL.

5 WAYS WITH MÂCHE

Sweet, nutty, and a little bit wild-tasting, mâche is a multi-tasker. Its delicate round leaves are good with spring's new little vegetables, but its hearty texture lets mâche work equally well as a cooking green. Here are some ideas for cooking with mâche:

Wilted salad Mix with chopped bacon, sliced mushrooms, and a little balsamic vinegar.

Pasta Toss with cooked noodles, garlic sautéed in olive oil, toasted walnuts, and shredded parmesan.

Sauce for chicken or fish Blanch for 30 seconds (keep pushing the mâche under water), then purée with white wine vinegar and chopped garlic sautéed in olive oil.

Soup Purée with sautéed onions and some chicken broth, then heat with a white sauce seasoned with freshly grated nutmeg; top with cooked shrimp or crab.

Side dish Braise in a little chicken broth for about 2 minutes, then spritz with fresh lemon juice.

Curried spinach with fresh cheese (*saag paneer*)

SERVES 6

TIME 1½ hours, plus at least 3 hours to press paneer

Paneer is a simple cheese that is easy to make at home. Its fresh flavor highlights the warm spices of this classic North Indian dish. Because *saag paneer* needs to cook for a long time so its flavors can develop, don't use baby spinach, which will fall apart; instead, go for more mature leaves. You can find garam masala at Indian markets and well-stocked grocery stores.

8 cups whole milk
¼ cup plus 1 tsp. fresh lemon juice
5 tsp. salt, divided
4 lbs. spinach, washed well and heavy
    stems trimmed
8 garlic cloves, peeled
2 onions, roughly chopped
2 serrano chiles, seeds and ribs removed
1 piece fresh ginger (3 in.), peeled and roughly
    chopped
2 tbsp. vegetable oil
Seeds from 7 cardamom pods
3 whole cloves
2 dried bay leaves
1 cinnamon stick
2 tbsp. ground coriander
1 tbsp. ground cumin
1 tsp. turmeric
1 canned tomato, chopped
¼ cup plain whole-milk yogurt
2 tsp. garam masala

1. Line a colander with 2 layers of cheesecloth and set in sink. Bring milk to a boil in a large pot over medium-high heat, stirring occasionally to prevent scorching. Let it boil 30 seconds (remove from heat if it starts to boil over) and stir in ¼ cup lemon juice. The milk will curdle, separating into cheese curds and a clear yellow whey. Pour into cheesecloth-lined colander.

2. Rinse curds with cold water. Pull up edges of cheesecloth, gently squeeze out as much water as possible, and form curds into a 6-in. disk. Put cheesecloth-wrapped disk on a large plate, top with a large cutting board, and weigh down with a heavy pot. Put in refrigerator and let press at least 3 hours and up to overnight.

3. Meanwhile, bring a large pot of water to a boil. Fill a large bowl with ice water and set aside. To boiling water, add 3 tsp. salt and the spinach. Cook 1 minute, then drain and transfer spinach to ice water. Swirl around to cool spinach and drain again. Use your hands to squeeze water from spinach. Set aside.

4. Whirl garlic, onions, chiles, ginger, and ¼ cup water in a blender to make a paste. Set aside.

5. Heat oil in a medium pot over medium-high heat. Add cardamom, cloves, bay leaves, and cinnamon and cook until spices darken, about 2 minutes. Add reserved onion paste. Cook, stirring occasionally, until mixture thickens and darkens, about 15 minutes. If mixture starts to stick, add 1 tbsp. water at a time, stirring, to help loosen it.

6. Stir in coriander, cumin, and turmeric. Cook until fragrant, about 2 minutes. Add tomato and yogurt. Cook until thickened slightly, about 3 minutes. Stir in spinach and remaining 2 tsp. salt. Turn heat to low and cover. Cook, stirring occasionally, until flavors are blended, about 30 minutes.

7. Cut paneer into ½-in. cubes and gently stir into spinach mixture. Cook until paneer is heated through, about 2 minutes. Add garam masala and remaining 1 tsp. lemon juice. Adjust salt and lemon juice to taste. Serve hot, with flatbread or rice.

PER SERVING 337 CAL., 45% (153 CAL.) FROM FAT; 19 G PROTEIN; 17 G FAT (7.7 G SAT.); 33 G CARBO (6.9 G FIBER); 1,233 MG SODIUM; 47 MG CHOL.

Arugula pesto farfalle

SERVES 4
TIME 30 minutes

This recipe from reader Mary Hainley of West Linn, Oregon, is proof you don't have to sacrifice flavor for speed. Arugula, lemon zest, walnuts, gorgonzola, and raisins combine for a tasty interplay of peppery, sweet, rich, earthy, and toasty.

12 oz. farfalle pasta

2 cups baby arugula

1 tbsp. *each* finely shredded lemon zest and minced garlic

1 cup walnut pieces, toasted (see Flavor Note, below), divided

3 tbsp. olive oil

½ tsp. kosher salt

¼ tsp. freshly ground black pepper

¾ cup crumbled gorgonzola cheese

½ cup golden raisins

1. Cook pasta according to package directions.
2. Whirl together arugula, lemon zest, garlic, ¼ cup walnuts, the oil, salt, and pepper in a food processor until blended, scraping down the bowl as needed.
3. Drain pasta, reserving about ¼ cup of cooking water. Return pasta to pot and add pesto, stirring to coat. Stir in remaining ¾ cup walnuts, the cheese, raisins, and reserved pasta water.

FLAVOR NOTE Toasting nuts increases their flavor and crunch. Spread the nuts in a single layer in a baking pan and toast in a 350° oven until golden, 5 to 15 minutes, depending on the type of nut.

PER 1½-CUP SERVING 740 CAL., 45% (335 CAL.) FROM FAT; 22 G PROTEIN; 37 G FAT (8.1 G SAT.); 84 G CARBO (6.5 G FIBER); 535 MG SODIUM; 19 MG CHOL.

Crisp lettuces with Asian noodles

SERVES 4
TIME About 35 minutes

Use crunchy lettuces like 'Sierra', a bronze-tinged iceberg cousin, and a red romaine like 'Ruben's Red'— or a mix of iceberg and romaine.

8 oz. capellini or angel hair pasta, broken into about 2-in. lengths

3 tbsp. seasoned rice vinegar

2 tbsp. peanut oil

1 tbsp. *each* toasted sesame oil and Asian chili oil

1 package (8 oz.) savory baked tofu, such as five-spice flavored, cut into ½-in. cubes

8 oz. crisp lettuces, cut crosswise into ¼-in.-wide strips

1 cup loosely packed cilantro

1 cup chopped salted roasted peanuts

Soy sauce

1. Cook pasta according to package directions; drain.
2. Meanwhile, stir together vinegar, peanut oil, sesame oil, and chili oil in a large serving bowl.
3. Add hot noodles to bowl. Gently stir with oil mixture, then add tofu, lettuces, cilantro, and peanuts and toss lightly to coat. Season each serving to taste with soy sauce.

PER SERVING 646 CAL., 50% (324 CAL.) FROM FAT; 29 G PROTEIN; 36 G FAT (5 G SAT.); 56 G CARBO (6.7 G FIBER); 623 MG SODIUM; 0 MG CHOL.

Lettuce fried rice with ham and eggs

SERVES 4

TIME 25 minutes

This is a wonderful way to make use of leftover ham.

1 tbsp. minced fresh ginger

2 tsp. minced garlic

2 tbsp. vegetable oil, divided

3 large eggs, lightly beaten

3/4 cup diced baked ham or Black Forest ham

4 cups cold cooked white rice

1 large head butter lettuce, chopped

1 tbsp. soy sauce, plus more for serving

1. Combine ginger and garlic. Put 1 tsp. of mixture in a 12-in. nonstick frying pan with 1 tbsp. oil and cook over medium-high heat until sizzling, about 2 minutes. Add eggs, then cook, stirring often, until set, 3 minutes; transfer from pan to a bowl.

2. Put remaining ginger mixture in pan with ham and stir-fry until garlic is softened, about 2 minutes. Add remaining 1 tbsp. oil and the rice and cook, stirring often, until hot, 3 to 4 minutes. Add lettuce and cook, tossing gently, until wilted, about 2 minutes. Stir in eggs. Season with soy sauce and serve more at the table if you like.

PER 1³/4-CUP SERVING 347 CAL., 31% (108 CAL.) FROM FAT; 14 G PROTEIN; 12 G FAT (2.3 G SAT.); 45 G CARBO (0.5 G FIBER); 565 MG SODIUM; 170 MG CHOL.

Spinach salad with sesame tofu

SERVES 4 as a main course
TIME 30 minutes

Instead of the usual chicken, steak, or shrimp, we used crunchy cubes of sautéed tofu for this salad. The spicy, tart dressing pulls it all together. Look for *furikake* (a Japanese sesame and seaweed blend) in the Asian foods section of most large supermarkets.

14 oz. firm tofu, cut into ½-in. slices
¼ cup plus 1½ tbsp. grapeseed or vegetable oil
½ cup cornstarch
¼ cup furikake or a mix of black and white
    sesame seeds
1 celery stalk
½ tart green apple, such as Granny Smith
8 to 10 radishes
1½ tsp. Asian chili garlic sauce
1½ tbsp. unseasoned rice vinegar
1½ qts. loosely packed baby spinach
½ tsp. kosher salt

1. Lay tofu between paper towels to dry. Heat ¼ cup oil in a large frying pan over medium-high heat until shimmering.
2. Spread cornstarch on a rimmed baking sheet and furikake on another. Stack tofu and cut into ½-in. cubes. Lightly toss tofu in cornstarch, then quickly but thoroughly roll and press in furikake. Fry in 2 batches until well browned and crunchy, about 20 minutes total, and drain on paper towels.
3. Slice celery, core and dice apple, and cut radishes into thin wedges. In a big salad bowl, whisk remaining 1½ tbsp. oil with chili garlic sauce and vinegar. Add celery, apple, radishes, spinach, salt, and tofu and toss to coat.

PER SERVING 379 CAL., 58% (219 CAL.) FROM FAT; 11 G PROTEIN; 25 G FAT (2.3 G SAT.); 29 G CARBO (5.1 G FIBER); 546 MG SODIUM; 0 MG CHOL.

PEAS

'Super Sugar Mel'

WHY GROW THEM

Bright green peas, with their fresh flavor and sweet crunch, are one of the most welcome signs of spring. They're delicious in all their guises—sturdy sugar snaps, translucent young snow peas, and delicate English (shelling) peas. Easy to grow, they're also a superb garden snack, snapped right off the vine—sweet and juicy.

EXTRA REWARD Pea shoots. You want only sweet, new growth. Take a bite of the shoots and tendrils—if they are tough and stringy, strip off the tender leaves and stems and discard the rest. Add pea shoots to stir-fries, soups, and pastas (cook just until they wilt), or salads.

WHEN TO HARVEST

When peas reach harvesting size, pick all the pods that are ready; if the seeds (the peas inside) are allowed to ripen, the plant will stop producing. The vines are brittle; steady them with one hand while picking with the other. **(Shelling peas)** Begin harvesting when the pods have swelled to almost a cylindrical shape but before they lose their bright green color. **(Edible-pod peas)** Pick snow peas when they're 2 to 3 inches long, before the seeds begin to swell; pick snap peas after the pods have filled out.

HOW TO KEEP

Eat both shelling and edible-pod peas immediately; like corn, they begin converting their sugar to starch as soon as they are picked. If you must keep them, refrigerate, unwashed, in a plastic bag up to 3 days.

'Oregon Giant'

Some of our favorite varieties

SHELLING PEAS

'Blauwschokkers' A beautiful purple-podded heirloom shelling pea, originally from Holland, with lovely flowers in pale and deep purple. The peas themselves are a vivid green, and are tasty but rather starchy; great for soup.

'Caselode' Very nice sweet flavor.

'Mr. Big' Extra-sweet, extra-big peas.

'Waverex' A petits pois variety, it produces 2- to 3-in.-long pods that each contain 6 to 9 small peas.

EDIBLE-POD PEAS

'Mammoth Melting Sugar' An heirloom sugar snap pea.

'Oregon Giant' A bush-type snow pea that produces extra-large pods.

'Super Sugar Mel' This sugar snap pea boasts sweet, crunchy pods.

'Super Sugar Snap', 'Sugar Ann', 'Sugar Sprint' These three varieties combine the qualities of shelling peas and edible-pod peas. You can eat the immature pods, peas and all, or wait for the peas to mature and harvest them for shelling.

Basic Ways to Cook

BLANCH Bring water to a boil in a large pot, then add peas. Cook just until they start to turn a brighter green, 15 to 30 seconds, then drain immediately. Rinse well under cold running water until cool, then drain again.

BOIL (Shelling peas) Boil 2 lbs. shelled peas, covered, in ½ in. water just until tender, 5 to 10 minutes. **(Edible-pod peas)** Boil 1 lb. peas, uncovered, in 3 qts. water until tender-crisp, about 30 seconds.

STEAM For either type of pea, arrange on a steamer rack and steam until shelling peas are tender, 8 to 12 minutes, or snow or sugar snap peas are tender-crisp, 3 to 5 minutes.

SAUTÉ (Shelling peas) Melt 1 to 2 tbsp. butter. Add up to 5 cups shelled peas and cook, stirring, 1 minute. Add 3 to 4 tbsp. liquid of your choice, cover, and cook just until tender, 2 to 3 minutes more. **(Edible-pod peas)** Melt 1 to 2 tbsp. butter. Add up to 5 cups snow or sugar snap peas and cook, stirring, 3 minutes. Add 1 tbsp. liquid of your choice, cover, and cook until tender-crisp, 30 seconds more.

Snow pea salad with sesame dressing

SERVES 4 to 6

TIME About 15 minutes, plus at least 1 hour to chill

Crunchy and easy to make, this is an excellent side for grilled foods with Asian flavors.

1 lb. snow peas, ends trimmed and blanched (page 119)

3 tbsp. vegetable oil

2 tbsp. soy sauce

1½ tbsp. toasted sesame oil

2 tsp. finely grated fresh ginger

1 tsp. sugar

½ tsp. hot Chinese mustard

2 tbsp. thinly sliced green onions, divided

1 tsp. sesame seeds

1. Stack several snow peas and slice on the diagonal into ¼-in.-wide strips. Repeat to slice remaining peas.

2. Whisk vegetable oil, soy sauce, sesame oil, ginger, sugar, and mustard in a large bowl until well combined. Add sliced snow peas and 1 tbsp. green onions; mix to coat. Cover and chill until cold, at least 1 hour or up to 1 day.

3. Just before serving, mound salad on a platter and sprinkle with remaining 1 tbsp. green onions and the sesame seeds.

PER SERVING 132 CAL., 75% (99 CAL.) FROM FAT; 2.5 G PROTEIN; 11 G FAT (1.4 G SAT.); 7.2 G CARBO (2 G FIBER); 352 MG SODIUM; 0 MG CHOL.

Icebox salad

SERVES 12 as a first course or side dish

TIME 45 minutes, plus at least 2 hours to chill

The top layers of chopped vegetables keep the dressing from soaking and wilting the bottom layer of lettuce. This salad improves after a few hours in the refrigerator; the dressing works its way into the peas, cucumbers, and radishes, the flavors meld, and the vegetables become sweeter.

2 cups plain low-fat yogurt

1 small head romaine lettuce

10 oz. sugar snap peas, ends trimmed

1 bunch radishes (about 12)

1 English cucumber

4 green onions

2 cups shelled fresh peas (about 2 lbs. in pod)

1¾ tsp. salt, divided

3 tbsp. olive oil

¼ tsp. freshly ground black pepper

2 tbsp. minced dill

4 large mint leaves, minced

½ cup finely chopped chives (about 1 bunch)

1. Line a fine-mesh strainer with 2 layers of cheesecloth and put strainer over a bowl. Put yogurt in strainer, cover with plastic wrap, and chill 30 minutes.

2. Tear romaine into bite-size pieces. Arrange evenly in a 9- by 13-in. baking pan or other 3-qt. dish.

3. Chop sugar snap peas and arrange evenly on top of lettuce. Trim and thinly slice radishes. Arrange them on top of sugar snap peas.

4. Peel cucumber, halve lengthwise, and, using a spoon, scoop out and discard pulpy flesh and small seeds in the center. Cut each in half lengthwise again and chop. Arrange cucumber on top of radishes. Trim green onions, thinly slice white and light green parts, and sprinkle evenly on top of cucumber.

5. Bring a large saucepan of water to a boil. Add shelled peas and 1 tsp. salt. Boil for 1 minute, drain, and plunge peas into ice water to stop cooking. Drain peas. Dry peas thoroughly on paper towels and sprinkle evenly over green onions.

6. Transfer yogurt to a bowl (discard liquid beneath strainer). Stir in oil, remaining ¾ tsp. salt, and the pepper, then stir in dill and mint. Spread yogurt mixture evenly over salad and sprinkle with chives. Cover with plastic wrap and chill for at least 2 hours and up to overnight. Serve cold, cut into 12 pieces.

PER SERVING 95 CAL., 39% (37 CAL.) FROM FAT; 4.7 G PROTEIN; 4.2 G FAT (0.8 G SAT.); 10 G CARBO (2.5 G FIBER); 205 MG SODIUM; 2.3 MG CHOL.

BASIC WAYS TO PREP

Shelling peas Break open the pod by squeezing one end; the pod should pop open at the seam. Then run your thumb down the opening to release the peas. One pound of peas in the pod yields approximately 1 cup shelled peas.

Edible-pod peas Cut or snap off ends and pull up sharply to remove any strings on the pea. Discard ends and strings.

Icebox salad

Grilled chicken and
pea shoot charmoula
sandwich

Pea pod soup with lemon crème fraîche

SERVES 4 to 6; makes 2 qts.
TIME 1½ hours

The fresh flavor of garden peas is accented here by the bright citrus punch of the lemon crème fraîche. If you can't find crème fraîche, substitute sour cream, omit the lemon juice, and add one more teaspoon lemon zest.

2 lbs. fresh peas in pod
2 tbsp. butter
1 cup *each* chopped shallots and dry white wine
1 qt. chicken broth
½ cup *each* basmati rice and crème fraîche
1 tsp. finely shredded lemon zest
2 tsp. fresh lemon juice
Salt and freshly ground black pepper

1. Cut off and discard tough ends from pods; pull off and discard strings. Shell peas. Reserve pods; blanch peas (page 119) and reserve.
2. Melt butter in a 4- to 5-qt. pan over medium heat. When it is foamy, add shallots and stir until limp, about 3 minutes. Add wine, increase heat, and boil, stirring, until about half the liquid has evaporated. Add pea pods, broth, and 3 cups water; reduce heat, cover, and simmer for 20 minutes. Add rice and cook until pods are tender, 25 minutes more.
3. Stir together crème fraîche and lemon zest and juice in a small bowl.
4. Working in small batches, transfer pod mixture to a blender; whirl until nearly smooth. (The tough bits of pea pods may catch on blade; stop motor and remove blender jar to clean blade.) Pour soup through a fine-mesh strainer into a 4- to 5-qt. pan, pressing on solids to extract liquid; discard solids.

5. Stir in half the lemon crème fraîche; add salt and pepper to taste. Set over medium heat and stir occasionally until soup is steaming. Add blanched peas. Ladle soup into bowls and top each with remaining lemon crème fraîche.

PER SERVING 250 CAL., 43% (108 CAL.) FROM FAT; 11 G PROTEIN; 12 G FAT (7.1 G SAT.); 26 G CARBO (2.7 G FIBER); 118 MG SODIUM; 27 MG CHOL.

Grilled chicken and pea shoot charmoula sandwiches

SERVES 4 to 5
TIME 25 minutes, plus at least 1 hour to marinate

Before grilling, the chicken is marinated in charmoula—a potent North African flavor paste made with cilantro, garlic, olive oil, and lemon juice.

½ cup extra-virgin olive oil
¼ cup fresh lemon juice
1 tsp. kosher salt
½ tsp. *each* freshly ground black pepper and ground cumin
2 tsp. smoked Spanish paprika (pimentón de La Vera; see Flavor Note, page 131)
2 garlic cloves, minced
⅓ cup chopped cilantro
1 lb. boned, skinned chicken breast halves
4 or 5 ciabatta or francese sandwich rolls (12 oz. total), split
1 carrot, cut into long shreds, preferably with a mandoline
1 qt. loosely packed tender pea shoots, separated into 4- to 5-in. pieces
⅓ cup mayonnaise

1. Stir together oil, lemon juice, salt, pepper, cumin, paprika, garlic, and cilantro in a medium bowl to make charmoula. Transfer 6 tbsp. to a small bowl and set aside.
2. Pull off tenders (the long, small, tenderloin muscles) from chicken. Add chicken (including tenders) to charmoula in medium bowl and turn to coat. Chill chicken and reserved charmoula, covered, about 1 hour and up to 1 day, turning chicken once.
3. Prepare a charcoal or gas grill for direct high heat (450° to 550°; you can hold your hand 5 in. above cooking grate only 2 to 4 seconds). Grill chicken, covered, turning over once, until cooked through, 4 to 10 minutes; discard marinade. Transfer chicken to a board, let it rest briefly, then slice diagonally. Grill rolls, cut side down, until toasted, 1 minute.
4. Spoon 2 tbsp. reserved charmoula into a clean medium bowl, add carrot and pea shoots, and toss gently. Spoon 1½ tbsp. more charmoula into a small dish and set aside. Whisk mayonnaise into charmoula remaining in small bowl and spread over cut sides of rolls.
5. Fill rolls with pea shoot salad and arrange chicken on top. Spoon about 1 tsp. reserved charmoula (from small dish) over chicken on each sandwich.

PER SANDWICH 635 CAL., 45% (285 CAL.) FROM FAT; 33 G PROTEIN; 32 G FAT (5.3 G SAT.); 61 G CARBO (1.9 G FIBER); 727 MG SODIUM; 58 MG CHOL.

GOOD FOR YOU
A lot of nutrition is packed into peas and their pods, including vitamins C and K, folate, and fiber.

Three peas with leeks,
mint, and cream
RECIPE P. 126

Ravioli with snap peas,
pea shoots, and minty
pea shoot pesto
RECIPE P. 126

Three peas with leeks, mint, and cream

SERVES 4 to 6
TIME About 30 minutes

Using all three types of peas makes this side special, but it's also delicious with any single type or two combined. Serve with salmon or a simple roast chicken. (Photo on page 124.)

8 oz. sugar snap peas
4 oz. snow peas
1 cup shelled fresh peas (about 1 lb. in pods)
1 leek (white and pale green parts only), halved lengthwise
2 tbsp. butter
1/2 cup whipping cream
Salt and freshly ground black pepper
1/4 cup slivered mint, divided

1. Trim sugar snap and snow peas, then blanch (page 119) along with shelled fresh peas.
2. Rinse leek well, flipping layers under running water to remove grit. Thinly slice crosswise.
3. Melt butter in a large frying pan over medium heat. When it's foamy, add leek and stir until soft, about 5 minutes. Pour in cream, increase heat to medium-high, and stir often until liquid is reduced by about half, 3 to 4 minutes. Add salt and pepper to taste.
4. Add all the peas and half the mint and stir just until heated through, about 1 minute. Pour into a serving bowl and sprinkle with remaining mint.

PER SERVING 147 CAL., 61% (90 CAL.) FROM FAT; 3.6 G PROTEIN; 10 G FAT (6.2 G SAT.); 11 G CARBO (2.8 G FIBER); 52 MG SODIUM; 32 MG CHOL.

Scallop and snow pea stir-fry

SERVES 4
TIME 20 minutes

Creamy scallops and crisp snow peas make a wonderful contrast of tastes and textures in a dish that comes together in just minutes.

1 tbsp. vegetable oil
2 tbsp. *each* minced garlic and fresh ginger
1 lb. large sea scallops, halved crosswise
8 oz. snow peas, ends trimmed
1/2 cup reduced-sodium chicken broth
3 tbsp. reduced-sodium soy sauce
2 tbsp. chopped green onions
About 6 oz. thin dried Asian egg or wheat noodles, cooked according to package directions and drained

Heat oil in a large wok or nonstick frying pan over medium-high heat. Add garlic and ginger and cook, stirring, until fragrant, about 30 seconds. Add scallops and stir to coat with garlic mixture, then cook 1 minute. Mix in snow peas and cook 1 minute. Stir in broth and soy sauce and cook just until simmering. Sprinkle with green onions and mix with noodles.

PER SERVING 315 CAL., 16% (49 CAL.) FROM FAT; 27 G PROTEIN; 5.4 G FAT (0.5 G SAT.); 43 G CARBO (7.4 G FIBER); 708 MG SODIUM; 37 MG CHOL.

Ravioli with snap peas, pea shoots, and minty pea shoot pesto

SERVES 4
TIME 30 minutes

Both sugar snap peas and their tender young shoots are combined with fresh mint and cheese ravioli for an easy and original dinner. (Photo on page 125.)

1 small garlic clove, peeled
4 oz. parmesan cheese, cut into chunks
1 1/2 qts. loosely packed tender pea shoots, separated into 4- to 5-in. pieces, divided
1/2 cup *each* loosely packed mint and extra-virgin olive oil
1 lb. fresh cheese ravioli
2 cups sugar snap peas, ends trimmed

1. Mince garlic in a food processor. Add parmesan and whirl until grated. Add 2 cups pea shoots, the mint, and oil; pulse until coarsely puréed. Scrape into a small bowl and press plastic wrap against pesto.
2. Cook ravioli according to package directions, adding snap peas during last 2 minutes. Drain; return to pot. Whisk pesto, then gently toss three-quarters of it with pasta. Add remaining pea shoots and toss gently. Serve immediately, with remaining pesto if you like (or save it for a sandwich).

PER SERVING 842 CAL., 40% (338 CAL.) FROM FAT; 38 G PROTEIN; 39 G FAT (13 G SAT.); 96 G CARBO (4.3 G FIBER); 827 MG SODIUM; 84 MG CHOL.

Scallop and snow
pea stir-fry

PEPPERS

Jalapeños

WHY GROW THEM

Growing your own sweet peppers and hot peppers (chiles) is all about experimentation. Bell peppers alone come in a rainbow of colors—green, red, orange, purple, and white. Some start out one color, then turn another as they ripen; others, like 'Golden Bell', keep their color through to harvest. There are other sweet peppers you can try growing, like the banana (also known as sweet Hungarian wax) pepper and pimiento. As for chiles, they grow in an astounding range of flavors, heat levels, shapes, sizes, and colors, making them incredibly fun and interesting to grow.

WHEN TO HARVEST

Most peppers, sweet and hot, can be picked green after they have reached a good size, but their flavor typically becomes fuller and sweeter as the fruit ripens to its mature color, which varies by variety. For instance, the serrano, when harvested green, has a lively, almost citrusy zing; if picked red, its flavor is warm and ripe. Pick pimientos only when red-ripe. Poblanos should be harvested green. To harvest any kind of pepper or chile, snip the stem with hand pruners or scissors.

HOW TO KEEP

Refrigerate, unwashed, in a plastic bag up to 5 days.

PRESERVING THE HARVEST

FREEZE Roast peppers (see left). Once they have cooled completely, arrange them in a single layer in a resealable plastic bag. Seal the bag; then seal in a second bag. Freeze for up to 6 months.

DRY Pick your chiles when they are fully ripe. Rinse and pat dry. *To air-dry:* Using a needle and strong thread (fishing line works well too), pierce chiles through the base of the stem and space out along the length of the thread. (The New Mexican *ristra* style—chiles threaded so they overlap—works well in that state's arid climate, but in more humid areas, the chiles will rot.) Leave enough thread on either end to tie to shelving or some other support, so the chiles hang like a necklace. Hang in a well-ventilated spot out of the sun and let the chiles dry until they have withered. Small chiles are ready when they are brittle, at least 2 weeks. Anchos (dried poblanos) should be taken down when they are evenly darkened, fully wrinkled, and leathery but still supple, 2 to 3 weeks. *To dry in a dehydrator:* Arrange chiles in a single layer on dehydrator trays. Dehydrate small chiles until they are brittle, 1 to 2 days. Anchos should be leathery but still supple, which will take 2 days. Store dried chiles in airtight containers. They keep, at room temperature, for several months.

GROUND Make your own ground chile powder: Stem the dried chiles, then pulverize them in a cleaned coffee grinder. Store in an airtight container in a dry, dark spot.

Basic Ways to Cook

ROAST This works well with both sweet peppers and chiles. Preheat the broiler. Put the peppers/chiles on a rimmed baking sheet lined with foil. Place about 4 in. from the heat source and broil, turning as needed, until blackened all over, at least 15 minutes. Remove from the broiler, cover with a kitchen towel, and let cool until the peppers/chiles can be handled. Gently pull off and discard the blackened skins. Use as directed in your recipe or, if freezing for future use (see right), you can remove the stems and seeds and cut roasted peppers into strips. If you're roasting poblanos, we recommend leaving them whole with the seeds, so they can be prepped in different ways.

SAUTÉ Cut about 1 lb. sweet peppers into ¼-in. strips. Melt or heat 2 tbsp. butter or olive oil in a wide frying pan over medium heat. Add peppers and cook, stirring, until tender, 10 to 15 minutes.

STIR-FRY Cut bell peppers into 1-in. squares. Stir-fry up to 5 cups, using 1 to 2 tbsp. oil, for 1 minute. Add 2 to 3 tbsp. liquid, cover, and cook until peppers are tender, 3 to 5 minutes more.

Some of our favorite varieties

SWEET PEPPERS

'Apple' and 'Red Heart' Two favorite pimiento varieties. Pimientos are smaller than bells, but juicier and sweeter.

'Carmen' An early Italian sweet pepper; as it matures from green to red, it gets even sweeter, which is when it's best sliced in salads.

'Miniature Yellow Bell' The perfect size for a bite-size stuffed pepper hors d'oeuvre.

'Tequila' Watch this bell pepper's color shift from yellow to purple to red as it matures.

HOT PEPPERS (CHILES)

Jalapeño Indispensable workhorse of the Mexican kitchen. When dried and smoked, it's called a chipotle.

'Mariachi' A nice choice if you like just a little bit of heat, plus the chiles turn from creamy yellow to bright red when ripe.

Poblano This broad-shouldered, mildly spicy pepper is a must if you are a fan of Mexican and Southwestern cooking. When it is dried, it's called an ancho.

Serrano These slender chiles are hotter than jalapeños and extremely versatile in the kitchen.

'Trinidad Perfume' One of the less incendiary habanero varieties.

Roasted green chile and tomatillo salsa

MAKES About 2 cups
TIME 20 minutes

Chipotle chiles provide the fire for this green salsa. Roasting the poblano, tomatillos, garlic, and onion adds an additional layer of smoky flavor.

1 white onion, quartered
1 poblano chile or 2 'Anaheim' chiles (5 oz. total)
1 lb. tomatillos, husked
3 large garlic cloves, peeled
2 or 3 canned chipotle chiles, plus 1 tbsp. sauce
    from can
¼ cup loosely packed cilantro
1 tbsp. fresh lime juice
Salt

1. Preheat broiler. Put onion, poblano, tomatillos, and garlic on a baking sheet. Broil 4 to 5 in. from heat, turning once, until blackened, 8 to 10 minutes total. Let cool.
2. Peel, stem, and seed fresh chile and cut into chunks. Whirl onion, chile, tomatillos, garlic, chipotle chiles with sauce, cilantro, and lime juice in a blender or food processor until coarsely puréed. Season to taste with salt.

PER ¼-CUP SERVING 40 CAL., 16% (6.3 CAL.) FROM FAT; 1.5 G PROTEIN; 0.7 G FAT (0.1 G SAT.); 8.2 G CARBO (1.9 G FIBER); 165 MG SODIUM; 0 MG CHOL.

Roasted red pepper–tomato soup

SERVES 10 to 12
TIME 30 minutes

Guests can sip this festive, zesty first-course soup from small cups or glasses.

3 red bell peppers (1½ lbs.), seeds and ribs removed, halved
3 tbsp. olive oil
1 onion (7 oz.), chopped
2 garlic cloves, minced
1 can (28 oz.) whole 'San Marzano' or other pear or plum tomatoes
1 tbsp. paprika such as pimentón de La Vera (see Flavor Note, right)
3 cups vegetable or chicken broth
2 tsp. fresh lemon juice
Salt and freshly ground black pepper
Crème fraîche or plain yogurt
Chopped flat-leaf parsley for garnish

1. Preheat broiler. Place red pepper halves, cut side down, in a baking pan and broil 4 to 5 in. from heat until skins are black and blistered, about 8 minutes. Let cool, uncovered, 10 to 15 minutes. Peel peppers and place in a bowl, reserving any juices.
2. Heat oil in a 3- to 4-qt. pan over medium heat. Add onion and cook, stirring often, until soft, about 5 minutes. Add garlic and cook, stirring, until translucent, 1 to 2 minutes. Add roasted peppers and tomatoes, along with their juices, and paprika. Bring to a low simmer and cook, stirring occasionally, about 3 minutes.
3. Purée soup in a blender or food processor in small batches until smooth. Return purée to pan and stir in broth and lemon juice. Stir over medium heat until hot. Season with salt and pepper to taste. Ladle into cups or bowls and garnish with a dollop of crème fraîche or yogurt and a sprinkling of parsley.

FLAVOR NOTE Pimentón de La Vera is a Spanish paprika that adds a smoky, sweet intensity, but Hungarian or regular paprika works too.

PER SERVING 72 CAL., 47% (34 CAL.) FROM FAT; 1.5 G PROTEIN; 3.8 G FAT (1.5 G SAT.); 9.3 G CARBO (1.5 G FIBER); 127 MG SODIUM; 0 MG CHOL.

Smoky five-pepper cheese dip

SERVES 8
TIME 35 minutes

This nod to nacho cheese dip lets you make good use of garden-fresh bell peppers and chiles—amped up with smoky chipotles (smoke-dried jalapeños).

1½ tsp. vegetable oil
½ cup chopped onion
½ *each* red and green bell pepper, seeds and ribs removed, chopped
1 jalapeño chile, seeds and ribs removed, minced
1 'Fresno' or red jalapeño chile, seeds and ribs removed, minced
2 tbsp. flour
½ cup milk
4 oz. *each* sharp cheddar and jack cheese, shredded (about 3 cups total)
2 canned chipotle chiles, chopped, plus 1 tbsp. sauce from can
¾ tsp. kosher salt
Tortilla chips

1. Heat oil in a large, heavy-bottomed saucepan over medium heat. Cook onion, bell peppers, and fresh chiles, stirring often, until softened, about 5 minutes. Add flour and stir until peppers are coated and flour is yellow, about 1 minute.
2. Add milk, stirring constantly until incorporated, then add ¾ cup water, stirring constantly until thickened and hot (the mixture will look pasty at first).
3. Sprinkle in half the cheeses, stirring until melted and smooth. Repeat with remaining cheeses. Add chipotle chiles and their sauce and salt and mix until blended. Serve with tortilla chips.

TIMESAVER TIP This recipe can be made up to two days ahead and refrigerated. Bake at 400°, covered, stirring once, until warm and smooth, about 20 minutes.

PER ¼-CUP SERVING 146 CAL., 63% (92 CAL.) FROM FAT; 8 G PROTEIN; 10 G FAT (5.6 G SAT.); 5.1 G CARBO (0.8 G FIBER); 415 MG SODIUM; 29 MG CHOL.

HOW TO WORK WITH CHILES

A chile's heat comes from capsaicin (cap-*say*-i-sin), a compound found primarily in its veins but also where the seeds and flesh touch the veins. If you have a sensitivity to capsaicin or are working with a lot of chiles or particularly potent ones, wear rubber gloves (also make sure your work area is well ventilated, otherwise you might find your chest tightening).

If the chiles burn your skin, rinse the area with rubbing alcohol. If juice sprays into your eyes or you touch your eyes with capsaicin-coated hands, flush them well with water. And if your mouth is burning from chile fire, never try to douse it with water, as capsaicin is not water soluble; try ice cream, milk, or yogurt. All contain casein, which washes away the capsaicin.

Fennel-pepper slaw

Fennel-pepper slaw

SERVES 6

TIME About 25 minutes, plus 1 hour to chill

This is a wonderful way to use a bounty of rainbow-colored bell peppers. We like this slaw after it has been chilled in its dressing overnight, but it's also good after just an hour.

3 tbsp. *each* fresh lemon juice and olive oil

1 tbsp. *each* Dijon mustard and honey

Salt and freshly ground black pepper

2 small heads fennel (about 1³/₄ lbs. total)

3 red, yellow, and/or orange bell peppers, seeds and ribs removed, slivered lengthwise

1. Whisk lemon juice, oil, mustard, and honey in a small bowl to blend. Add salt and pepper to taste.

2. Trim stalks from fennel; chop enough feathery green fronds to make 2 tbsp. and reserve. Cut heads in half lengthwise, then shave into paper-thin strips using a mandoline or cut into thin slivers.

3. Combine fennel and bell peppers in a medium bowl. Drizzle with dressing and mix gently to coat; cover and chill at least 1 hour and up to 1 day. Just before serving, sprinkle with reserved fennel fronds.

PER SERVING 114 CAL., 55% (63 CAL.) FROM FAT; 1.5 G PROTEIN; 7 G FAT (0.9 G SAT.); 13 G CARBO (3.6 G FIBER); 111 MG SODIUM; 0 MG CHOL.

Warm bell pepper, chickpea, and spinach salad with harissa

SERVES 6

TIME 1 hour

To create this bright-tasting but sultry salad, Dan Petrie, owner of Mise en Place SF, a San Francisco–based cooking-party business, starts with classic Moroccan roasted vegetables, then adds fresh spinach and a sherry vinaigrette.

VINAIGRETTE

1 tbsp. sherry vinegar

¹/₂ tbsp. Dijon mustard

¹/₄ tsp. *each* kosher salt and freshly ground black pepper

2 to 4 tsp. harissa (see Flavor Note, right)

3 tbsp. extra-virgin olive oil

SALAD

1 *each* medium red and yellow bell pepper

2 tbsp. olive oil

1 medium eggplant, cut into ¹/₂-in. cubes

1 can (15 oz.) chickpeas (garbanzos), rinsed and drained

³/₄ tsp. *each* kosher salt and freshly ground black pepper, plus more to taste

1 bag (6 oz.) baby spinach

12 large mint leaves, stacked and cut crosswise into thin ribbons

¹/₃ cup minced red onion, rinsed and drained

1. Preheat broiler. Make vinaigrette: Whisk vinegar, mustard, salt, pepper, and 2 tsp. harissa in a bowl. Gradually whisk in oil. Taste; add more harissa if you'd like a hotter dressing. Set aside.

2. Make salad: Put peppers on a baking sheet and broil, turning periodically, until charred on all sides, about 20 minutes. Place peppers in a paper bag about 15 minutes to allow trapped steam to loosen their skins. Remove charred skins, stems, and seeds; cut peppers into ¹/₂-in. pieces.

3. Meanwhile, heat oil in a large nonstick frying pan over medium heat. Add eggplant and cook, stirring often, until softened and beginning to color, about 12 minutes. Add chickpeas, 2 tbsp. water, salt, and black pepper; cook, stirring, to blend flavors, about 3 minutes. Stir in chopped peppers. Remove from heat and let stand until vegetables are warm but not hot.

4. Toss spinach, mint, and onion in a large bowl with half the vinaigrette. Add chickpea mixture, drizzle with additional dressing, and toss again to coat. Season to taste with more salt and pepper.

FLAVOR NOTE The heat level of harissa, a North African chile-and-spice paste, varies greatly from brand to brand, so try a little before using it. Look for it in the international food aisle of larger supermarkets.

PER SERVING 197 CAL., 59% (117 CAL.) FROM FAT; 4.6 G PROTEIN; 13 G FAT (1.7 G SAT.); 19 G CARBO (5.6 G FIBER); 360 MG SODIUM; 0 MG CHOL.

Green chile grits

SERVES 4
TIME 1 hour

The chiles give these grits, from reader Judy Johnston of Mesilla, New Mexico, some kick—but they are still creamy comfort food at its best.

3 'Anaheim' or green New Mexico chiles
4 cups chicken broth
1 cup quick-cooking grits
2 tbsp. butter
2 cups shredded cheddar cheese
2 large eggs, beaten

1. Preheat broiler. Place chiles in a baking pan and broil, turning once or twice, until skins are charred all over. Let sit until cool enough to handle, then peel skins and discard stems and seeds. Dice chiles.
2. Preheat oven to 350°. Grease a 2-qt. casserole.
3. Bring broth to a boil in a 3- or 4-qt. pan over high heat. Add grits, reduce heat to medium, and stir until broth is absorbed, 5 to 6 minutes. Stir in butter, cheese, and chiles.
4. In a small bowl, whisk ½ cup of the cooked grits into the beaten eggs. When blended, stir this mixture back into pan with rest of grits. Pour mixture into prepared casserole. Bake until just set, 25 to 30 minutes.

PER SERVING 494 CAL., 55% (270 CAL.) FROM FAT; 24 G PROTEIN; 30 G FAT (17 G SAT.); 33 G CARBO (2.3 G FIBER); 552 MG SODIUM; 185 MG CHOL.

GOOD FOR YOU
Peppers are full of vitamin C, and are the perfect healthy snack; 1 cup of sliced green peppers has only 18 calories.

Lamb stew with roasted red peppers

SERVES 6

TIME 2½ hours

This simple stew rewards a little bit of effort with deep layers of flavor.

3 lbs. lamb shoulder or other lamb stew meat, fat trimmed and cut into 1½-in. chunks

Salt and freshly ground black pepper

About 1 tbsp. olive oil

1 medium onion, chopped

2 tbsp. *each* minced garlic and paprika

2 tsp. ground cumin

1 cup Syrah or other dry red wine

About 1½ cups reduced-sodium beef broth

3 tbsp. tomato paste

3 red bell peppers, halved and seeded

¼ cup chopped flat-leaf parsley

3 tbsp. *each* chopped kalamata olives and capers

1. Sprinkle lamb with salt and pepper. Pour 1 tbsp. oil into a large pot over medium-high heat. Working in batches, add lamb in a single layer and brown all over. Transfer to a bowl and add more oil to pot as necessary.

2. Reduce heat to medium; if pan is dry, add a little more oil. Add onion and cook until softened, 5 minutes. Add garlic, paprika, and cumin and cook until fragrant, 2 minutes. Add wine, 1½ cups broth, and tomato paste; bring to a boil, stirring to scrape up browned bits. Add lamb and juices; cover and simmer, stirring occasionally, until lamb is very tender, 1½ to 1¾ hours.

3. Broil pepper halves until blackened all over. Remove from oven and let stand at least 10 minutes, then peel and thinly slice lengthwise. Mix parsley, olives, and capers in a small bowl.

4. Stir roasted peppers into lamb mixture. If stew is too thick, add a little more broth. Cook, uncovered, until heated through. Season to taste with more salt and pepper and top with parsley mixture.

PER SERVING 352 CAL., 43% (153 CAL.) FROM FAT; 39 G PROTEIN; 17 G FAT (5 G SAT.); 11 G CARBO (1.7 G FIBER); 578 MG SODIUM; 123 MG CHOL.

Chiles stuffed with almonds and raisins
RECIPE P. 138

Green chile
chicken enchiladas
RECIPE P. 138

Chiles stuffed with almonds and raisins

SERVES 5 or 6
TIME About 1¾ hours

This dish softens the chiles' heat with raisins, nuts, spices, and a slightly sweet tomato sauce. (Photo on page 136.)

15 to 18 green New Mexico or 'Anaheim' chiles
⅓ cup plus ¾ cup slivered almonds
1 tbsp. olive oil
8 large garlic cloves, peeled
¾ cup chopped onion
1 lb. ground beef
1½ tsp. salt, divided
1 tsp. *each* cinnamon, ground cumin, and freshly
    ground black pepper
⅓ cup raisins
½ cup plain dried bread crumbs
2 tbsp. chopped oregano
8 oz. queso fresco (see Flavor Note, right), crumbled
1 can (28 oz.) crushed tomatoes
2 tbsp. honey

1. Slice off chile stems. With a spoon or melon baller, scoop out seeds and ribs from chiles (avoid slitting chiles); set chiles aside. Preheat oven to 375°.
2. Toast almonds in a large frying pan over medium-low heat, stirring often, until golden brown and fragrant, 8 to 10 minutes. Transfer to a bowl and set aside.
3. Add oil to pan and increase heat to medium-high. Mince 4 garlic cloves and add to pan along with onion. Cook, stirring, until onion is translucent, 3 minutes. Add beef, 1 tsp. salt, the cinnamon, cumin, and pepper and cook, breaking up beef with a wooden spoon, until beef is cooked through, about 10 minutes. Add raisins and cook, stirring, 3 minutes. Add bread crumbs, oregano, ⅓ cup toasted almonds, and queso fresco. Cook, stirring, 2 minutes; remove from heat.

4. Carefully pack each chile with filling. Arrange chiles in a large baking pan and bake until chiles are browned and beginning to blister, 35 to 45 minutes.
5. Meanwhile, make sauce: In a large frying pan over medium heat, bring tomatoes, honey, remaining 4 garlic cloves, and remaining ½ tsp. salt to a gentle simmer. Cook until most of the liquid is evaporated, about 15 minutes. Stir in remaining ¾ cup toasted almonds. Transfer to a blender, add ½ cup water, and whirl sauce until very smooth, about 1 minute. Drizzle sauce over chiles and serve warm.

FLAVOR NOTE Queso fresco is a mild, crumbly Mexican cheese sold in Latin markets and some supermarkets. You can substitute farmer's cheese or feta.

PER 3-CHILE SERVING 568 CAL., 52% (297 CAL.) FROM FAT; 31 G PROTEIN; 33 G FAT (11 G SAT.); 40 G CARBO (4.4 G FIBER); 1,202 MG SODIUM; 76 MG CHOL.

Green chile chicken enchiladas

SERVES 5; makes 10 enchiladas
TIME 50 minutes

This is simple, earthy, and delicious. Its heat depends on the chiles; go with Anaheims if you scorch easily. (Photo on page 137.)

2 tbsp. olive oil
1 tbsp. butter
5 large garlic cloves, finely chopped
1 lb. green New Mexico chiles, roasted (page 129),
    skins, stems, and seeds removed, and chopped
½ tsp. *each* salt and freshly ground black pepper
3 cups reduced-sodium chicken broth, divided
10 (7 to 8 in.) corn tortillas
2 cups coarsely shredded cheddar or jack cheese,
    divided
2½ cups shredded cooked chicken
Sour cream

1. Preheat oven to 400°.

2. Heat oil and butter in a large frying pan over medium heat. Add garlic and cook until fragrant, about 30 seconds. Add chiles, salt, and pepper. Cook, stirring occasionally, 3 minutes. Add 1 cup broth and simmer until reduced by one-third, about 10 minutes.
3. Meanwhile, prepare tortillas: In a small frying pan, bring remaining 2 cups broth to a gentle simmer. Working one at a time, very briefly dip tortillas into broth to barely soften. Transfer each tortilla to a large baking sheet (you may need 2 or 3 sheets). Do not overlap or tortillas will stick.
4. Divide 1¼ cups cheese equally among tortillas and top each with shredded chicken, dividing evenly. Wrap tortilla around filling and transfer, seam side down, to a 9- by 13-in. baking dish.
5. Pour chile sauce over enchiladas and top with remaining ¾ cup cheese. Bake until cheese is bubbling and browned, 15 to 20 minutes. Serve with sour cream.

TIMESAVER TIP Baked enchiladas can be frozen for up to 1 month.

PER 2-ENCHILADA SERVING 526 CAL., 50% (261 CAL.) FROM FAT; 32 G PROTEIN; 29 G FAT (13 G SAT.); 38 G CARBO (4.2 G FIBER); 1,402 MG SODIUM; 117 MG CHOL.

Grilled chicken kebabs with romesco sauce

SERVES 4
TIME 40 minutes

Romesco sauce has its roots in the Spanish province of Catalonia. Although the mixture has lots of variations, most combine roasted red peppers, nuts, garlic, and crusty bread to make a thick sauce that often tops grilled fish. It's a tasty way to make use of a freezer stash of roasted peppers.

2 lbs. boned, skinned chicken breasts, cut into
   1½-in. cubes
½ cup chopped cilantro
8 tbsp. extra-virgin olive oil, divided
2 tbsp. fresh lime juice
2 tsp. plus 1 tbsp. minced garlic
1 tsp. *each* kosher salt and smoked Spanish paprika
   (pimentón de La Vera; see Flavor Note, page 131)
½ tsp. freshly ground black pepper
¾ cup peeled roasted red peppers (page 129)
¼ cup whole almonds or hazelnuts, toasted
   (see Flavor Note, below)
1 slice crusty bread, toasted and cut into cubes
1 tbsp. sherry vinegar
2 bunches green onions, root ends trimmed

1. If using wood skewers, soak in cold water at least 30 minutes before using. In a large bowl or resealable plastic bag, combine chicken, cilantro, 3 tbsp. oil, the lime juice, 2 tsp. garlic, the salt, paprika, and black pepper. Toss to coat, then marinate in refrigerator 25 minutes.

2. Meanwhile, put roasted peppers, nuts, bread, vinegar, remaining 1 tbsp. minced garlic, and 4 tbsp. oil in food processor and whirl until puréed; sauce will be thick.

3. Prepare a charcoal or gas grill for direct medium-high heat (about 450°; you can hold your hand 5 in. above cooking grate only 4 to 5 seconds). Thread chicken onto skewers, discarding marinade. Drizzle green onions with remaining 1 tbsp. oil. Lay skewers on grill (cover if using gas) and cook 4 minutes. Turn skewers over, then lay green onions on grill. Cook until chicken is browned and cooked through and onions are charred in places, about 4 minutes

4. Transfer skewers and green onions to a platter and serve hot, accompanied by sauce.

FLAVOR NOTE Nuts develop greater flavor and more crunch when they're toasted. Spread the nuts on a baking pan in a single layer and toast in a 350° oven until golden, 5 to 15 minutes, depending on the type of nut.

PER SERVING 533 CAL., 47% (252 CAL.) FROM FAT; 56 G PROTEIN; 28 G FAT (4.2 G SAT.); 14 G CARBO (2.9 G FIBER); 495 MG SODIUM; 132 MG CHOL.

Grilled chicken kebabs with romesco sauce

POTATOES

'Yukon Gold'

WHY GROW THEM

Potatoes are a bit of an undertaking, but it's so much fun to experiment with all the varieties that are available. You can choose your type (dry and starchy versus dense and waxy), color (from the familiar buff to gold, red, and purple/blue; you can select varieties whose color is only skin deep or those colored through and through), and shape (round, cylindrical, or fingerlike).

EXTRA REWARD Your own new potatoes. New potatoes are just immature potatoes harvested when the plant flowers. They're extra sweet because their sugar has not yet converted to starch, as it has in mature tubers. And their skins are as delicate as tissue paper.

WHEN TO HARVEST

For new potatoes, dig when the plants begin to bloom; for mature potatoes, dig when the plants die down. Where the ground doesn't freeze, late potatoes can remain in the ground until needed. Dig before warmer temperatures start them growing again. No matter when you harvest, dig carefully to avoid bruising or cutting the tubers.

HOW TO KEEP

New potatoes, because of their tender, thin skins and higher moisture, are quite perishable; eat within 2 days of harvest. Mature potatoes that are free of defects are the best keepers; store them in a cool (40°), dark, dry place. If you will be storing your mature potatoes for a prolonged period, it helps to cure them first before storage: Spread them out in a single layer, at room temperature, in a dark, well-ventilated place for 2 weeks. This will toughen their skins and help them last longer. **IMPORTANT NOTE** Do not store potatoes with apples or members of the onion family, as they emit ethylene gas, which will make the potatoes sprout.

'All Blue'

Some of our favorite varieties

'All Blue' A gorgeous potato with a delicate white layer under the skin. The color lightens when cooked, but is still blue.

'Butte' and 'Russet Burbank' Good choices for baking and mashing, as each cooks up light and fluffy.

'Carola' If you like creamy, potato-based soups, this variety falls apart nicely when cooked.

'Reddale' A waxy, moist potato perfect for boiling, stews, and potato salad.

'Rose Finn Fingerling' and 'Banana Fingerling' Both have good flavor and dense, fine texture.

'Yukon Gold' The best all-purpose potato, this spud has buttery, sweet flesh that's equally suited to boiling and baking.

Basic Ways to Cook

BAKE Russets are best for baking; they'll have a crisp, slightly shriveled skin and fluffy interior. Pierce skin in several places with a fork. Bake on a rack in a 400° oven until potatoes feel soft when squeezed, 45 to 60 minutes.

ROAST Toss whole or cut-up potatoes on a baking sheet with just enough olive oil to coat, season generously with salt and pepper, and roast in a 400° oven until well browned and tender. Total time will depend on the size of the potatoes, but generally at least 45 minutes.

MASH Peel the potatoes or leave the skins on. Cut large potatoes into chunks, put in a saucepan, cover with water, and salt generously. Bring to a boil, reduce heat, and simmer until tender. Drain well, then return to the still-hot pot, off the stove, to let potatoes dry for a couple of minutes. For the best results, use a potato masher or ricer (it looks like a giant garlic press) to mash potatoes. An electric mixer also works, but be careful not to overbeat waxy varieties. And don't use a food processor unless you want glue. Stir in the liquid of your choice (the kind and amount will determine how rich your mash is and its consistency). Season with salt and pepper.

STEAM This works nicely for fingerlings and other small thin-skinned potatoes. Arrange whole potatoes of no more than 3-inch diameter on a rack. Steam until tender when pierced, 30 to 35 minutes.

FRY We think russets make the best fries. For each serving, peel 1 large russet and cut into ¼-in.-wide strips; place in ice water until ready to fry. Heat 2 in. vegetable oil to 380°. Drain potatoes and pat dry. Fry until well browned, 5 to 7 minutes. Scoop out with a slotted spoon, drain on paper towels, and sprinkle with salt.

**Baby vegetable salad
with cornichons**
RECIPE P. 144

**Chanterelle potato
salad with pancetta,
shallots, and thyme**
RECIPE P. 144

Baby vegetable salad with cornichons

SERVES 4 to 6
TIME 40 minutes

Creamy young potatoes, tiny carrots, and crunchy peas star in this remake of a favorite Russian dish called Salade Olivier. (Photo on page 142.)

1 lb. small red and yellow fingerling potatoes (about 16)
1 bunch baby carrots with tops (about 8), trimmed
1 cup sugar snap peas (5 oz.), ends trimmed
2 tbsp. red wine vinegar
½ cup cornichon pickles
⅓ cup fat-free Greek-style yogurt
2 tbsp. mayonnaise
½ tsp. kosher salt
¼ tsp. freshly ground black pepper
⅓ cup loosely packed flat-leaf parsley, finely chopped

1. Pour about 1 in. water into a large pot and set a steamer basket (see Quick Tip, right) in bottom. Bring to a boil. Add potatoes to basket, reduce heat, and simmer until tender when pierced, 15 to 20 minutes. Remove potatoes as each is done, then steam carrots until just tender, 5 to 7 minutes. Remove carrots and steam pea pods until tender-crisp, about 5 minutes. With each vegetable, transfer to an ice bath to stop cooking, then drain and dry on paper towels.

2. When potatoes are cool enough to handle (but still warm), halve each lengthwise and transfer to a large bowl. Sprinkle with vinegar and let stand 5 minutes. Halve carrots lengthwise and add to potatoes along with cornichons and pea pods.

3. Combine yogurt, mayonnaise, salt, and pepper in a small bowl and stir to combine. Pour dressing over vegetables and very gently toss to coat (try not to crush the potatoes). Transfer to a platter and sprinkle with parsley.

QUICK TIP Potatoes cook most evenly in a steamer basket, but if you don't have one, fill a pot halfway with water and boil potatoes.

PER SERVING 96 CAL., 18% (17 CAL.) FROM FAT; 3.4 G PROTEIN; 1.9 G FAT (0.3 G SAT.); 17 G CARBO (2.5 G FIBER); 374 MG SODIUM; 1.3 MG CHOL.

GOOD FOR YOU
Potatoes are a good source of potassium and an excellent source of fiber when eaten with the skins on. They also deliver a fair amount of vitamins C and B₆.

Chanterelle potato salad with pancetta, shallots, and thyme

SERVES 8
TIME 55 minutes

Potato salad goes uptown in this recipe from Dory Ford, former executive chef at Monterey Bay Aquarium's Portola Restaurant. You'll have about 1 cup vinaigrette left over; it's excellent on any salad and on fish, and keeps up to two weeks, chilled. (Photo on page 143.)

¼ cup white wine vinegar
⅔ cup vegetable oil
⅔ cup extra-virgin olive oil, or more as needed to dress potatoes
2 shallots, 1 chopped, 1 minced
2 tsp. kosher salt, divided
12 oz. fresh chanterelle mushrooms or 10 oz. fresh shiitake mushrooms
6 oz. slab pancetta or thick-cut bacon, diced
3 lbs. baby 'Yukon Gold' potatoes, halved lengthwise (if potatoes are longer than 2 in., cut into quarters)
4 medium garlic cloves, minced
2 tsp. thyme leaves
¾ tsp. freshly ground black pepper, divided
2 tbsp. butter
⅓ cup Chardonnay or other white wine
2 tbsp. chopped tarragon
1 tbsp. chopped chives

1. Put vinegar, both oils, the chopped shallot, and ½ tsp. salt in a blender and whirl at medium speed until mixture is pale yellow and emulsified. Set aside.

2. Preheat oven to 375°. Wipe chanterelles with a damp cloth or scrape with a knife to remove dirt; cut away dry, woody parts. Tear mushrooms into 1-in. pieces.

3. Cook pancetta in a large frying pan over medium-high heat until crisp and browned, about 7 minutes. Transfer with a slotted spoon to paper towels, reserving drippings (add olive oil if needed to make 3 tbsp.).

4. Toss potatoes with reserved pancetta drippings, garlic, thyme, 1 tsp. salt, and ½ tsp. pepper. Divide potatoes between two 9- by 13-in. baking pans. Bake, stirring every 10 minutes, until tender, well browned, and crisp, 25 to 35 minutes. Remove from oven and keep warm.

5. Melt butter in a large frying pan over medium-high heat. Add minced shallot and cook until soft, 1 minute. Add mushrooms and cook, stirring occasionally, until browned, 5 to 6 minutes. Add wine and remaining ½ tsp. salt and ¼ tsp. pepper; scrape up browned bits from bottom of pan and cook until liquid evaporates, about 2 minutes.

6. Toss together potatoes, mushrooms, pancetta, tarragon, and chives in a large bowl. Drizzle with ½ cup vinaigrette. Serve warm.

PER SERVING 385 CAL., 58% (225 CAL.) FROM FAT; 8.1 G PROTEIN; 25 G FAT (8 G SAT.); 34 G CARBO (2.5 G FIBER); 680 MG SODIUM; 20 MG CHOL.

'Yukon Gold' and fresh herb potato salad

SERVES 8 to 10
TIME 1 hour

This tangy salad from Oregon cookbook author Janie Hibler is all about good potatoes, olive oil, and herbs.

4 lbs. 'Yukon Gold' potatoes (about 3 in. wide)
6 tbsp. fruity extra-virgin olive oil
3 tbsp. Champagne vinegar
3/4 tsp. kosher salt, plus more to taste
1½ tbsp. *each* chopped basil and flat-leaf parsley
1 tbsp. minced chives
Freshly ground black pepper

1. Pour about 1 in. water into a large pot and set a steamer basket (see Quick Tip, below) in bottom. Bring to a boil. Add potatoes to basket, reduce heat, and simmer, covered, until tender when pierced, 25 to 30 minutes. Pour potatoes into a colander in the sink, rinse with cool water, and let stand until cool enough to handle.
2. Peel potatoes and slice crosswise into ½-in.-thick pieces. Put in a large serving bowl.
3. Whisk together oil, vinegar, and salt in a small bowl and drizzle over warm potatoes. Sprinkle with herbs and add pepper and additional salt to taste, mixing gently to coat.

TIMESAVER TIP You can prepare the salad up to 1 day ahead and refrigerate (the salad will become even more flavorful); before serving, bring to room temperature, then stir.

QUICK TIP Potatoes cook most evenly in a steamer basket, but if you don't have one, fill a pot halfway with water and boil potatoes.

PER SERVING 208 CAL., 37% (76 CAL.) FROM FAT; 3.9 G PROTEIN; 8.4 G FAT (1.2 G SAT.); 29 G CARBO (2 G FIBER); 97 MG SODIUM; 0 MG CHOL.

Golden olive oil–roasted potatoes

SERVES 8

TIME About 1¼ hours, plus overnight to chill

Nothing more than good olive oil and crunchy sea salt turn potatoes into an irresistible holiday side dish. It's from Maria Helm Sinskey, cookbook author and co-owner of Robert Sinskey Vineyards.

5 lbs. large 'Yukon Gold' potatoes

3 tbsp. extra-virgin olive oil

½ tbsp. sea salt such as fleur de sel, plus more to taste

1. Peel potatoes and cut into 1½-in. cubes. Put in a large bowl, cover with cold water, and refrigerate overnight (see Flavor Note, below). Drain.

2. Preheat oven to 475°. Bring a large pot of lightly salted water to a boil over high heat. Add potatoes and cook until barely tender when pierced, about 10 minutes. Pour into a colander and let drain and dry 10 minutes.

3. Set potatoes in a single layer in a large rimmed baking pan. Drizzle evenly with oil and sprinkle with salt; stir gently to coat. Bake potatoes until golden brown, 25 to 30 minutes, turning halfway through baking.

4. Mound hot potatoes on a platter or in a shallow serving bowl; season with more salt to taste.

FLAVOR NOTE Soaking the potatoes at least a day (and up to 2 days) ahead makes them even crisper on the outside and creamier in the middle.

PER SERVING 255 CAL., 18% (47 CAL.) FROM FAT; 6 G PROTEIN; 5.2 G FAT (0.8 G SAT.); 45 G CARBO (3 G FIBER); 383 MG SODIUM; 0 MG CHOL.

Browned butter and hazelnut mashed potatoes

SERVES 8
TIME 30 minutes

Save this indulgent recipe for a special-occasion dinner (it's great with turkey). Browning the butter gives it toasty flavor notes that are further accented by the hazelnuts.

3 lbs. 'Yukon Gold' or russet potatoes, unpeeled, cut into 1-in. chunks
1 cup hazelnuts, coarsely chopped
½ cup unsalted butter
1 cup milk, warmed to steaming
1 container (7 oz.) plain Greek-style yogurt
2 tsp. kosher salt
½ tsp. freshly ground black pepper

1. Put potatoes in a large pot and cover with cold water. Cover pot and bring to a boil over high heat. Reduce heat to medium and cook until potatoes are tender when pierced, about 15 minutes. Drain; return to pot.

2. Meanwhile, toast hazelnuts in a large dry frying pan over medium heat, stirring often, until fragrant, about 5 minutes. Add butter and cook, stirring frequently, until butter is golden brown and flecked with brown bits and hazelnuts are dark brown, about 5 minutes. Pour hot hazelnuts into a bowl; set aside.

3. Mash hot potatoes. Add milk, yogurt, salt, and pepper, mashing to blend. Transfer potatoes to a serving bowl and spoon about half the warm hazelnuts over the top; serve the rest on the side.

PER SERVING 384 CAL., 55% (212 CAL.) FROM FAT; 8.9 G PROTEIN; 24 G FAT (10 G SAT.); 35 G CARBO (3.4 G FIBER); 511 MG SODIUM; 38 MG CHOL.

Kale colcannon
RECIPE P. 150

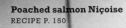

Poached salmon Niçoise
RECIPE P. 150

Grilled fingerlings with dill

SERVES 12

TIME 45 minutes

Never thought of grilling potatoes? It's a particularly tasty way to prepare newly dug fingerlings.

6 lbs. fingerling potatoes, halved lengthwise (if very small, keep whole)
¼ cup extra-virgin olive oil
1½ tsp. kosher salt
1 tsp. freshly ground black pepper
¼ cup butter, softened
¼ cup roughly chopped dill
Coarse sea salt, for finishing (optional)

1. Prepare a charcoal or gas grill for direct medium heat (350° to 450°; you can hold your hand 5 in. above cooking grate only 5 to 7 seconds). In a large bowl, toss potatoes with oil, kosher salt, and pepper.
2. Set out 4 sheets heavy-duty foil (each about 12 by 26 in.). Oil foil; divide potatoes among sheets, arranging them, cut side down, in a single layer on the short half of each sheet. Fold other half of each sheet over potatoes and crimp edges to seal.
3. Grill packets, crimped side up, covered, rotating their position on the grill halfway through, until potatoes are tender when pierced through foil, about 20 minutes. Open packets; if potatoes aren't brown on cut side, cook longer.
4. Transfer potatoes to a large bowl. Toss with butter and dill. Arrange on a platter; sprinkle with coarse sea salt if you like.

TIMESAVER TIP You can grill the potatoes up to 3 days ahead; remove them from the foil and chill. Reheat in an oiled baking pan in a 450° oven until hot, about 15 minutes, then proceed with step 4.

PER SERVING 233 CAL., 33% (77 CAL.) FROM FAT; 4.4 G PROTEIN; 8.7 G FAT (3.1 G SAT.); 36 G CARBO (3.9 G FIBER); 281 MG SODIUM; 10 MG CHOL.

Kale colcannon

SERVES 4 to 6

TIME About 40 minutes

Colcannon is one of the genius ways that the Irish have with potatoes—mashing them up with milk, good butter, and cooked kale or cabbage. It is simple but delicious. (Photo on page 148.)

1½ lbs. 'Yukon Gold' potatoes, unpeeled, cut into large, evenly sized chunks
½ lb. Tuscan kale, tough ribs removed and leaves coarsely chopped
About ⅓ cup whole milk, warmed
2 tbsp. unsalted butter, plus more for serving (optional)
¾ tsp. fine sea salt

1. Put potatoes in a saucepan, cover with about 1 in. cold water, and bring to a boil over high heat. Reduce the heat and simmer, covered, until potatoes are tender, about 20 minutes.
2. Meanwhile, pour about ½ in. water into another saucepan and set a steamer basket in bottom. Bring to a boil. Add kale to basket, reduce heat, and simmer, covered, turning kale occasionally with tongs, until tender, about 20 minutes.
3. Drain potatoes, return them to pan, and add milk, butter, and salt. Mash with a potato masher, keeping potatoes slightly chunky. Add kale and stir to combine. Stir in a little more milk if mixture seems too thick.
4. Serve colcannon with more butter if you like.

PER ¾-CUP SERVING 145 CAL., 27% (39 CAL.) FROM FAT; 3.8 G PROTEIN; 4.4 G FAT (2.7 G SAT.); 23 G CARBO (1.7 G FIBER); 309 MG SODIUM; 12 MG CHOL.

Poached salmon Niçoise

SERVES 6 to 8

TIME About 1 hour

We've included this recipe in the potato section, but it truly celebrates all the bounty of the garden, with its flavorful combination of potatoes, ripe tomatoes, tender haricots verts, and fresh herbs. (Photo on page 149.)

2 dried bay leaves
1 tbsp. kosher salt
10 black peppercorns
2 cups dry white wine
2 lbs. skin-on wild salmon fillet pieces (1 to 1½ in. thick)
3 garlic cloves, minced
1 tbsp. whole-grain mustard
5 tbsp. Champagne vinegar
⅔ cup extra-virgin olive oil
2 tbsp. *each* chopped flat-leaf parsley and basil
Sea salt
2 large bunches watercress, ends trimmed, leaving stems intact
10 small yellow-skinned new potatoes, boiled until tender and cut in half
4 hard-cooked eggs, cut into quarters
¼ lb. haricots verts or regular green beans, ends trimmed, boiled until tender-crisp
½ cup pitted Niçoise olives
3 Roma tomatoes, cut into lengthwise wedges

1. Put bay leaves, kosher salt, peppercorns, and wine in a large roasting pan. Add salmon and enough water to cover.
2. Remove salmon and set aside; bring liquid to a boil, covered. Reduce to a simmer, then gently slide salmon into liquid and simmer 10 to 15 minutes, covered, until it is just opaque.
3. Meanwhile, whisk together garlic, mustard, and vinegar in a small bowl. Gradually whisk in oil, then herbs and sea salt to taste.

4. Using 2 spatulas, transfer salmon to a cooling rack set on a rimmed baking sheet and chill 10 minutes. Discard poaching liquid.

5. Break salmon into large pieces, discarding skin. Arrange watercress on a very large serving platter and top with fish, potatoes, eggs, green beans, olives, and tomatoes. Drizzle dressing over everything and serve with crusty bread.

PER SERVING 547 CAL., 51% (277 CAL.) FROM FAT; 35 G PROTEIN; 32 G FAT (4.8 G SAT.); 30 G CARBO (4.5 G FIBER); 396 MG SODIUM; 178 MG CHOL.

Molten cheese gnocchi

SERVES 6 to 8 as a main course or 10 to 12 as a first course; makes about 100 gnocchi
TIME About 3 hours

Think of molten chocolate cake and you'll get the idea here: Each gnocchi has a melted cheese center. It's easy to pop down several before your brain registers how rich they are, so try savoring them slowly.

2 lbs. russet potatoes (3 large), scrubbed clean

4 cups (about 9 oz.) finely grated aged gouda cheese (such as Winchester Sharp), divided

¾ cup whipping cream

1 large egg, lightly beaten

1 tsp. salt

1 to 2 cups all-purpose flour

1½ tbsp. butter, melted

1 tsp. freshly ground black pepper

2 tbsp. finely chopped flat-leaf parsley

1. Preheat oven to 350°. Set potatoes on a baking sheet and slash each deeply lengthwise down center. Bake potatoes until tender and slightly dried out, 1¼ to 1½ hours.

2. Mix together 3 cups cheese and the cream in a small bowl. Set aside.

3. As soon as potatoes are cool enough to handle, peel them; discard peels. Put potatoes through a potato ricer into a large bowl (see Quick Tip, far right). Mix in egg, salt, and 1 cup

Molten cheese gnocchi

flour, adding just enough additional flour to make the dough pliable and not sticky (too much flour will make gnocchi heavy). Turn out onto a floured work surface; with floured hands, knead dough 10 to 12 times.

4. Divide dough and cover one batch with a damp kitchen towel. Roll other batch into a ¾-in.-thick rope and cut into ¾-in.-long pieces. Roll each piece into a ball, then flatten into a 2-in. circle.

5. Bring a large pot of salted water to a boil. Meanwhile, top each dough circle with ½ tsp. cheese-cream mixture. Gather up dough around filling and pinch to close, then roll into a small, smooth ball. Repeat rolling, filling, and forming with second batch of dough.

6. Preheat broiler with rack 4 in. below heating element. Divide melted butter between two 2-qt. casserole dishes. Working in batches, drop gnocchi into boiling water, being careful not to

crowd them. Boil gnocchi until they rise to the surface, 4 to 5 minutes; cook 8 to 10 seconds longer, then transfer with a slotted spoon to casserole dishes, making sure water drains off from gnocchi first.

7. Turn gnocchi to coat in butter. Sprinkle with pepper and remaining 1 cup cheese and broil until browned on top, 5 minutes. Sprinkle with parsley right before serving.

TIMESAVER TIP The gnocchi can be made through step 5 and kept for a month, frozen in resealable plastic freezer bags (freeze in a single layer on a cookie sheet to harden, then transfer to bags).

QUICK TIP If you don't have a ricer, you can use the fine disk on a food mill, but it will take longer and the gnocchi won't be as fluffy.

PER MAIN-COURSE SERVING 443 CAL., 47% (207 CAL.) FROM FAT; 16 G PROTEIN; 23 G FAT (14 G SAT.); 43 G CARBO (2.9 G FIBER); 686 MG SODIUM; 113 MG CHOL.

RADISHES

'Champion'

WHY GROW THEM

They're easy, gratifyingly fast-growing, and so good when picked while young, juicy, and sweet. If you're going to grow your own, strike out and experiment with the many different varieties available, from the classic short, round red radish to the long, narrow, sweet varieties called breakfast radishes, to the Asian varieties, which include daikon and the distinctive red-heart radish—also known as watermelon radish for its stunning deep pink interior.

EXTRA REWARD Radish greens. Don't throw those radish tops away—they make a wonderful (and nutritious) addition to soups and stir-fries; you can also sauté or braise them with other greens as a side dish. And they're good in salads too (toss with dressing at the last minute, since they wilt quickly).

WHEN TO HARVEST

Pick as soon as radishes reach full size (many mature about 3 weeks after sowing, but some varieties are slower), when you see their little shoulders pushing above the soil. If you leave them in the ground too long, they will turn woody and too pungent to eat.

HOW TO KEEP

Refrigerate, unwashed, in a plastic bag up to 1 week.

'Cherry Belle'

Some of our favorite varieties

'Champion' A good all-around red radish with a perfect ball shape and plenty of leafy greens.

'Cherry Belle' An early-bearing variety best harvested when the weather is still cool.

Daikon These giant Asian radishes (they can reach a foot or more) look like long white icicles. Crisp and mild.

'Easter Egg II' This seed mix blends pink-, rose-, purple-, and white-skinned radishes. All have crisp, juicy white flesh.

'French Dressing' and 'Red Flame' Both varieties are the sweet, long, narrow, white tipped type known as breakfast radishes.

'Misato Rose Flesh' This long, narrow radish is green outside and pink inside.

Watermelon An heirloom originally from China, this whitish green radish has a gorgeous fuchsia interior that is juicy, mild, and sweet. Great for cooking, pickling, or eating raw.

Basic Ways to Cook

PICKLE For a fast, lively condiment, make this quick pickle: Slice radishes thinly (enough to make 1 cup loosely packed). Mix 2 tbsp. sugar and 1 tsp. salt with ½ cup unseasoned rice vinegar, ¼ cup white wine vinegar, and ½ cup water until dissolved. Add 5 to 6 black peppercorns. Pour over radishes and let sit at least 1 hour and up to 4 days.

ROAST This works especially well with watermelon radishes. Cut 1 lb. trimmed radishes into wedges. Mix radishes with 2 tbsp. olive oil and put in a 2-qt. baking dish. Roast radishes in a 375° oven, stirring occasionally, until fork tender, about 1 hour. Drizzle with another 1 tbsp. oil and sprinkle with 1 tsp. coarse sea salt.

STIR-FRY Add thinly sliced radishes when stir-frying. Cook until tender-crisp, 4 to 6 minutes.

Radishes, fresh
butter, and salt

GOOD FOR YOU
If you're looking for a super
low-cal snack, turn to radishes.
One radish has only about a
calorie.

Radishes, fresh butter, and salt

SERVES 6
TIME About 5 minutes

This classic country French hors d'oeuvre could not be easier. When both the radishes and butter are very fresh, it is delicious.

24 juicy, just-picked radishes
Unsalted butter, best quality possible
Fine sea salt

Cut the bigger radishes in half and leave smaller ones whole. Serve with butter, salt, and a butter knife or two for spreading.

PER SERVING (4 RADISHES AND ³/₄ TSP. BUTTER) 28 CAL., 93% (26 CAL.) FROM FAT; 0.15 G PROTEIN; 2.9 G FAT (1.8 G SAT.); 0.61 G CARBO (0.28 G FIBER); 7.4 MG SODIUM; 7.6 MG CHOL.

Whole-leaf radish and herb salad

SERVES 4 to 6
TIME About 20 minutes, plus 30 minutes to chill

Instead of lettuces, this salad has lots of just-picked herbs plus radish leaves, which have a lovely, fresh, "green" taste.

3 cups loosely packed small, tender radish leaves (or use larger tender leaves torn into pieces)
2 cups *each* quartered radishes and loosely packed small flat-leaf parsley leaves
³/₄ cup *each* loosely packed small dill sprigs, chervil sprigs, and tarragon leaves
1½ tsp. red wine vinegar
½ tsp. fine sea salt, plus more to taste
3 tbsp. extra-virgin olive oil

1. Combine the radish leaves, radishes, parsley, dill, chervil, and tarragon in a large serving bowl. Cover and chill for about 30 minutes to crisp the leaves.
2. Whisk together vinegar and salt in a small bowl, then whisk in oil to make a dressing. Drizzle dressing over salad and toss gently to coat evenly. Season to taste with salt.

PER SERVING 99 CAL., 67% (66 CAL.) FROM FAT; 3 G PROTEIN; 7.7 G FAT (1.1 G SAT.); 6 G CARBO (1.8 G FIBER); 234 MG SODIUM; 0 MG CHOL.

Watermelon-radish salad

SERVES 6
TIME At least 15 minutes

Also known as red-heart or rose-heart radish, the sweet watermelon radish is an Asian variety. You might even find it sold as red daikon. It is an absolute stunner when cut in half, and that's the prettiest way to serve it, thinly sliced across to see its gorgeous interior.

1 watermelon radish (about 12 oz.)
¹/₃ cup seasoned rice vinegar
1 tsp. black sesame seeds (optional)

1. Peel radish; if it is wider than 3 in., cut in half lengthwise. Slice crosswise as thinly as possible. Mix with vinegar.
2. Cover and chill at least 10 minutes or up to 1 hour, stirring occasionally. Sprinkle with sesame seeds if you like and serve.

PER SERVING 21 CAL., 2.4% (0.5 CAL.) FROM FAT; 0.3 G PROTEIN; 0.1 G FAT (0 G SAT.); 5 G CARBO (0.9 G FIBER); 273 MG SODIUM; 0 MG CHOL.

Watermelon-radish salad

ANOTHER WAY WITH RADISHES

Radishes with nori vinaigrette, crème fraîche, and salt

Try this starter from Jeremy Fox, former executive chef of Ubuntu restaurant, in Napa. Grind nori in a clean coffee grinder; then blend with Dijon and stone-ground mustards, extra-virgin olive oil, and sherry vinegar. Serve as a dip for radishes, along with crème fraîche, and salt (Fox likes Hawaiian black salt).

SUMMER SQUASH

Zucchini

WHY GROW THEM

A good question, considering zucchini is the classic vegetable-that-ate-my-garden plant. The key to growing summer squash is to not let your eyes get too big for your refrigerator, and just put in a plant or two. And remember that summer squash isn't just about zucchini—there are also the very beautiful and tasty pattypan and crookneck types. Grow your own so you can pick them at their flavorful best, while they're still small and their skin is tender. You can even enjoy them as baby vegetables, picked when they're only a couple of inches long, with the blossom attached.

EXTRA REWARD Squash blossoms. These beautiful flowers can be battered and fried, stuffed and fried, sautéed, or added raw to any number of recipes. When you can find them at markets, they are most often zucchini blossoms, but the flowers of all squash plants (summer and winter varieties) are edible, and growing your own lets you try different types.

WHEN TO HARVEST

(Squash) When they are the size you prefer, use pruners to cut the stems close to the fruit (be careful of the prickly stems). **(Squash blossoms)** Pick flowers in the morning, snipping them off the vine when they're cool, fresh, and still open; they will wilt as the day progresses. Eat them that day if possible or no later than the next. If you're looking forward to a harvest of squash, be sure to pick only male flowers, which won't have a baby squash attached to them.

'Trombetta di Albenga'

Some of our favorite varieties

'Benning's Green Tint' and 'Sunburst' These pattypan squash varieties are, respectively, lime green and brilliant yellow. Both produce small squash with tender skins, delicate flavor, and few seeds and are perfect for stuffing.

'Condor' This is a more compact-growing bush variety of zucchini.

'Trombetta di Albenga' This variety produces huge, pale green zucchini that can curve like trombones. They taste sweet and mild, stay crunchy even when cooked, and all the seeds are concentrated in the bulbous end, so most of what you get is seed-free.

Basic Ways to Cook

STIR-FRY Cut squash into ¼-in.-thick slices. Stir-fry up to 5 cups, using 1 tbsp. oil, for 1 minute. Add 2 to 4 tbsp. liquid of your choice, cover, and cook just until tender-crisp, 3 to 4 minutes more.

STEAM This works nicely for whole baby squash, but you can also do it with ¼-in.-thick slices. Arrange squash in a steaming basket, put in a saucepan filled with 1 in. of boiling water, and cover. Steam until tender when pierced, 10 to 12 minutes for whole squash, 4 to 7 minutes for slices.

GRILL Leave smaller squash (1 in. or less in diameter) whole; cut larger squash in half lengthwise. Brush with olive oil or a basting sauce or marinade and grill over direct medium heat (350° to 450°; you can hold your hand 5 in. above cooking grate only 5 to 7 seconds), turning frequently, until browned, crisp-edged, and tender when pierced, 10 to 15 minutes.

HOW TO KEEP

(Squash) Refrigerate, unwashed, in a plastic bag up to 5 days. **(Squash blossoms)** Keep in a plastic bag in the refrigerator until ready to use. To clean, dunk them in cold water several times, then gently pat dry. Check inside for ants or other critters and brush them out gently.

PRESERVING THE HARVEST

FREEZE You can freeze whole young squash, cut into ½-inch-thick slices, or shredded zucchini for use throughout the winter in baking breads, cakes, and cookies. For sliced squash, blanch in boiling water for 3 minutes, drain, plunge into cold water to cool, drain again, pack in resealable plastic bags with ½-inch headspace, and freeze. For shredded zucchini, steam in small amounts in a fine-mesh metal colander until translucent, 1 to 2 minutes. Pack in plastic bags, leaving ½-inch headspace. Seal bags, plunge into cold water to cool, pat dry, and freeze.

Creamy basil zucchini soup
RECIPE P. 160

Squash blossom,
avocado, and butter
lettuce salad
RECIPE P. 160

Grilled vegetable meze plate

SERVES 4
TIME 30 minutes

Reader Joel Hash of San Francisco gives thin ribbons of garden-fresh summer squash and peppers a turn on the grill for a twist on traditional crudités and dip.

4 tbsp. extra-virgin olive oil, divided

1 tbsp. minced garlic

Juice of 1 lemon, divided

½ tsp. kosher salt

About 1½ lbs. green zucchini, thinly sliced lengthwise

About 1 lb. yellow zucchini, thinly sliced lengthwise

2 red bell peppers (8 oz. each), quartered and seeds and ribs removed

1 large red onion, cut into 8 wedges

2 tbsp. chopped oregano

8 oz. hummus

1 cup mixed olives

Pita wedges or chips

1. Prepare a charcoal or gas grill for direct high heat (450° to 550°; you can hold your hand 5 in. above cooking grate only 2 to 4 seconds). Mix 2 tbsp. oil, the garlic, half the lemon juice, and the salt in a large bowl. Add vegetables and toss to coat.

2. Grill vegetables, turning once, until softened and grill marks appear, about 10 minutes.

3. Divide vegetables among 4 plates. Drizzle with remaining 2 tbsp. oil and remaining lemon juice. Sprinkle with oregano. Serve with hummus, olives, and pita.

PER SERVING 366 CAL., 61% (224 CAL.) FROM FAT; 9.3 G PROTEIN; 26 G FAT (3.3 G SAT.); 30 G CARBO (8.9 G FIBER); 928 MG SODIUM; 0 MG CHOL.

Creamy basil zucchini soup

SERVES 4 to 6
TIME 45 minutes

Reader Daniela F. Thompson of Lafayette, California, got this recipe from her mother, who was a teacher. The students' parents would bring her mom pounds of zucchini, and this soup was a way to use up all that squash. In summertime, Daniela likes to serve her mother's soup with sliced tomatoes and hunks of baguette. (Photo on page 158.)

1 tbsp. olive oil

1 large yellow onion, chopped

2 lbs. zucchini, sliced ¼ in. thick

4 cups reduced-sodium chicken broth

1 cup loosely packed basil, plus more for garnish

2 tbsp. crème fraîche or sour cream, plus more for garnish

¼ tsp. chili powder, plus more for garnish

Kosher salt

1. Heat oil in a large saucepan over medium heat. Add onion and cook until translucent, about 5 minutes. Add zucchini and cook another 2 minutes; add broth and basil. Reduce heat to a simmer and cook 20 minutes.

2. Purée soup in batches in a blender. Pour soup through a fine-mesh strainer into a bowl, using a ladle to push any solid bits through. Add crème fraîche and chili powder. Season with salt to taste.

3. Divide soup among bowls and garnish each with a little additional crème fraîche, a sprinkle of chili powder, and a few basil leaves.

PER 1½-CUP SERVING 101 CAL., 45% (45 CAL.) FROM FAT; 5.5 G PROTEIN; 5 G FAT (1.7 G SAT.); 11 G CARBO (2.5 G FIBER); 440 MG SODIUM; 4.7 MG CHOL.

Squash blossom, avocado, and butter lettuce salad

SERVES 4 to 6
TIME 10 minutes

The avocado adds a rich creaminess to this simple—and beautiful—salad. (Photo on page 159.)

1 tbsp. fresh lemon juice

5 tbsp. extra-virgin olive oil

1 tsp. Dijon mustard

½ tsp. *each* kosher salt and freshly ground black pepper

1 butter lettuce head, torn into large pieces

2 cups small squash blossoms, stems removed, divided

3 tbsp. roasted, unsalted sunflower seeds

1 avocado, peeled, pitted, and sliced

Whisk together lemon juice, oil, mustard, salt, and pepper in a large bowl. Add lettuce, 1½ cups blossoms, the sunflower seeds, and avocado and lightly toss with dressing until coated. Sprinkle remaining ½ cup blossoms on top of salad.

PER SERVING 187 CAL., 89% (166 CAL.) FROM FAT; 1.9 G PROTEIN; 19 G FAT (2.6 G SAT.); 5.2 G CARBO (3.2 G FIBER); 184 MG SODIUM; 0 MG CHOL.

Smoked trout and vegetable salad

SERVES 4

TIME 45 minutes

This first-course salad is a picture of summertime freshness, with the bright yellow of the crookneck squash and tomatoes specked with vibrant green parsley vinaigrette.

1 cup chopped flat-leaf parsley

7 tbsp. olive oil

2 tbsp. plus 1 tsp. fresh lemon juice

½ tsp. finely shredded lemon zest

¼ tsp. kosher salt, plus more to taste

¾ lb. 'Yukon Gold' potatoes, boiled in water
   to cover until tender, drained, and cut into
   ¼-in.-thick slices

½ lb. yellow crookneck squash, very thinly sliced

3 medium yellow tomatoes, cut into wedges

Freshly ground black pepper

8 oz. smoked trout, broken into flakes

1. Whirl parsley in a blender with oil, 2 tbsp. lemon juice, the lemon zest, and salt until smooth and emulsified.

2. Gently toss potatoes and squash in a large bowl with some of dressing. In another bowl, toss tomato wedges with remaining 1 tsp. lemon juice, adding salt and pepper to taste.

3. Divide vegetables and trout among 4 plates. Add more dressing to taste if you like.

PER SERVING 422 CAL., 59% (247 CAL.) FROM FAT; 21 G PROTEIN; 28 G FAT (4.4 G SAT.); 24 G CARBO (3.2 G FIBER); 147 MG SODIUM; 81 MG CHOL.

Summer squash carpaccio and shaved cheese salad

SERVES 4

TIME 30 minutes

Sliced paper-thin, the squash get a lively flavor punch from peppery arugula, refreshing mint, and tangy sheep's-milk cheese. Cookbook author Janet Fletcher gave us this recipe.

3 tbsp. pine nuts
1½ tbsp. fresh lemon juice
1 small garlic clove, minced
1 tsp. Thai or Vietnamese fish sauce (*nam pla* or *nuoc mam*)
3 tbsp. extra-virgin olive oil
Kosher salt and freshly ground black pepper
1 lb. small summer squash, preferably both green and yellow, 4 to 5 in. long
2 cups loosely packed baby arugula
12 large mint leaves, coarsely chopped
2 to 3 oz. aged sheep's-milk cheese

1. Preheat oven to 350°. Toast pine nuts in a pie pan until golden, shaking occasionally, 5 to 8 minutes; set aside. Combine lemon juice, garlic, and fish sauce in a large bowl. Whisk in oil. Add salt and pepper to taste.
2. Trim ends from squash. With a cheese plane or mandoline, shave squash thinly lengthwise.
3. Mix squash in bowl with dressing. Let stand for 5 minutes to soften. Add arugula and mint. With a cheese plane, shave as much cheese over salad as you like. Add 2 tbsp. pine nuts and toss. Add more salt and pepper to taste, then transfer to a platter. Sprinkle with remaining pine nuts and serve immediately.

PER SERVING 306 CAL., 77% (236 CAL.) FROM FAT; 14 G PROTEIN; 27 G FAT (9.4 G SAT.); 5.9 G CARBO (1.8 G FIBER); 521 MG SODIUM; 34 MG CHOL.

Grilled yellow squash and zucchini pasta salad

SERVES 15
TIME About 1¼ hours

Here's a way to use summer's abundant squash that's perfect for a potluck picnic.

16 oz. farfalle (bow-tie) pasta
1 lb. yellow crookneck squash, cut into 1-in. chunks
1 lb. zucchini, halved lengthwise and cut into 1-in. chunks
½ cup olive oil, divided
Salt
2 tbsp. Champagne vinegar
½ tsp. freshly ground black pepper, plus more to taste
2 tbsp. chopped oregano
¼ to ½ cup pine nuts, toasted (see Flavor Note, right)
¼ cup chopped pitted kalamata olives

1. Cook pasta in a large pot of boiling salted water until tender to the bite, 9 to 12 minutes or according to package directions. Drain and rinse thoroughly under cold water until completely cool (see Timesaver Tip, right).
2. Prepare a charcoal or gas grill for direct medium heat (350° to 450°; you can hold your hand 5 in. above cooking grate only 5 to 7 seconds). Thread squash and zucchini chunks onto 10- to 12-in. metal skewers and place on a baking sheet. Brush vegetables with ¼ to ⅓ cup oil on all sides and sprinkle with salt to taste. Transfer to grill and cook, turning occasionally, until vegetables are very tender, 10 to 15 minutes.
3. Meanwhile, whisk together remaining oil, the vinegar, and pepper in a small bowl.
4. With a fork, push vegetables off skewers back onto baking sheet and toss them in oil left there. In a large bowl, toss together pasta, vegetables, oregano, pine nuts, and olives. Add dressing and salt and pepper to taste; toss. Serve warm or cold.

FLAVOR NOTE Toasting pine nuts increases their flavor and crunch. Spread them in a pie pan and toast in a 350° oven until golden, shaking occasionally, 5 to 8 minutes.

TIMESAVER TIP The ingredients can be prepped and the pasta cooked a day ahead of time and chilled (add 1 tbsp. extra-virgin olive oil to the cooked pasta). Toss everything together just before serving.

PER 1-CUP SERVING 207 CAL., 41% (86 CAL.) FROM FAT; 5.1 G PROTEIN; 9.5 G FAT (1.3 G SAT.); 26 G CARBO (1.4 G FIBER); 212 MG SODIUM; 0 MG CHOL.

Pattypan squash with eggs

SERVES 8
TIME About 1 hour

You may find that your squash—depending on shape—can't hold a whole egg. No problem; just scoop out some of the white.

8 pattypan squash (each 5 in. across)
About 2 tbsp. olive oil, divided
1 medium onion, finely chopped
1 tsp. sea salt, divided
3 garlic cloves, minced
1 tsp. minced thyme
8 large eggs

1. Preheat oven to 375°. Cut tops (stem ends) off squash and reserve. Scoop out and discard insides of squash, leaving a shell at least ¼ in. thick. Brush squash and tops with about 1 tbsp. oil, set on a baking sheet, and bake until tender when pierced with a fork, about 15 minutes.
2. Meanwhile, heat remaining 1 tbsp. oil in a large frying pan over medium-high heat. Add onion and ¾ tsp. salt. Cook, stirring often, until onion is soft, 3 to 5 minutes. Add garlic and cook, stirring, until fragrant, 30 seconds. Add thyme and cook, stirring, 30 seconds more.

Pattypan squash with eggs

3. Set squash tops aside. Divide onion mixture evenly among the squash. Crack 1 egg into each squash, lifting out any white that doesn't fit. Sprinkle eggs with remaining ¼ tsp. salt. Bake until eggs are set, 15 to 20 minutes. Serve immediately, with tops set to the side.

TIMESAVER TIP You can bake the empty squash cups up to 4 hours ahead and keep at room temperature, covered.

PER SQUASH 165 CAL., 48% (80 CAL.) FROM FAT; 10 G PROTEIN; 8.9 G FAT (2.1 G SAT.); 14 G CARBO (3.9 G FIBER); 366 MG SODIUM; 212 MG CHOL.

Shrimp-and-
zucchini skewers
with noodle salad

End-of-summer pasta

SERVES 6

TIME About 1 hour, plus 45 minutes to marinate

Reader Lea Black of North Tustin, California, put together this grilled chicken and summer vegetable pasta.

1 cup olive oil, divided
⅓ cup reduced-sodium soy sauce
¼ cup balsamic vinegar
3 tbsp. Dijon mustard
6 garlic cloves, minced
1½ lbs. boned, skinned chicken breast halves
1 lb. zucchini
2 red bell peppers (12 oz. total)
1 red onion (12 oz.)
2 portabella mushroom caps (7 oz. total)
1 lb. dried penne pasta
1½ cups freshly grated parmesan cheese
Salt and freshly ground black pepper
½ cup slivered basil leaves

1. Whisk ⅔ cup oil in a bowl with the soy sauce, vinegar, mustard, and garlic. Reserve ½ cup marinade for basting vegetables; pour the rest into a 1-gal. resealable plastic bag.
2. Cut chicken lengthwise into 1-in.-wide strips and add to bag. Seal bag and turn to coat. Chill about 45 minutes.
3. Meanwhile, slice zucchini lengthwise into ¼-in.-thick strips. Stem and seed bell peppers; quarter lengthwise. Peel onion and slice crosswise into ¼-in.-thick rounds. Brush vegetables, including mushrooms, with reserved marinade.
4. Prepare a charcoal or gas grill for direct high heat (450° to 550°; you can hold your hand 5 in. above cooking grate only 2 to 4 seconds).
5. Cooking in batches if necessary, lay vegetables and chicken (discard marinade) on grill; close lid on gas grill. Cook, turning once, until vegetables are slightly charred and chicken is no longer pink in center (cut to test), 6 to 10 minutes. Let cool a few minutes. Chop vegetables and chicken into 1-in. pieces.
6. Meanwhile, in a 6- to 8-qt. pan over high heat, bring 4 qts. water to a boil. Add pasta, stir, and cook, uncovered, until barely tender to bite, 9 to 13 minutes. Drain.
7. Mix pasta in a large bowl with remaining ⅓ cup oil, the parmesan, half the chopped vegetables and chicken, and salt and pepper to taste. Top with remaining vegetables and chicken. Garnish with basil.

PER SERVING 872 CAL., 44% (387 CAL.) FROM FAT; 49 G PROTEIN; 43 G FAT (9.6 G SAT.); 69 G CARBO (4.2 G FIBER); 1,165 MG SODIUM; 85 MG CHOL.

Shrimp-and-zucchini skewers with noodle salad

SERVES 4

TIME 40 minutes

Reader Letty Ernst of San Francisco created this refreshing summer combo of grilled shrimp with a Vietnamese-style salad of lettuce, mint, cilantro, and cold rice noodles.

3 garlic cloves, finely chopped
Finely shredded zest and juice of 1 lime
1½ tsp. Thai or Vietnamese fish sauce (*nam pla* or *nuoc mam*)
¾ tsp. Asian chili garlic sauce
2½ tbsp. soy sauce
½ tsp. minced fresh ginger
¼ cup olive oil
1 lb. (about 24) large shrimp, peeled and deveined
½ lb. zucchini, halved lengthwise and sliced ½ in. thick
2 oz. flat rice-stick noodles
2 tbsp. seasoned rice vinegar
4 cups loosely packed torn butter or red-leaf lettuce
¼ cup *each* thinly sliced mint, chopped cilantro, and thinly sliced red onion

1. Whisk together garlic, lime zest and juice, fish sauce, chili garlic sauce, soy sauce, ginger, and oil in a small bowl. Toss shrimp and zucchini in a medium bowl with ¼ cup sauce mixture.
2. Prepare a charcoal or gas grill for direct medium heat (350° to 450°; you can hold your hand 5 in. above cooking grate only 5 to 7 seconds). Cook noodles according to package directions. Drain, rinse under cold water, and chill until ready to use.
3. Thread shrimp and zucchini alternately on 8 metal skewers (8 to 10 in.). Using tongs and a wad of oiled paper towels, oil cooking grate. Grill skewers, turning once, until shrimp are cooked through and zucchini is tender-crisp, about 7 minutes total.
4. Whisk vinegar into small bowl of sauce mixture to make salad dressing. In a medium bowl, toss lettuce, rice noodles, mint, cilantro, and onion with dressing until coated. Divide salad among 4 plates and set skewers alongside each serving.

PER SERVING 340 CAL., 42% (142 CAL.) FROM FAT; 27 G PROTEIN; 16 G FAT (2.3 G SAT.); 22 G CARBO (2.5 G FIBER); 1,100 MG SODIUM; 172 MG CHOL.

GOOD FOR YOU
Summer squash is low in calories (1 cup of sliced raw squash contains only 19 calories).

Chocolate zucchini rum cake

SERVES 16 to 20; makes 1 tube cake
TIME 1½ hours

This boozy, tender, and extremely chocolaty cake from reader Andee Zetterbaum of Modesto, California, gets some of its moistness from the zucchini, but otherwise the vegetable is undetectable. It's a fine use of zucchini that has perhaps grown a little too big.

¾ cup butter, at room temperature,
    plus more for pan
2 cups granulated sugar
3 large eggs
2 cups loosely packed shredded zucchini
⅓ cup rum, brandy, or water
2½ cups flour, plus more for pan
1 cup *each* semisweet chocolate chips and
    chopped walnuts
½ cup unsweetened cocoa powder
    (not Dutch-processed)
2½ tsp. baking powder
1½ tsp. baking soda
1 tsp. salt
¾ tsp. cinnamon
¼ cup milk

RUM GLAZE (optional)
1⅔ cups powdered sugar
3 tbsp. rum

1. Preheat oven to 350°. Generously butter and flour a nonstick 10-cup plain or fluted tube pan (angel food cake pan). In a large bowl, with a mixer on medium speed, beat butter and granulated sugar until smoothly blended. Beat in eggs, one at a time, until fluffy. With a wooden spoon, stir in zucchini and rum.
2. Mix flour with chocolate chips, walnuts, cocoa, baking powder and soda, salt, and cinnamon in a medium bowl. Stir flour mixture and milk into egg mixture until well blended. Pour batter into prepared tube pan and spread evenly.
3. Bake until cake begins to pull away from pan sides and springs back when firmly pressed in center, 55 to 60 minutes. Let cool in pan on a rack about 15 minutes. Invert cake onto rack and let cool completely.
4. Make glaze if using: Mix powdered sugar and rum together in a medium bowl until smooth. Drizzle glaze over cake.

TIMESAVER TIP You can make the cake in advance; it will keep up to 2 days at room temperature and up to 1 week, chilled.

PER SERVING 296 CAL., 44% (130 CAL.) FROM FAT; 4.5 G PROTEIN; 15 G FAT (6.7 G SAT.); 40 G CARBO (2.2 G FIBER); 343 MG SODIUM; 50 MG CHOL.

Zucchini cookies

MAKES 5 dozen cookies
TIME 1 hour

You can't taste the zucchini in these cookies from reader Jacob Gross of Lompoc, California, but it adds a nice moist texture.

1 cup butter, at room temperature,
    plus more for pan
1½ cups sugar
2 large eggs
1 tsp. vanilla extract
2 cups grated zucchini
2¾ cups flour
2 tsp. baking powder
1 tsp. *each* cinnamon and salt
1 cup *each* chopped walnuts, semisweet chocolate
    chips, and sweetened flaked coconut
½ cup raisins

1. Preheat oven to 350°. Butter a large baking sheet.
2. Cream together butter and sugar in a large bowl until light and fluffy. Beat in eggs and vanilla. Stir in zucchini.
3. Whisk flour in a medium bowl with baking powder, cinnamon, and salt. Add to zucchini mixture. Stir in walnuts, chocolate chips, coconut, and raisins.
4. Drop cookie dough by tablespoonfuls onto prepared baking sheet. Bake until lightly browned, 15 to 20 minutes, then transfer to a rack to cool. Repeat with remaining dough.

PER COOKIE 106 CAL., 48% (51 CAL.) FROM FAT; 1.3 G PROTEIN; 5.7 G FAT (2.9 G SAT.); 13 G CARBO (0.6 G FIBER); 93 MG SODIUM; 15 MG CHOL.

WINTER SQUASH

'Jarrahdale' pumpkin

WHY GROW THEM

Growing your own opens you up to the incredible variety of shapes, colors, and sizes of these edible members of the gourd family. From the tiny 'Jack Be Little' pumpkin to the small acorn and buttercup types to the enormous Hubbard squash, you will find greens, yellows, oranges, buff, even blue, along with all sorts of striped, striated, and speckled combinations. The cooked texture of winter squash and pumpkins can be dense and dry or moist and custardy or crisp-tender (in the case of the strands of spaghetti squash), and most everything in between, with flavors ranging from lightly sweet to honey sweet.

EXTRA REWARD Squash blossoms. Normally you think of summer squash, particularly zucchini, when you think of squash blossoms, but winter squash (including pumpkins) also produce edible flowers. They can be enjoyed in all the same ways: battered and fried, stuffed and fried, sautéed, or eaten raw in soups or salads.

WHEN TO HARVEST

(Squash) Winter squash should stay on the vine until thoroughly hardened; harvest them, using pruners, with an inch of stem. **(Squash blossoms)** Pick flowers in the morning, snipping them off the vine when they're cool, fresh, and still open; they will wilt as the day progresses. Eat them that day if possible or no later than the next. If you're looking forward to a harvest of squash, be careful to pick only male flowers, which won't have baby squash attached to them.

HOW TO KEEP

(Squash) Store in a cool place (about 55°) until ready to use; they will keep up to 2 months. **(Squash blossoms)** Keep in a plastic bag in the refrigerator until ready to use. To clean, dunk them in cold water several times, then gently pat dry. Check inside for any critters.

PRESERVING THE HARVEST

FREEZE Frozen cooked winter squash is great to have on hand for a quick side-dish purée or as the base for a creamy soup. Steam or roast the squash or pumpkins until soft. Seed if necessary, then remove flesh from rind and let cool. Pack in resealable plastic freezer bags, leaving ½-inch headspace. Seal and freeze.

Basic Ways to Cook

GRILL Try this with smaller squash like kabocha or acorn. Cut in half, scoop out the seeds, and cut into ½-in.-thick slices. Brush with olive oil or your favorite basting sauce or marinade and grill over direct medium heat (350° to 450°; you can hold your hand 5 in. above cooking grate only 5 to 7 seconds), turning only once, until browned, crisp-edged, and tender when pierced, 10 to 12 minutes.

MICROWAVE Poke squash all over with a fork. Microwave on high 5 to 10 minutes, depending on size. Fork should easily pierce peel and flesh. If it doesn't, microwave squash in 1-minute intervals until it does. Let sit until cool enough to handle, cut in half lengthwise, scoop out seeds, and proceed with recipe. Works for all varieties.

ROAST/BAKE Cut squash in half lengthwise. Using a soup spoon, scoop out and discard seeds. Place squash, cut side down, on a greased baking sheet and bake at 375° until tender when pierced with a fork, 15 to 45 minutes, depending on size. **(Spaghetti squash)** Pierce shell in several places to let steam escape. Place whole squash on baking sheet; bake at 350° for 45 minutes. Turn squash over and bake until squash gives to pressure, 15 to 45 minutes more, depending on size.

STEAM Peel, seed, and cut or slice squash and put in a steamer basket. Steam, covered, over 1 in. boiling water until tender, 10 to 20 minutes, depending on size of pieces. Best for squash that is smooth-skinned and easily peeled, such as butternut and kabocha.

Some of our favorite varieties

Acorn A good all-around squash. Generally on the small side, it's ideal for stuffing.

Butternut Easy to peel, with lots of rich-tasting, deep orange flesh and very few seeds; the most versatile of the winter squash.

Delicata Small, oblong, and festively striped. Sweet yellow flesh cooks up to be nutty and pleasantly dry.

Kabocha Roundish and dark green outside with dense, smooth, dark orange flesh inside that hints of caramel.

Pumpkin What's a garden without a pumpkin? But why not make it interesting and try an offbeat variety like 'Sugar Pie', which is mild and dry and great for curries, or the Australian heirloom 'Jarrahdale'—a space gobbler, but voluptuous and sweet, and it stores well for months?

Spaghetti It's all about texture with this mild squash: When cooked, scrape it with a spoon, and the flesh separates into juicy, pastalike strands.

**Roasted squash
soup with sage**

1. Preheat oven to 375°. Cut off top third of each squash. Scoop out seeds from squash bottoms and tops; discard. Trim just enough off bottom of each squash so it sits straight.
2. Set squash bottoms and tops on 2 large baking sheets and drizzle with about 2 tbsp. oil, rubbing it over insides and rims. Bake until flesh is soft and golden brown, but before squash start collapsing, 45 to 55 minutes.
3. Meanwhile, heat remaining 2 tbsp. oil in a large pot over medium heat; add onion, paprika, chopped sage, and ½ tsp. salt and cook until golden brown, about 5 minutes. Add garlic and cook 2 minutes more.
4. Scoop cooked flesh from squash into pot, leaving enough flesh so that squash keep their shape. Pave over any holes in squash "bowls" with some cooked squash and keep squash bowls warm.
5. Add 5 cups broth, remaining 1 tsp. salt, and the pepper to pot. Bring to a boil; reduce heat and simmer 5 minutes. Add salt to taste.
6. Purée soup in batches in a blender, adding more broth if soup is too thick (cover top with a towel to keep hot soup from spurting out). Reheat in pot. Stir in crème fraîche and more broth if necessary.
7. Ladle soup into squash bowls and top with sage leaves.

PER SERVING 251 CAL., 49% (122 CAL.) FROM FAT; 6.1 G PROTEIN; 14 G FAT (4.8 G SAT.); 30 G CARBO (8.3 G FIBER); 285 MG SODIUM; 13 MG CHOL.

Roasted squash soup with sage

SERVES 8

TIME 2 hours

Served in its own edible "bowl," this soup always makes an impression.

8 medium acorn squash (roundish)

4 tbsp. mild olive oil, divided

1 medium yellow onion, chopped

1 tsp. smoked Spanish paprika (pimentón de La Vera; see Flavor Note, page 131)

2 tbsp. chopped sage, plus several leaves for garnish

1½ tsp. coarse sea salt, divided, plus more to taste

2 garlic cloves, chopped

5 to 6 cups reduced-sodium chicken broth

½ tsp. freshly ground black pepper

½ cup crème fraîche

HOW TO CUT WINTER SQUASH

Some winter squash have incredibly hard skins, and cutting them can be difficult. It helps to soften them up a little first: Poke the squash in several places with a knife tip or skewer, then microwave for 1 to 2 minutes, or until it's slightly more tender when poked with a knife tip. Use a large, heavy knife to cut the tenderized squash, and tap the knife into the flesh with a mallet if necessary.

Spiced pumpkin
soup with ginger
browned butter
RECIPE P. 173

Spaghetti squash
with jalapeño cream

Spaghetti squash with jalapeño cream

SERVES 8

TIME 1¼ hours

We've tossed spaghetti squash with a spicy cream sauce and baked it, mac-'n'-cheese-style, for a warming, hearty side dish that doubles easily and reheats beautifully. Keep this one in mind for Thanksgiving.

1 spaghetti squash (about 3 lbs.)

2 cups milk

2 to 3 jalapeño chiles, stems, seeds, and ribs removed, chopped

2 tbsp. butter, plus more for pan and baking dish

3 tbsp. flour

1 tsp. salt

1 cup shredded jack cheese

1. Preheat oven to 375°. Cut squash in half lengthwise and use a spoon or melon baller to remove seeds and surrounding fiber. Put squash, cut side down, on a lightly buttered baking sheet and bake until tender when flesh is pierced with a fork, 30 to 40 minutes. Or poke several holes in skin of squash with a fork and microwave it on high 10 minutes. Squash should be tender when pierced with a fork; if it isn't, microwave on high in 1-minute intervals until tender. Let cool.

2. Meanwhile, in a medium saucepan over medium heat, warm milk and jalapeños until bubbles form along edge of pan. Remove mixture from heat and let sit 15 minutes. Strain and discard jalapeños.

3. When squash is cool enough to handle, use a large spoon to scrape strands out of skin and into a large bowl.

4. Melt 2 tbsp. butter in a medium saucepan over medium-high heat. Whisk in flour and salt and cook, whisking, until flour smells cooked (like pie crust), about 3 minutes. Slowly pour in jalapeño-infused milk while whisking. Reduce heat to medium and continue whisking until mixture thickens slightly, about 3 minutes. Pour mixture over squash and stir to combine. Transfer mixture to a buttered 2-qt. baking dish. Sprinkle with jack cheese and bake until bubbling and brown on top, about 30 minutes.

PER SERVING 168 CAL., 53% (89 CAL.) FROM FAT; 6.7 G PROTEIN; 9.9 G FAT (5.7 G SAT.); 14 G CARBO (2 G FIBER); 447 MG SODIUM; 31 MG CHOL.

Spiced pumpkin soup with ginger browned butter

SERVES 8

TIME 1¾ hours

Warm spices and caramelized onions underscore the natural sweetness of pumpkin and butternut squash in this comforting dish. The easy swirl of ginger butter at the end adds a bit of flavor and a lot of style. (Photo on page 171.)

2 lbs. 'Sugar Pie' or other baking pumpkin

2 lbs. butternut or acorn squash

8 cups reduced-sodium chicken broth, divided

7 tbsp. butter, divided

2 medium onions, chopped

1 tsp. salt, plus more to taste

4 garlic cloves, chopped

2 tbsp. plus 1 tsp. finely grated fresh ginger

1 tsp. ground ginger

¼ tsp. freshly grated nutmeg

⅛ tsp. *each* ground cloves and freshly ground cardamom seeds (from about 4 pods)

2 carrots, chopped

½ cup firmly packed light brown sugar

1. Preheat oven to 375°. Cut pumpkin and squash in half lengthwise. Scoop out seeds and any stringy parts. Put flesh side up in a large roasting pan with 1 cup broth. Cover pan with foil and bake until vegetables are tender when pierced with a fork, about 1 hour.

2. Meanwhile, melt 3 tbsp. butter in a large pot over medium heat. Add onions and salt. Cook, stirring occasionally, until onions are soft and start to look creamy, about 5 minutes. Reduce heat to low or medium-low and cook onions, stirring every few minutes, until they turn a caramel color and become quite sweet, about 30 minutes. Set aside.

3. When pumpkin and squash are tender, scoop out flesh and set aside; discard skins. Reserve any liquid in bottom of pan.

4. Return pot with onions to medium-high heat. Add garlic and 2 tbsp. fresh ginger. Cook, stirring, until fragrant, about 2 minutes. Add ground ginger, nutmeg, cloves, and cardamom. Cook, stirring, 1 minute. Add remaining 7 cups broth, the carrots, cooked pumpkin and squash, and reserved liquid from roasting pan. Bring to a boil, then reduce heat and simmer until carrots are tender, about 15 minutes.

5. Whirl vegetables in a blender (in batches) until completely smooth. (For a silky smooth soup, you can pour puréed soup through a fine-mesh strainer.) Return to pot and stir in brown sugar. Season to taste with salt. Keep warm over low heat.

6. Put a small bowl or measuring cup next to stove. Melt remaining 4 tbsp. butter in a small frying pan over medium-high heat. Add remaining 1 tsp. fresh ginger. Cook, stirring occasionally, until butter starts to foam. Stir mixture constantly until it starts to brown. Pour mixture into waiting bowl or measuring cup. Divide soup among 8 bowls and serve hot, with a swirl of ginger browned butter in each serving.

PER SERVING 248 CAL., 36% (90 CAL.) FROM FAT; 5.6 G PROTEIN; 10 G FAT (6.3 G SAT.); 37 G CARBO (3.2 G FIBER); 982 MG SODIUM; 27 MG CHOL.

GOOD FOR YOU

Winter squash is an excellent source of fiber and a good source of potassium and vitamin C.

**Cashew, coconut,
and pumpkin curry**
RECIPE P. 176

Stuffed kabocha squash with Arabic lamb stew
RECIPE P. 176

Cashew, coconut, and pumpkin curry

SERVES 4
TIME 50 minutes

Dense, smooth 'Sugar Pie' pumpkin or kabocha or butternut squash work best here, because they won't fall apart when cooked. You can find curry leaves in Indian markets. (Photo on page 174.)

1 pumpkin or other orange-fleshed squash (3 lbs.), peeled and cut into 1½-in. chunks (1½ qts.)
1 tsp. kosher salt, divided, plus more to taste
3 tbsp. vegetable oil, divided
1 onion, halved and cut into half-moons
1 or 2 red or green serrano chiles, minced
1 cinnamon stick (2½ in. long)
20 fresh curry leaves or 6 bay leaves
1 tsp. *each* cumin seeds and turmeric
1 can (14.5 oz.) coconut milk
1 cup salted roasted cashews
1 tbsp. fresh lemon juice
Steamed basmati rice

1. Sprinkle pumpkin with ½ tsp. salt. Heat 1 tbsp. oil in a large nonstick frying pan over medium-high heat. Brown half the pumpkin in oil, turning once, 6 to 8 minutes; reduce heat if pumpkin starts getting dark. Transfer to a bowl and repeat with another 1 tbsp. oil and remaining pumpkin.
2. Meanwhile, heat remaining 1 tbsp. oil in another large frying pan over medium heat. Cook onion, stirring occasionally, until deep golden, 12 to 15 minutes. Transfer half to the nonstick frying pan and reserve other half in a bowl.
3. Add chiles, cinnamon, and curry leaves to onion in pan. Cook, stirring often, until curry leaves are very fragrant, about 2 minutes. Add cumin seeds, turmeric, and remaining ½ tsp. salt and cook, stirring, until spices are fragrant, about 1 minute.

4. Return pumpkin to nonstick frying pan (with onion) and add coconut milk. Bring to a boil over high heat, then cover, reduce heat, and simmer until pumpkin is tender, 5 to 10 minutes. Stir in cashews and lemon juice, and add more salt to taste. Top curry with reserved onion and serve with rice.

PER SERVING 546 CAL., 79% (430 CAL.) FROM FAT; 9.9 G PROTEIN; 48 G FAT (23 G SAT.); 29 G CARBO (3.2 G FIBER); 498 MG SODIUM; 0 MG CHOL.

Stuffed kabocha squash with Arabic lamb stew

SERVES 6
TIME 3 hours

This warmly spicy stew is made with the spice blend known as *baharat*. Though the exact mix can vary, it usually contains allspice, black pepper, cinnamon, coriander, nutmeg, and cloves. Look for it at a Middle Eastern food market or online. (Photo on page 175.)

3 tbsp. olive oil, divided
1 lb. lamb stew meat, cut into 1½-in. chunks
1 tsp. kosher salt, divided
½ tsp. freshly ground black pepper, divided
¾ lb. shallots, cut in half if large
About 2¼ cups reduced-sodium chicken broth, divided
2 tbsp. *baharat*
¼ cup white basmati rice, rinsed
1½ cups coarsely chopped tomatoes
1 kabocha squash (3½ to 4 lbs.)
1½ tbsp. sliced chives

1. Heat 1 tbsp. oil in a 5- to 6-qt. pan over high heat. Sprinkle lamb with ¾ tsp. salt and ¼ tsp. pepper, then brown in oil, stirring occasionally, 6 to 8 minutes. Transfer lamb to a bowl.

2. Reduce heat to medium-high. Add shallots, 1 tbsp. oil, and ¼ cup broth to pan; stir to loosen browned bits from bottom of pan. Cook, stirring occasionally, until shallots are browned, 7 to 10 minutes; add a splash of water if drippings start to get dark. Return meat to pan and sprinkle with baharat. Add 2 cups more broth, stirring to loosen browned bits again. Cover, bring to a boil, then reduce heat and simmer 1 hour, adding another ¼ cup broth if pan starts to dry. Stir in rice and tomatoes and return to a boil.
3. Meanwhile, preheat oven to 375°. With a short knife, carefully cut around squash stem to make a 4-in. lid. Pry out lid with a table knife. Scrape out and discard seeds from lid and squash. Brush interior of squash and inside of lid with remaining 1 tbsp. oil, then sprinkle them with remaining ¼ tsp. *each* salt and pepper, tipping squash to coat evenly. Set squash on a rimmed baking sheet. Prick with a fork in a couple of spots near top.
4. Fill squash with as much stew as fits. Set lid in place and bake until squash is just tender inside when pierced, 70 minutes to 1½ hours. Meanwhile, spoon remaining stew into a small loaf pan, cover with foil, and bake 1 hour.
5. Stir chives into stew in pan and squash. Transfer squash to a platter using 2 wide spatulas (squash may split a little; this is okay). Use a big metal spoon to scoop squash and stew into soup bowls, adding stew from pan.

PER SERVING 326 CAL., 33% (109 CAL.) FROM FAT; 22 G PROTEIN; 12 G FAT (3.1 G SAT.); 36 G CARBO (4.5 G FIBER); 542 MG SODIUM; 48 MG CHOL.

Whole-wheat lasagna with butternut squash and kale

SERVES 8

TIME About 2 hours

Full of the satisfying flavors of autumn, this lasagna is made with whole-wheat noodles, which add a slight nuttiness. It's even better the next day.

4 tbsp. olive oil, divided

1 medium red onion, sliced

3 garlic cloves, 1 minced, 2 peeled and left whole

2 cans (14 oz. each) crushed tomatoes

1 tsp. dried oregano

1 tsp. *each* salt and freshly ground black pepper, divided, plus more to taste

1 butternut squash (about 2 lbs.), peeled and cut into ½-in. cubes (6 cups)

½ tsp. dried thyme

1 lb. 'Lacinato' kale (often sold as dinosaur or Tuscan kale), rinsed well

9 whole-wheat lasagna noodles (about 8 oz.)

About 2 cups (1 carton, 15 oz.) part-skim-milk ricotta cheese

⅛ tsp. ground nutmeg

2 cups shredded mozzarella cheese, divided

1. Preheat oven to 400°. Heat 2 tbsp. oil in a 2- to 3-qt. saucepan over medium heat. Add onion and minced garlic; cook, stirring occasionally, until onion is soft and translucent, 5 minutes. Add tomatoes, oregano, and ½ tsp. *each* salt and pepper. Reduce heat and simmer until thick and flavors are combined, about 30 minutes. Set aside.

2. While sauce is cooking, in a 12- by 15-in. baking pan, sprinkle squash with thyme, remaining 2 tbsp. oil, and salt and pepper to taste. Add garlic cloves and toss squash mixture to coat with oil. Bake until soft, 10 to 15 minutes. Bring 3 qts. salted water to a boil in a large pot.

3. Meanwhile, reduce oven temperature to 350°. Transfer squash and garlic to a food processor and purée until smooth.

4. Tear kale leaves from center ribs and discard ribs. Boil leaves until soft, 5 to 8 minutes. Drain; let cool. Squeeze out as much water as possible and chop finely.

5. Bring another 3 qts. salted water to a boil in same pot. Add noodles and cook until tender to the bite, about 10 minutes. Drain; rinse with cold water.

6. Mix ricotta, nutmeg, 1 cup mozzarella, and remaining ½ tsp. *each* salt and pepper in a medium bowl.

7. Coat bottom of a 9- by 13-in. pan with one-third of tomato sauce (about 1½ cups). Lay 3 noodles in a single layer over sauce.

Top noodles with squash, spreading evenly. Sprinkle half the kale evenly over squash. Arrange 3 more noodles on kale and top with ricotta, spreading evenly. Top with remaining kale and noodles. Cover noodles with remaining tomato sauce and sprinkle with remaining 1 cup mozzarella.

8. Bake lasagna until juices are bubbling and cheese is melted, about 30 minutes. Let stand 10 minutes before slicing.

TIMESAVER TIP You can assemble and chill the lasagna a day ahead, but add 10 to 15 minutes to the baking time. You can also freeze the lasagna, wrapped well in plastic wrap, for up to 1 month and bake it frozen (add 1¼ hours to the oven time).

PER 4½-IN.-SQUARE SERVING 424 CAL., 38% (162 CAL.) FROM FAT; 20 G PROTEIN; 18 G FAT (7.4 G SAT.); 51 G CARBO (8 G FIBER); 659 MG SODIUM; 39 MG CHOL.

2. Reduce oven temperature to 325°. Butter an 8-in. square baking pan and set aside.

3. Combine flour, allspice, cinnamon, nutmeg, baking powder, salt, baking soda, and pepper in a small bowl. Set aside.

4. Cream together butter and brown sugar with a mixer in a large bowl until smooth and a bit fluffy. Add eggs one at a time, beating for 30 seconds after each addition. Mix in vanilla.

5. Add half the flour mixture to the butter mixture and stir to combine. Stir in the 1 cup mashed squash. Add remaining flour mixture and stir just enough to combine. Pour batter into prepared pan and bake until a toothpick inserted in center comes out clean, 50 to 60 minutes. Serve plain or with a dusting of powdered sugar or a dollop of whipped cream.

QUICK TIPS Whole-wheat pastry flour is sold at natural-food and specialty baking stores, as well as at Whole Foods Market. Serve extra mashed squash hot with butter, salt, and pepper; stir into soups or stews; or freeze for future cakes.

PER SERVING 417 CAL., 30% (126 CAL.) FROM FAT; 6.9 G PROTEIN; 14 G FAT (8 G SAT.); 70 G CARBO (5.3 G FIBER); 401 MG SODIUM; 85 MG CHOL.

Butternut squash spice cake

SERVES 8
TIME 1½ hours

Remarkably moist and tender, this cake gets its warmth from spices like cinnamon, nutmeg, allspice, and a hint of black pepper. Whole-wheat pastry flour adds nutrients without compromising taste or texture.

1 small butternut squash
2 cups whole-wheat pastry flour (see Quick Tips, above right)
1 tsp. *each* ground allspice, cinnamon, freshly grated nutmeg, and baking powder
¾ tsp. salt
½ tsp. baking soda
¼ tsp. freshly ground black pepper
½ cup unsalted butter, softened
1½ cups firmly packed light brown sugar
2 large eggs
1 tsp. vanilla extract
Powdered sugar or whipped cream (optional)

1. Preheat oven to 350°. Cut squash in half lengthwise and remove seeds. Place squash halves, cut side up, on a baking pan, then cover with foil and bake until tender when pierced with a fork, 20 to 30 minutes. Uncover and let sit until cool enough to handle, then use a spoon to scoop cooked squash from peel. Mash with a fork. Measure out 1 cup of squash and set aside any remaining for future use (see Quick Tips, above right).

Pumpkin gingersnap ice cream

SERVES 8; makes 1 qt.
TIME About 45 minutes, plus 2½ hours to freeze

Harder cookies—like Nabisco's—keep the most crunch (softer ones will dissolve).

2 cups whipping cream
½ cup milk
1 cup firmly packed light brown sugar
1 cup Homemade Pumpkin Purée (recipe follows)
1 tsp. *each* cinnamon, ground ginger, and vanilla extract
¼ tsp. salt

½ cup coarsely crushed gingersnaps

2 tbsp. bourbon (optional)

1. Whisk cream, milk, brown sugar, pumpkin purée, cinnamon, ginger, vanilla, and salt in a bowl to blend. Strain into an ice cream maker and freeze according to manufacturer's directions.

2. Scrape ice cream into a bowl and stir in gingersnaps and bourbon if using. Freeze, covered, until scoopable, 2½ hours and up to 1 week (gingersnaps soften somewhat after 1 day).

PER ½-CUP SERVING 371 CAL., 58% (216 CAL.) FROM FAT; 2.6 G PROTEIN; 24 G FAT (14 G SAT.); 39 G CARBO (0.6 G FIBER); 162 MG SODIUM; 84 MG CHOL.

Homemade pumpkin purée

MAKES 1½ to 2 cups (from a 2-lb. pumpkin)

TIME 1 hour

This purée has a concentrated caramelized flavor, making it particularly good for desserts. It freezes well.

1 'Sugar Pie' pumpkin or other deep orange–fleshed squash (about 2 lbs. or larger)

1 to 2 tsp. vegetable oil

1. Preheat oven to 375°. Cut pumpkin through the top, using a large, heavy knife and a mallet to tap knife through flesh. Scoop out and discard seeds. Rub inside of pumpkin with oil. Set pumpkin, cut side down, on a rimmed baking sheet. Bake until very soft when pierced, 45 to 75 minutes.

2. Scoop flesh into a food processor; whirl until smooth. If purée is watery, drain in a strainer 30 minutes.

PER ¼-CUP SERVING 28 CAL., 29% (8 CAL.) FROM FAT; 0.8 G PROTEIN; 1 G FAT (0.1 G SAT.); 5.2 G CARBO (0.4 G FIBER); 0.8 MG SODIUM; 0 MG CHOL.

TOMATOES

'Roma' tomatoes on the vine and a mix of heir-looms in the colander

WHY GROW THEM

Nothing beats the flavor of a just-picked sun-ripened tomato. If all you've ever had are store-bought tomatoes, growing your own will be a revelation. The level of acidity will vary with the varieties you choose to grow, but some types are nearly as sweet as candy, with a yielding texture that makes a mockery of bland, mealy supermarket tomatoes. Growing your own—whether you start with plants or seeds—also allows you to experience the range of tomato flavors, textures, colors, and sizes available, from 2-pound heirloom to cherry tomatoes.

EXTRA REWARD Green tomatoes, picked when full-size but not yet colored, have a tanginess that lends itself to pickling, or to breading and frying.

WHEN TO HARVEST

Tomatoes are best when allowed to fully ripen on the vine (unless you want green tomatoes). Be aware that some varieties ripen from the bottom up and may still have slightly green shoulders when ripe. A tomato that is ready to be picked will usually yield when gently pulled by hand. You can also snip the fruit from the stem with scissors or pruners.

Tomatoes will continue to ripen once picked, so don't leave tomatoes on the vine if a hard frost is coming. Any in the intermediate light green phase will ripen fully indoors. In fact, if you like, you can pull up the entire plant and hang it upside down in a frost-free garage or porch.

HOW TO KEEP

If possible, don't put tomatoes in the refrigerator, or at least only briefly, and bring them back to room temperature before slicing. If refrigerated more than a few days under 50°, a tomato gets mealy and loses its smell (which affects how we taste it). Keep your harvested ripe tomatoes at room temperature or cool room temperature and out of the sun. Arrange them in a single layer, sturdier (stem) side down, so they don't bruise.

PRESERVING THE HARVEST

FREEZE Either slow-roast (see recipe, page 196) and freeze, or freeze ripe unpeeled tomatoes in a single layer until frozen solid, then double-bag in resealable plastic freezer bags. The thawed tomatoes will have lost their firmness, but they'll still taste good and will be fine for sauce. You can also make sauce and bank that in the freezer as well; see our recipes on page 195.

CAN See our recipe for Canned Heirloom Tomatoes (page 196).

DRY Slice large tomatoes thinly; halve cherry tomatoes or leave whole. Arrange in a single layer in a dehydrator and leave until dry, from 8 hours to 1 day, depending on moisture level. Pack in an airtight container and keep in a cool, dark spot for up to 6 months, or in the refrigerator.

Basic Ways to Cook

ROAST Core big tomatoes, cut in half, and squeeze out juice and seeds. Roast, drizzled with olive oil and sprinkled with salt or other seasonings, at 400° for 20 to 25 minutes. For concentrated flavor, slow-roast them (see recipe, page 196).

PURÉE Remove skins first by slicing an X at the blossom end, plunging in boiling water until the skins loosen (20 to 30 seconds), then cooling. Peel, core, seed (if you like), and purée in a blender. Use as a base for sauces, soups, or cocktails.

GRILL Slice big tomatoes into thick slices, brush with oil, and grill over direct medium heat (350° to 450°; you can hold your hand 5 in. above cooking grate only 5 to 7 seconds) 8 to 12 minutes, turning once with a wide metal spatula.

Some of our favorite varieties

'Brandywine' This heirloom is a great favorite around the country, and no wonder—it produces tomatoes with a beautiful magenta-purple color and a sweet, creamy texture that just begs to be enjoyed straight off the vine.

'Early Girl' Your best bet for an early-season tomato.

'Green Zebra' We love this purposefully green tomato for its tart, citrusy flavor.

'Hillbilly' An heirloom that dates back to 1880. It's a super slicing tomato, producing 1- to 2-pound heavily ribbed fruits. The flesh is orange-yellow mottled with red, and has an almost peachlike texture.

'Kellogg's Breakfast' Electric orange, sweet-tart flesh, and tender texture.

'Roma' Their dense, meaty flesh is ideal for cooking and canning.

'Sun Gold' Deep yellow cherry tomatoes, with fabulous flavor and juiciness.

'Sweet 100' The quintessential red cherry tomato—juicy and with a good balance of acidity and sweetness.

Filo tomato tart
RECIPE P. 184

Tomato salad with chile and lime
RECIPE P. 184

Filo tomato tart

MAKES About 20 (3 in.) squares
TIME 45 minutes

This tart from reader Sandy McKee of Omaha, Nebraska, is stunning and simple—a winner as a party hors d'oeuvre or a picnic main dish. Be sure to cut the tomatoes very thinly so the juice evaporates while baking; otherwise, the dough will be soggy. (Photo on page 182.)

7 sheets filo dough, thawed
5 tbsp. unsalted butter, melted
7 tbsp. grated parmesan, divided
1 cup *each* very thinly sliced onion and shredded
    mozzarella cheese
8 'Roma' tomatoes, cut into ⅛-in.-thick slices
1 tbsp. fresh thyme leaves
Salt and freshly ground black pepper

1. Preheat oven to 375°. Line a large baking sheet with parchment paper and spray paper with cooking-oil spray (or brush lightly with vegetable oil). Lay 1 sheet filo on paper and brush lightly with a little melted butter. Sprinkle all over with 1 tbsp. parmesan. Repeat layering 5 more times (with filo, butter, and parmesan), pressing each sheet firmly so it sticks to sheet below. Lay the last filo sheet on top, brush with remaining melted butter, and sprinkle on remaining 1 tbsp. parmesan.
2. Scatter onion across filo, top with mozzarella, and arrange tomato slices in a single layer, overlapping slightly. Sprinkle with thyme and salt and pepper to taste.
3. Bake until filo is golden brown, 30 to 35 minutes. Cool 10 minutes, then serve.

PER SQUARE 76 CAL., 60% (46 CAL.) FROM FAT; 2.5 G PROTEIN; 5.1 G FAT (2.9 G SAT.); 5.2 G CARBO (0.5 G FIBER); 88 MG SODIUM; 14 MG CHOL.

Caramelized tomato bruschetta

SERVES 6
TIME 40 minutes

When cherry tomatoes ripen in the garden, it can almost be too much of a good thing in a short period of time. This appetizer, inspired by a technique in *Seven Fires: Grilling the Argentine Way* by Francis Mallmann, is a tasty way to make use of them. If you have the real estate on your grill, you can do steps 2 and 3 at the same time.

1 slender baguette (8 oz.)
3 tbsp. extra-virgin olive oil, divided
1 pt. large cherry tomatoes, halved
¼ tsp. *each* kosher salt and freshly ground
    black pepper, plus more to taste
¾ cup whole-milk ricotta cheese
1 cup loosely packed small basil leaves

1. Prepare a charcoal or gas grill for direct medium heat (350° to 450°; you can hold your hand 5 in. above cooking grate only 5 to 7 seconds). Cut 18 thin slices from baguette, each 3 to 4 in. wide. Save remaining bread for another use. Set baguette slices on a tray to carry to grill and brush all over with about 1 tbsp. oil.
2. Grill bread with lid down, turning once with tongs, until browned, 1 to 3 minutes total. Transfer to a platter.
3. Heat a large cast-iron skillet or other oven-proof frying pan on cooking grate with grill lid down until water dances when sprinkled on skillet, 8 to 10 minutes. Add 1½ tbsp. oil and spread with a heat-proof brush. Pour tomato halves into pan, then quickly turn with tongs so all are cut side down. Sprinkle with salt and pepper. Cook with grill lid down, without stirring, until juices evaporate and tomatoes

are blackened on cut side, 10 to 15 minutes. Gently loosen tomatoes from pan with a wide metal spatula as they're done and transfer to a bowl.
4. Spoon ricotta into a bowl; drizzle remaining ½ tbsp. oil on top. Put basil in another bowl. Set out toasts with tomatoes, ricotta, and basil so people can build their own bruschetta. Season with more salt and pepper to taste.

PER SERVING 216 CAL., 45% (98 CAL.) FROM FAT; 8.2 G PROTEIN; 11 G FAT (3.6 G SAT.); 22 G CARBO (1.7 G FIBER); 321 MG SODIUM; 16 MG CHOL.

Tomato salad with chile and lime

SERVES 8
TIME 25 minutes

This salad pleasantly reminds us of fresh salsa. We especially like it with beef fajitas or pork or shrimp tacos. (Photo on page 183.)

2 lbs. ripe tomatoes
1 large mild green chile, such as poblano
3 tbsp. olive oil
2 tbsp. fresh lime juice
½ tsp. salt, plus more to taste
¼ tsp. dry mustard

1. Core and halve tomatoes. Remove seeds (either scoop them out with a spoon or hold a half in your hand and squeeze out the seeds) and cut tomatoes into bite-size pieces. Put tomatoes in a large bowl.
2. Remove stem and seeds from chile. Finely chop chile and add to tomatoes. Set aside.
3. In a small bowl, whisk together oil, lime juice, salt, and mustard until emulsified.
4. Drizzle dressing over tomatoes and chiles and toss gently to combine. Add more salt to taste if you like. Serve at room temperature.

PER SERVING 72 CAL., 68% (49 CAL.) FROM FAT; 1.1 G PROTEIN; 5.4 G FAT (0.7 G SAT.); 6 G CARBO (1.5 G FIBER); 155 MG SODIUM; 0 MG CHOL.

Fresh Bloody Mary

MAKES 1 generous serving
TIME 10 minutes

We tested this full-flavored revisiting of the Bloody Mary with the heirloom tomato 'Kellogg's Breakfast'. One look at its OJ-colored flesh and juice, and you know where the name comes from. With a bright, tart taste, this beefsteak tomato has lots of juice and few seeds, which makes it perfect for juicing.

½ lb. 'Kellogg's Breakfast' or other yellow
    heirloom tomatoes
¼ cup gin or vodka
1 tbsp. fresh lemon juice
¼ tsp. Worcestershire
¼ tsp. salt, or to taste
Pinch to ⅛ tsp. celery seed
Hot sauce
Ice
Celery stick or green onion
Freshly ground black pepper

1. Cut tomatoes in half crosswise and press, cut side down, through a colander or a coarse-mesh strainer set over a bowl to collect juice; discard skins.
2. Mix ¾ cup juice (save rest for another use) with gin, lemon juice, Worcestershire, salt, celery seed, and hot sauce to taste. Pour into an ice-filled glass.
3. Garnish with a celery stick or green onion. Sprinkle with pepper to taste.

PER GENEROUS SERVING 182 CAL., 2% (4.5 CAL.) FROM FAT; 2.1 G PROTEIN; 0.5 G FAT (0.1 G SAT.); 13 G CARBO (3.8 G FIBER); 665 MG SODIUM; 0 MG CHOL.

Spicy tomato shorba

SERVES 6 as a first-course soup
TIME 1 hour

This aromatic Indian soup is traditionally served hot, but we've chilled our version to make a refreshing first course for summer.

4½ lbs. ripe tomatoes
2 tsp. vegetable oil
1 tsp. *each* garam masala and ground cumin
½ cup chopped red onion
2 tsp. minced garlic
1 serrano chile, seeds and ribs removed, chopped
2 tbsp. finely grated fresh ginger
1 to 1½ cups reduced-fat coconut milk
3 tbsp. tomato paste
2 tbsp. fresh lemon juice
1 tbsp. sugar
1½ tsp. kosher salt
½ cup chopped cilantro, plus small cilantro leaves

1. Dip tomatoes with a slotted spoon in a pan of boiling water until skins pull off easily with a knife tip, 15 seconds. Cool, peel, core, quarter, and seed.

2. Warm oil in a frying pan over medium heat. Add spices and stir until fragrant, 1 minute.

3. Purée onion in a blender with garlic, chile, ginger, 1 cup coconut milk, the tomato paste, and spice mixture. Add half the tomatoes and their juices and whirl until very smooth. Pour into a stainless steel bowl. Set aside 2 tomato pieces. Purée remaining tomatoes and add to bowl along with lemon juice, sugar, and salt. Stir to combine.

4. Nest bowl in ice water; stir often until cold, 15 minutes. Stir in chopped cilantro and more coconut milk if you like. Chop reserved tomato.

5. Ladle cold soup into bowls; top with chopped tomato and cilantro leaves.

PER 1-CUP SERVING 144 CAL., 31% (44 CAL.) FROM FAT; 3.4 G PROTEIN; 5 G FAT (2.7 G SAT.); 20 G CARBO (3.6 G FIBER); 1,293 MG SODIUM; 0 MG CHOL.

GOOD FOR YOU

Tomatoes are a good source of both fiber and vitamin C, plus 1 large tomato has only 32 calories. Also, their abundant lycopene, a type of antioxidant, may defend against cancer by protecting the DNA.

Tiered tomato soup

SERVES 6 to 8 as a first-course soup
TIME About 30 minutes, plus 1 hour to chill

This soup is a glory of flavor and color, with a ruby red stratum of tomato soup crowning a bright green layer of avocado soup. Clear, straight-sided glasses or wineglasses (12 to 16 oz. each) show off the layers best.

2 lbs. ripe tomatoes
3 to 4 tbsp. white wine vinegar, divided
Salt
2 firm-ripe avocados (8 oz. each)
¾ cup reduced-sodium chicken broth
¼ cup sour cream
3 tbsp. fresh lime juice
1 cucumber (12 oz.)
3 tbsp. minced shallots
1 tsp. minced tarragon

1. Core tomatoes; cut into chunks. Whirl in a blender or food processor until smooth, then rub through a fine-mesh strainer into a bowl; you should have about 3 cups. Discard residue. Season purée with 2 to 3 tbsp. vinegar and salt. Cover and chill until cold, at least 1 hour.
2. Pit and peel avocados; cut into chunks. In a blender or food processor, whirl avocados, broth, sour cream, and lime juice until smooth. Add salt to taste. Cover surface with plastic wrap (this will prevent discoloration) and chill until cold, at least 1 hour.
3. Peel cucumber; cut in half lengthwise and scoop out and discard seeds. Cut into ⅛-in. dice; you should have about 1 cup. In a small bowl, mix cucumber, shallots, 1 tbsp. vinegar, and tarragon. Cover and chill until cold, at least 30 minutes.
4. Stir avocado soup and pour into glasses. Whisk tomato soup and gently pour over avocado. Top with cucumber mixture.

PER SERVING 117 CAL., 65% (76 CAL.) FROM FAT; 2.5 G PROTEIN; 8.4 G FAT (2.1 G SAT.); 11 G CARBO (2.4 G FIBER); 31 MG SODIUM; 3.5 MG CHOL.

Paprika tomatoes with poached eggs (*shakshouka*)

SERVES 2
TIME 45 minutes

Traditionally, cooks in Tunisia and Israel use a lot of olive oil when making this one-pan tomato and egg dinner, but we've cut the oil way back in our lighter version. Feel free to add more oil if you like. Serve with crusty bread.

1½ tsp. coriander seeds
1 tsp. cumin seeds
1½ tbsp. paprika
½ tsp. kosher salt, plus more to taste
3 large garlic cloves, peeled
1 large poblano chile, seeds and ribs removed, chopped
2 tbsp. extra-virgin olive oil, divided
2 tbsp. tomato paste
1½ lbs. ripe 'Roma' tomatoes, halved lengthwise
4 large eggs
Freshly ground black pepper

1. Put coriander, cumin, paprika, and salt in a mortar and pound until crushed; or seal in a plastic bag and crush with a rolling pin. Add garlic and pound into a paste. Set aside.
2. Cook chile in 1 tbsp. oil in a 10-in. frying pan over medium heat, stirring often, until well browned, 10 to 12 minutes. Add spice mixture and tomato paste and cook, stirring, until fragrant, 1 minute. Stir in ¾ cup water, then tomatoes. Cook, turning tomatoes occasionally, until softened, 10 to 20 minutes; add more water, ¼ cup at a time, if mixture starts to get dry (you should see juices).
3. Make 4 depressions in tomato mixture with a wooden spoon and crack an egg into each. Season with salt and pepper. Cover and cook until eggs are set but yolks are still runny, about 5 minutes.

4. Drizzle the shakshouka with 1 tbsp. oil (or more if you like), then scoop onto plates and serve with crusty bread.

PER SERVING 372 CAL., 53% (198 CAL.) FROM FAT; 19 G PROTEIN; 22 G FAT (4.8 G SAT.); 30 G CARBO (6.6 G FIBER); 598 MG SODIUM; 424 MG CHOL.

Tomato breakfast toasts

MAKES 8 slices
TIME 20 minutes

Yes, tomatoes are good even first thing in the morning—as you'll see when you taste this savory play on French toast from reader Teresa Cruz Carns of Pacifica, California. It's great with bacon on the side.

2 large ripe tomatoes
4 large eggs
½ cup low-fat milk
1 tsp. Dijon mustard
½ tsp. *each* salt and minced thyme
¼ tsp. *each* freshly ground black pepper
    and dry mustard
8 slices sourdough bread (about ½ in. thick)
2 tsp. olive oil
8 slices gruyère or white cheddar cheese

1. Cut tomatoes into ⅛- to ¼-in.-thick slices and lay on paper towels (to soak up some of their juices). Set aside.
2. Whisk together eggs, milk, Dijon mustard, salt, thyme, pepper, and dry mustard in a medium bowl. Soak each bread slice in egg mixture for about 30 seconds.
3. Heat oil in a large frying pan over medium-high heat. Working in batches of 4 slices, cook bread until browned on one side, 1 minute. Turn bread over and top with 1 slice tomato and 1 slice cheese. Reduce heat to low, cover pan, and cook until cheese melts, about 2 minutes.

PER SLICE 259 CAL., 49% (126 CAL.) FROM FAT; 15 G PROTEIN; 14 G FAT (6.7 G SAT.); 18 G CARBO (1.8 G FIBER); 458 MG SODIUM; 138 MG CHOL.

Bart's ultimate BLT

MAKES 1 sandwich
TIME 15 minutes

"When the first of the tomatoes come in, I have to have a BLT. It is the quintessential tomato dish," says Bart Hosmer, a senior culinary director at Marriott International. When he was the executive chef at Parcel 104 restaurant in Santa Clara, California, Bart would take his staff out to a farm to pick tomatoes and cook with them right there in the field. This recipe was born during one of those field trips.

2 slices (¼ to ½ in. thick) artisan levain or
    sourdough bread
2 tbsp. Basil Aioli (recipe follows)
3 slices applewood-smoked thick-cut bacon,
    cooked until crisp
1 ripe medium tomato, sliced
⅓ cup loosely packed arugula leaves
2 oz. fresh mozzarella cheese, sliced
Salt and freshly ground black pepper

Spread one side of each slice of bread with basil aioli. Stack one slice with bacon, tomato slices, arugula, and mozzarella. Sprinkle with salt and pepper to taste. Top with second slice of aioli-laden bread. Eat with gusto.

PER SANDWICH 792 CAL., 69% (549 CAL.) FROM FAT; 29 G PROTEIN; 61 G FAT (18 G SAT.); 34 G CARBO (4 G FIBER); 1,203 MG SODIUM; 130 MG CHOL.

Basil aioli

MAKES 1 cup
TIME 30 minutes

This vibrant green, flavorful mayonnaise is also delicious as a vegetable dip or spread on toasts or crackers. If you are concerned about salmonella or bacteria in raw eggs, use ½ cup pasteurized whole eggs (available at some grocery stores) in place of the egg yolks.

1 cup loosely packed basil leaves
½ cup *each* extra-virgin olive oil and canola oil
2 large egg yolks
2 garlic cloves, minced
½ tsp. *each* dry mustard, fresh lemon juice,
    salt, and freshly ground black pepper

1. Bring a large pot of salted water to a boil. Dunk basil leaves into boiling water for 20 seconds. Drain and squeeze out as much excess water as possible.
2. Whirl blanched basil with olive and canola oils in a blender. Empty into a measuring cup or small pitcher; set aside.
3. Whisk egg yolks in a medium bowl with garlic, mustard, lemon juice, salt, and pepper. Whisk in a drop of the basil oil; continue adding drops of oil, whisking until mixture thickens to a mayonnaise-like consistency. Continuing to whisk, pour in remaining basil oil in a very thin stream. Season with additional salt and pepper to taste. Aioli keeps, covered and chilled, up to 2 days.

PER TBSP. 132 CAL., 99% (131 CAL.) FROM FAT; 0.6 G PROTEIN; 14.5 G FAT (1.7 G SAT.); 0.7 G CARBO (0.4 G FIBER); 74 MG SODIUM; 27 MG CHOL.

Denver summer relish

MAKES 3 cups
TIME 30 minutes

Former *Sunset* food editor Jerry Di Vecchio came up with this recipe after visiting her daughter, Angela, who lives in Denver with her family and has a bountiful supply of backyard tomatoes. The relish is good in toasted brie cheese sandwiches or alongside pork chops, and will keep in an airtight container in the refrigerator for up to three weeks.

1 lb. 'Roma' tomatoes, cored and cut into ¼-in. dice
2 cups diced (¼ in.) onions
1 cup *each* golden raisins and sugar
1 cup white vinegar (distilled, unseasoned rice,
    or white-wine)
2 tbsp. minced fresh ginger
2 jalapeño chiles, seeds and ribs removed,
    chopped
Salt

1. Put tomatoes, onions, raisins, sugar, vinegar, ginger, and chiles in a large saucepan and bring to a boil over high heat, stirring often, until mixture is reduced to 3 cups, about 20 minutes.
2. Let cool at least 20 minutes. Season to taste with salt; stir and serve.

PER TBSP. 31 CAL., 0% FROM FAT; 0.3 G PROTEIN; 0 G FAT; 7.9 G CARBO (0.4 G FIBER); 1.5 MG SODIUM; 0 MG CHOL.

Tomatoes in spicy yogurt sauce

SERVES 4 to 8 as a side dish
TIME 30 minutes

The tomatoes are warmed, but not fully cooked, in the sauce, leaving their softly solid texture intact. For this recipe, you want a tomato variety that is still firm when ripe, such as 'Early Girl'. Serve the tomatoes alongside broiled, grilled, or steamed fish, and be sure to have plenty of rice to soak up the sauce.

8 ripe but firm tomatoes (about 2 lbs.)
1 tsp. vegetable oil
2 tsp. cumin seeds
1 tsp. brown mustard seeds
2 tbsp. butter, cut into small pieces
¼ tsp. *each* ground turmeric and cayenne
6 garlic cloves, minced
2 serrano chiles, seeds and ribs removed, finely chopped
1 tsp. salt
1 cup plain whole-milk yogurt
Cilantro sprigs (optional)

1. Bring a large pot of water to a boil. Meanwhile, fill a large bowl with cold water and a few ice cubes and set near the pot. Put each tomato in boiling water for 10 seconds, then use a slotted spoon to transfer to ice water. Drain and pat dry. Core and peel tomatoes (leave them whole). Set aside.
2. Heat oil in a large frying pan over high heat. When hot, add cumin and mustard seeds and reduce heat to medium-high. Cover and cook until seeds start to pop, about 2 minutes. Remove cover and add butter. When butter is melted, add turmeric and cayenne and cook, stirring, until fragrant, about 1 minute. Add garlic, chiles, and salt; cook, stirring, until fragrant, about 1 minute. Reduce heat to low. Add yogurt and stir in one direction until smooth. Add tomatoes. Gently stir to coat with sauce. Cook until tomatoes are just warm, about 5 minutes.
3. Top with cilantro if you like and serve warm, with plenty of sauce.

PER TOMATO 78 CAL., 56% (44 CAL.) FROM FAT; 2.2 G PROTEIN; 4.9 G FAT (2.5 G SAT.); 7.5 G CARBO (1.5 G FIBER); 344 MG SODIUM; 11 MG CHOL.

Spiced grilled chicken with yellow tomato salsa

SERVES 4
TIME 40 minutes, plus at least 30 minutes for salsa to marinate

The combination of tomato and mango may seem surprising, but the pickling ingredients bring them together in an enticing way.

YELLOW TOMATO SALSA
½ lb. firm-ripe yellow tomatoes, cut in wedges
½ medium serrano chile, very thinly sliced (see Flavor Note, below)
¾ cup chopped mango
2 tbsp. finely chopped red onion
1½ tsp. minced fresh ginger
1 tbsp. olive oil
1 tsp. cracked coriander seeds
1 tbsp. firmly packed light brown sugar
2 tbsp. unseasoned rice vinegar
½ tsp. kosher salt
1 green onion, sliced diagonally

CHICKEN
4 chicken breast halves with bones and skin
Olive oil
Unseasoned rice vinegar
Salt and freshly ground black pepper

1. Combine tomatoes, chile, mango, red onion, and ginger in a medium bowl.
2. Warm oil in a small saucepan over medium-high heat. Add coriander seeds and cook, stirring, until medium brown, about 1 minute. Remove from heat and carefully stir in brown sugar, vinegar, and salt.
3. Pour warm spice mixture over tomato mixture and let stand 30 to 60 minutes for flavors to develop.
4. Meanwhile, grill chicken: Prepare a charcoal or gas grill for direct medium-high heat (450°; you can hold your hand 5 in. above cooking grate only 4 to 5 seconds). Rub chicken with oil, a splash of vinegar, and salt and pepper to taste. Grill chicken, turning often, until an instant-read thermometer registers 160° at thickest part, 20 to 30 minutes.
5. Stir green onion into salsa and serve with chicken.

FLAVOR NOTE You can control the heat of the salsa by choosing to either include or discard the seeds and white veins of the serrano.

PER SERVING 214 CAL., 32% (69 CAL.) FROM FAT; 24 G PROTEIN; 7.7 G FAT (1.3 G SAT.); 12 G CARBO (1.5 G FIBER); 334 MG SODIUM; 71 MG CHOL.

Fresh tomato sauce

Fresh tomato sauce

MAKES Enough sauce for ½ lb. spaghetti
TIME 45 minutes

This sauce is a great way to preserve your summer tomato harvest: Double or triple the recipe (leave out the basil), let it cool completely, then ladle into plastic freezer bags in convenient amounts and freeze for up to six months. If you prefer a smooth sauce, either peel the tomatoes before chopping them or run the sauce through a food mill before stirring in the basil.

2 lbs. very ripe tomatoes
2 garlic cloves, thinly sliced
3 tbsp. olive oil
1 tsp. salt, plus more to taste
10 basil leaves

1. Core and halve tomatoes. Remove seeds (either scoop them out with a spoon or hold a half in your hand and squeeze out the seeds) and cut tomatoes into ½-in. dice. Set aside.

2. In a 10- to 12-in. frying pan over low heat, cook garlic in oil until it is soft and fragrant, about 5 minutes.

3. Add tomatoes and salt and increase heat to medium-high. Cook until tomatoes give off their liquid and start to bubble. Reduce heat to medium-low or low, so sauce gently simmers. Cook, uncovered and undisturbed, until oil separates from sauce and most of liquid has evaporated, about 30 minutes.

4. Meanwhile, chop basil. When sauce is done, stir in basil and add salt to taste.

PER ½-CUP SERVING 54 CAL., 72% (39 CAL.) FROM FAT; 0.8 G PROTEIN; 4.3 G FAT (0.6 G SAT.); 4.1 G CARBO (1.1 G FIBER); 241 MG SODIUM; 0 MG CHOL.

VARIATIONS

Butter it up Use unsalted butter in place of the olive oil and a chopped medium onion in place of the garlic.

Explore the herb patch Try ½ to 1 tsp. minced oregano, marjoram, rosemary, or thyme instead of basil.

Add some heat Toss in 2 or 3 dried arbol chiles with the garlic for a slightly spicy version. Remove chiles before serving.

Pick more produce At the beginning of step 3, add one peeled and chopped medium eggplant and cook until soft, about 10 minutes, before adding the tomatoes.

Cherry tomato sauce

MAKES About 1¾ cups
TIME About 1 hour, 10 minutes

We created this recipe especially for cherry tomatoes. The sauce has a rustic character and nice crunch from the tomato seeds and skins. Like Fresh Tomato Sauce (left), it freezes well: Make it without the herbs (add those when you're reheating). Let cool, then pack into sturdy plastic containers or resealable plastic bags and freeze for up to five months.

1 qt. cherry tomatoes
1 tbsp. *each* minced garlic and extra-virgin
   olive oil
1 tsp. honey
½ tsp. *each* crushed dried red serrano or arbol
   chile and fine sea salt
1 tsp. *each* chopped basil and oregano

1. Pulse tomatoes in a food processor to chop coarsely. Heat garlic and oil in a medium saucepan over medium heat, stirring, 1 minute. Stir in tomatoes, honey, chile, and salt. Bring mixture to a boil over high heat. Reduce heat to low and simmer, uncovered, stirring often, until very thick, 50 to 60 minutes.

2. Stir in basil and oregano and use right away, or cool, cover, and refrigerate.

PER ¼-CUP SERVING 42 CAL., 50% (21 CAL.) FROM FAT; 0.78 G PROTEIN; 2.3 G FAT (0.29 G SAT.); 4.7 G CARBO (1.1 G FIBER); 164 MG SODIUM; 0 MG CHOL.

HOW TO SEED A TOMATO

When you don't want all the juice, just intense tomato flavor, seed your tomato by halving it crosswise and scooping out the jellylike seed sections with a grapefruit spoon.

1. Preheat oven to 250°. Core all tomatoes except cherry tomatoes. Cut small tomatoes in half, keep cherry tomatoes whole, and cut medium and large tomatoes into 1½-in.-thick wedges. Arrange tomatoes, cut side up and packed tightly together, on rimmed nonreactive or foil-lined baking sheets.

2. Mix oil and garlic in a small bowl, then drizzle over tomatoes. Sprinkle with salt and oregano.

3. Roast tomatoes, switching pans to a different oven rack every 2 hours, until they have wrinkled and shrunk by more than half but are still slightly moist, 6 to 8 hours. If roasting cherry tomatoes, begin checking after 5 hours.

4. Let tomatoes cool completely, then transfer to a sturdy airtight container and store in refrigerator for up to 1 week or in freezer up to 5 months.

PER ¼-CUP SERVING 54 CAL., 59% (32 CAL.) FROM FAT; 1.2 G PROTEIN; 3.8 G FAT (0.54 G SAT.); 5.2 G CARBO (1.6 G FIBER); 147 MG SODIUM; 0 MG CHOL.

Slow-roasted tomatoes for the freezer

MAKES 8 cups
TIME About 8 hours

These slow-roasted tomatoes add deep, tomatoey flavor to any dish long after summer has gone. Any variety or size of tomatoes will work. Roast tomatoes of the same size together so they cook evenly.

10 lbs. tomatoes
½ cup extra-virgin olive oil
3 garlic cloves, finely chopped
2 tsp. fine sea salt
¼ cup chopped oregano

Canned heirloom tomatoes

MAKES 6 to 7 qts.
TIME 3 hours

For this extra-easy recipe, adapted from the USDA *Complete Guide to Home Canning* (*uga.edu/nchfp/index.html*), you just squish raw, skinned tomatoes into jars. The cold-pack technique may cause fruit and liquid to separate a bit during processing, but the results still taste delicious.

IMPORTANT NOTE It's essential for food safety that when working with plain tomatoes (recipes without added vinegar), you acidify them with bottled (not fresh) lemon juice or citric acid, each of which has a standardized acidity, and that you do not increase the amount of herbs or add any other ingredients. Buy citric acid in your market's baking aisle.

17 lbs. ripe yellow or red heirloom tomatoes
14 tbsp. bottled ReaLemon lemon juice
   or 3½ tsp. citric acid such as Fruit Fresh
   (see Important Note, above)
7 tsp. salt (optional)
7 thyme sprigs (3 to 4 in. long; optional)

1. Follow the directions in "Canning ABCs: Get Ready" (page 278), using 7 wide-mouthed quart-size jars, plus matching rings and lids.

2. Meanwhile, peel tomatoes: Fill a large saucepan three-quarters full of water and bring to a boil over high heat. Cook one layer of tomatoes at a time in water, just until skins split or will peel easily with a knife, 20 to 40 seconds. Remove from water with slotted spoon; let cool, then core, pull off skins, and trim any brown areas, working over a bowl to catch juice.

3. Put 2 tbsp. lemon juice or ½ tsp. citric acid in each jar. Add 1 tsp. salt if you like. Follow the directions in "Canning ABCs: Fill and Seal Jars" (page 278), cutting tomatoes to fit through jar openings if needed, and pushing them into jars to fill compactly; leave ½-in. headspace. Pushing will create juice; if needed, add more juice from bowl so tomatoes are covered. Using handle of a fork, poke 1 thyme sprig down side of each jar if you like. Release air, wipe rims, and seal with lids and rings as directed.

4. Process as directed in "Canning ABCs: Process Jars" (page 279), boiling for 1 hour and 25 minutes (add 5 minutes for every 3,000 ft. in altitude above sea level). It's okay if jars leak a little.

5. Turn off heat and let jars stand in water in canner for 5 minutes. Cool, check seals, and store as directed (up to 1 year).

PER ½-CUP SERVING 28 CAL., 13% (3.6 CAL.) FROM FAT; 1.1 G PROTEIN; 0.4 G FAT (0.1 G SAT.); 6.3 G CARBO (1.6 G FIBER); 14 MG SODIUM; 0 MG CHOL.

Oregano

Herbs

HERBS

Thyme

WHY GROW THEM

Fresh herbs add bright punches of flavor to any dish, and growing your own allows you to use them with abandon. It's also an opportunity to experiment with herbs you're not likely to find even in a farmers' market. Lemon balm, pineapple sage, Thai basil—your choices are almost limitless.

EXTRA REWARD Herb blossoms. And we're not talking just lavender. Think sage, chives, thyme, oregano—all of these produce lovely flowers that you can pick and add to soups and salads (and to bouquets for the table). What do they taste like? The herb itself, only spicier.

WHEN TO HARVEST

(Fresh herbs) Though it varies somewhat from herb to herb, in most cases, harvest the leaves as you need them. Pinching them off the top will help keep plants bushy. **(Seeds)** *For dill and fennel:* Tie small bags over seed heads when seeds begin to turn brown. Leave them in place for a week or so. Give each seed head a good shake before removing the bag (you may need to strip fennel seeds by hand). *For coriander (cilantro):* Pull up whole plants when fruits (which look like seeds) begin to turn gray-brown. Put plants headfirst into bags and shake them.

HOW TO KEEP

Rinse herbs under cold running water, then shake off excess moisture, wrap in a dry cloth or paper towel, and refrigerate in a plastic bag for up to 4 days (1 week for parsley). Hardier herbs (rosemary, parsley, thyme, oregano) can be kept in a glass of water (stems in, like a bouquet) and chilled at least 1 week.

Basic Ways to Prepare

FRESH HERB MAYONNAISE Add ½ cup chopped herbs of your choice (only ¼ cup if using tarragon) and 2 tsp. fresh lemon juice to 1 cup mayonnaise. Mix well, cover, and refrigerate at least overnight and up to 1 month.

WHIPPED HERB BUTTER In a blender or food processor, combine 1 cup softened butter, 2 tsp. fresh lemon juice, and about ⅓ cup chopped herbs. Whirl until thoroughly blended. Cover and refrigerate at least overnight and up to 2 weeks.

PESTO If you've got a bounty of fresh herbs, pesto is a wonderful way to make use of it. See recipes on pages 214 and 215, and feel free to experiment with other herbs.

PRESERVING THE HARVEST

FREEZE Blanch herbs 20 seconds in boiling water to preserve their color somewhat, pat dry, and freeze in resealable plastic freezer bags. Frozen herbs will become limp when thawed, so do not thaw them before adding to the food you are cooking.

DRY Give herbs a good rinsing in a sinkful of water, then shake off as much water as possible. Tie handful-size bunches together at the cut end with kitchen twine, leaving a length of string hanging. In a spot that is out of the sun and relatively dust-free, hang the bunches, allowing plenty of space for air to circulate. When the leaves are completely dry and crumbly, 1 to 2 weeks, you can strip them from the stems (do this over a large bowl). Pick out any pieces of stem, then crumble the leaves with your hands (in the case of chives, you may need to chop or snip them). Pack in airtight containers and store at room temperature in a dark place for up to 1 year. Or, dry herbs using a dehydrator; it takes about 1 day (follow manufacturer's instructions).

'Genovese' basil

Some of our favorite varieties

Basil For many gardeners, summer isn't summer without basil. We particularly like 'Genovese'; its spicy-sweet leaves make wonderful pesto.

Peppermint In Thai and Vietnamese cooking, it is used almost as a salad green, adding a shocking and welcome coolness. Try other mint types, like orange and chocolate (see recipe on page 216). Peppermint is much stronger than ordinary grocery-store spearmint.

Thyme We love French thyme, but you can also have fun experimenting with other kinds, including lemon thyme and caraway thyme.

See "Herbal Teas to Grow and Drink" on page 202 for other herbs we love to grow.

Herbal teas to grow and drink

You won't find most of these herbs at the market, so pull out your trowel! All grow well in pots or the ground and need well-draining soil, full sun, and regular water until established. (They're perennials except as noted.)

ANISE HYSSOP (*Agastache foeniculum*) Try both the licorice-tasting blossoms and leaves of 'Golden Jubilee'.

BEE BALM (*Monarda didyma*) Its mildly citrus-flavored pink, red, or pure white blossoms look spectacular in a mug or cup.

CHAMOMILE Snip the fragrant, mellow blossoms of this annual herb to use fresh or dried.

FEVERFEW (*Chrysanthemum parthenium*) We like bushy 'Golden Feather' for its chartreuse leaves (which can be bitter); for brewing tea, use the mildly herbaceous flowers.

LAVENDER Though it's compact, silvery 'Thumbelina Leigh' English lavender produces plenty of blossoms for steeping.

LEMON BALM (*Melissa officinalis*) In the same family as mint, this bushy plant tastes like mint plus citrus.

LEMONGRASS (*Cymbopogon citratus*) Its flavor is concentrated in the base; harvest by separating a stalk, roots and all, from the clump. Annual except in mildest climes.

LEMON VERBENA (*Aloysia triphylla*) Intensely flavored and highly fragrant. Prune to contain this rambling shrub, which grows up to 6 feet.

NUTMEG GERANIUM (*Pelargonium fragrans* 'Nutmeg') It's all about the aromatic leaves, which really do taste (as well as smell) of nutmeg. Annual except in mildest climes.

Flowering bee balm

SERVES 1

TIME 5 minutes

Pour 1 cup hot water into a glass or mug. Put 1 bee balm blossom on top and steep about 2 minutes (blossom will wilt as it stands).

NUTRITIONAL DATA UNAVAILABLE

Sunset Palmer

SERVES 2

TIME 25 minutes

Put 2 stalks lemongrass, trimmed and chopped; ½ cup *each* lemon verbena and lemon balm leaves; and finely shredded zest of 1 lemon in a teapot. Pour in 2 cups boiling water; steep 20 minutes. Strain, then stir in 1 tbsp. sugar. Divide between 2 ice-filled glasses. Top each with ½ cup cooled brewed English breakfast tea. Garnish with lemon verbena leaves.

PER SERVING 32 CAL., 0.9% (0.3 CAL.) FROM FAT; 0.1 G PROTEIN; 0 G FAT; 8.3 G CARBO (0.1 G FIBER); 0.6 MG SODIUM; 0 MG CHOL.

Garden chai

SERVES 2

TIME 20 minutes

Put ¼ cup nutmeg geranium leaves and 3 anise hyssop flowers in a teapot. Pour in 1 cup boiling water; steep 15 minutes. Strain and divide between 2 mugs. Pour ½ cup *each* hot brewed English breakfast tea and warm plain soy milk into each mug. Stir in sugar to taste.

PER SERVING 114 CAL., 17% (19 CAL.) FROM FAT; 4 G PROTEIN; 2.1 G FAT (0.3 G SAT.); 20 G CARBO (0.7 G FIBER); 62 MG SODIUM; 0 MG CHOL.

Blossom tisane

SERVES 1

TIME 5 minutes

Put 10 *each* fresh chamomile and feverfew flowers and 20 individual buds from a fresh lavender blossom into a teapot. Pour in 1 cup hot water; steep 3 to 4 minutes. Pour tea into a mug along with flowers.

PER SERVING 2 CAL., 10% (0.2 CAL.) FROM FAT; 0 G PROTEIN; 0 G FAT; 0.5 G CARBO (0 G FIBER); 2.4 MG SODIUM; 0 MG CHOL.

Blossom tisane

Sunset Palmer

Garden chai

**Flowering
bee balm**

Strawberry basil rosé

Strawberry-basil rosé

SERVES 1

TIME About 5 minutes

An invigorating combination.

2 large strawberries
2 tbsp. Herb-Infused Simple Syrup (recipe follows), made with basil
Ice
About 5 oz. chilled dry rosé
½ tbsp. fresh lemon juice
Basil sprig

Combine strawberries and simple syrup in a chilled highball glass. With a wooden spoon, break strawberries into large chunks. Fill glass about halfway with ice, pour rosé and lemon juice over ice, and stir. Garnish with basil sprig.

PER SERVING 220 CAL., 0.7% (1.5 CAL.) FROM FAT; 0.5 G PROTEIN; 0.2 G FAT (0 G SAT.); 29 G CARBO (1.1 G FIBER); 8.2 MG SODIUM; 0 MG CHOL.

Simple syrup

MAKES 1¼ cups

TIME About 3 minutes, plus 1 hour to chill

Combine 1 cup water and 1 cup sugar in a 2-qt. glass measuring cup. Microwave, stirring once, until sugar is dissolved, 2 minutes. Chill 1 hour.

HERB-INFUSED SIMPLE SYRUP When sugar is dissolved, stir in ½ cup loosely packed herb leaves, then chill. When cold, strain into another glass measuring cup; discard herbs.

PER SERVING 39 CAL., 0% FROM FAT; 0 G PROTEIN; 0 G FAT; 10 G CARBO (0 G FIBER); 0.1 MG SODIUM; 0 MG CHOL.

Rosemary-thyme mustard

MAKES 1 cup

TIME 10 minutes, plus at least 2 days for flavors to develop

This intensely herby mustard is from cookbook author and cooking show host Joanne Weir. Use it in vinaigrettes, rub it on roasts, or stir into stews halfway through cooking.

3 tbsp. yellow mustard seeds
1 tbsp. brown mustard seeds
3 tsp. minced thyme, divided
2 tsp. minced rosemary
⅓ cup cider vinegar
1 tsp. light brown sugar
¾ tsp. salt

1. Stir together both mustard seeds, 2 tsp. thyme, the rosemary, vinegar, and ⅓ cup water in a bowl until seeds are submerged. Let sit at room temperature, covered, 2 to 3 days.
2. Blend mustard mixture in a blender with brown sugar and salt until mixture is thick but coarse-textured. Stir in remaining 1 tsp. thyme.

PER 1-TSP. SERVING 5.1 CAL., 47% (2.4 CAL.) FROM FAT; 0.2 G PROTEIN; 0.3 G FAT (0 G SAT.); 0.4 G CARBO (0.1 G FIBER); 37 MG SODIUM; 0 MG CHOL.

Sweet onion and thyme dip

MAKES 2 cups

TIME 1 hour

Tangy, herby, and low fat.

2 cups finely chopped 'Maui' or other sweet onion
1 tbsp. olive oil
2 tsp. chopped thyme, plus thyme sprigs
¾ tsp. kosher salt
¼ tsp. freshly ground black pepper
1½ cups plain low-fat Greek-style yogurt

1. Cook onion in oil in a large frying pan over medium heat, stirring often, until golden, 12 to 15 minutes. Add chopped thyme, salt, and pepper and cook another minute. Let cool.
2. Stir in yogurt, transfer to a bowl, and chill at least 30 minutes. Garnish with thyme sprigs.

TIMESAVER TIP This can be made up to 4 days ahead and refrigerated.

PER 3-TBSP. SERVING 46 CAL., 39% (18 CAL.) FROM FAT; 3.1 G PROTEIN; 2.1 G FAT (0.6 G SAT.); 4 G CARBO (0.3 G FIBER); 158 MG SODIUM; 2.3 MG CHOL.

Tarragon bubble fling

SERVES 1

TIME About 2 minutes

The fresh, savory herbs infused in this sparkling-wine cocktail make it an ideal match for classic appetizers like herb-coated goat cheese and smoked salmon.

2 tbsp. Herb-Infused Simple Syrup (recipe at right), made with tarragon
About 4 oz. chilled blanc de blancs sparkling wine
Tarragon sprig

Pour syrup into a chilled Champagne flute, fill flute with sparkling wine, and garnish with tarragon sprig.

PER SERVING 194 CAL., 0% FROM FAT; 0.1 G PROTEIN; 0 G FAT; 28 G CARBO (0 G FIBER); 5.9 MG SODIUM; 0 MG CHOL.

Herbal vinegars

Herb-infused vinegars are easy to make, and they're pretty gifts.

Lemon verbena vinegar

Follow directions at right, but replace thyme sprigs with 2 or 3 lemon verbena sprigs (each 6 to 8 in. long); omit lemon zest if you like.

Lemon-thyme vinegar

Use a vegetable peeler to pare a thin spiral of zest 6 to 8 in. long from a lemon. With a chopstick or wooden skewer, push lemon zest and 6 thyme sprigs (each 3 in. long) into a clean 12- to 16-oz. bottle. Fill bottle with white wine vinegar (vinegar should cover herbs completely) and seal. Store in a cool, dark place for at least 1 week or up to 4 months.

Purple basil vinegar

Follow directions above, but replace thyme sprigs with 2 or 3 purple basil sprigs (each 4 to 6 in. long) and omit lemon zest.

Mini lamb meatballs with cilantro-mint chutney

MAKES 40
TIME 45 minutes

This meat mixture makes great burgers (try on naan bread, with the chutney and some tomato).

MEATBALLS
1½ tsp. cumin seeds, divided
1 tsp. *each* coriander and fennel seeds
½ tsp. *each* pepper, cayenne, cinnamon, and salt
¼ tsp. turmeric
1 lb. ground lamb (preferably grass-fed)
1 large egg, lightly beaten
1 tbsp. vegetable oil

CHUTNEY
3 tbsp. low-fat Greek-style yogurt
1 tsp. *each* minced serrano chile* and fresh ginger
½ tsp. salt
2 cups loosely packed cilantro
1 cup *each* loosely packed mint and
     chopped onion
About 1 tsp. fresh lemon juice

1. Toast cumin in a small frying pan over medium heat until fragrant, 3 to 5 minutes. Grind in a spice grinder, put 1 tsp. in a medium bowl, and reserve the rest for chutney. Grind coriander and fennel and add to bowl with remaining spices, salt, lamb, and egg. Mix gently. Chill mixture until firm, about 15 minutes.
2. Put all chutney ingredients and reserved cumin in a food processor and whirl until very smooth. Spoon into a serving bowl.
3. With wet hands, form chilled meat into 1-in. balls. Heat oil in a heavy 12-in. nonstick frying pan over medium heat. Brown meatballs all over, 8 to 10 minutes total; drain on paper towels. Serve with chutney.

For a milder chutney, seed chile before mincing.

PER 3-MEATBALL SERVING WITH 3 TSP. CHUTNEY 94 CAL., 60% (56 CAL.) FROM FAT; 7.1 G PROTEIN; 6.3 G FAT (2.2 G SAT.); 2.5 G CARBO (1.1 G FIBER); 204 MG SODIUM; 39 MG CHOL.

Mascarpone chive mashed potatoes

SERVES 10 to 12

TIME 1¼ hours

The secret to fluffy mashed potatoes is to dry them out before mashing.

5½ lbs. russet potatoes, peeled, cut in chunks
4 dried bay leaves
2¼ cups milk
12 ounces mascarpone cheese
¼ tsp. white pepper
1 bunch chives (1-in. diameter), snipped
Kosher salt

1. Simmer potatoes with bay leaves in a large pot of salted water until falling apart when poked, 20 to 25 minutes. Meanwhile, in a medium pot, whisk milk and mascarpone. Heat over low heat until simmering. Stir in pepper; keep warm.

2. Drain potatoes, discarding bay leaves. Return to pot over very low heat and cook, stirring, until dried and crumbling. Remove from heat. Beat with a mixer until smooth. Beat in mascarpone milk, a third at a time. Stir in chives and season to taste with salt.

PER SERVING 299 CAL., 45% (134 CAL.) FROM FAT; 7.6 G PROTEIN; 15 G FAT (8 G SAT.); 36 G CARBO (2.6 G FIBER); 203 MG SODIUM; 40 MG CHOL.

GOOD FOR YOU
Parsley and basil are both good sources of vitamin K, so use them liberally.

Salt-crusted beets
with avocado, lavender,
and thyme

Minty tabbouleh with preserved lemon

SERVES 8

TIME About 1 hour

Tabbouleh gets a zingy makeover, thanks to mint and preserved lemon. Our version complements grilled meats of all sorts.

1 cup bulgur wheat

1 tsp. salt, plus more to taste

2 cups loosely packed mint (from about 2 bunches), divided

¼ cup *each* extra-virgin olive oil and fresh lemon juice (from about 2 lemons)

2 garlic cloves, minced

1 tsp. freshly ground black pepper, plus more to taste

2 preserved lemons (see Flavor Note, above right)

2 qts. loosely packed flat-leaf parsley (from about 4 bunches)

1. Put bulgur and salt in a large bowl. Pour 1½ cups boiling water over bulgur, cover bowl, and let sit 20 minutes.

2. Meanwhile, in a blender or food processor, whirl 1 cup mint, the oil, lemon juice, garlic, and pepper until smooth, scraping down sides as necessary. Pour dressing over bulgur, stir to combine, cover, and chill at least 30 minutes and up to overnight.

3. Remove and discard seeds and pulp from preserved lemons. Rinse rind and chop finely. Stir into bulgur mixture. Finely chop parsley and remaining 1 cup mint (or pulse them in batches in a food processor). Add to bulgur mixture and stir to combine thoroughly. Add more salt or pepper to taste.

FLAVOR NOTE Preserved lemon is a salty, tangy condiment traditionally used in Middle Eastern and North African cooking. Use our recipe on page 249 to make your own (it's easy) or look for it in well-stocked supermarkets or specialty-foods stores.

TIMESAVER TIP This recipe can be prepared up to 2 days ahead and refrigerated.

PER SERVING 165 CAL., 42% (69 CAL.) FROM FAT; 5.1 G PROTEIN; 7.7 G FAT (1.1 G SAT.); 23 G CARBO (9.4 G FIBER); 623 MG SODIUM; 0 MG CHOL.

Salt-crusted beets with avocado, lavender, and thyme

SERVES 6

TIME About 2½ hours

Jeremy Fox, former executive chef of Ubuntu restaurant in Napa, roasts beets in an aromatic salt crust that infuses the kitchen and the beets with the fragrance of flowers and herbs. We've highlighted them in this simple salad.

4 large egg whites, beaten to blend

1 box (3 lbs.) plus ¼ tsp. kosher salt

⅓ cup chopped plus ½ tsp. minced thyme

¼ cup plus ¼ tsp. minced dried lavender

2 tbsp. black peppercorns

3 *each* medium red and golden beets (1¾ lbs. total without tops), trimmed and gently scrubbed (see Flavor Note, right)

3 tbsp. extra-virgin olive oil

1 tbsp. Champagne vinegar

1 tsp. minced shallot

¼ tsp. freshly ground black pepper

1 firm-ripe avocado, cut into small wedges

2 cups (1¼ oz.) loosely packed mâche

1. Preheat oven to 425°. In a large bowl, combine egg whites, 3 lbs. salt, ⅓ cup chopped thyme, ¼ cup lavender, the peppercorns, and ½ cup water, mixing with your hands until salt is evenly coated and feels like wet sand.

2. Spoon enough of salt mixture into a 9- by 13-in. baking pan to make a ¼-in. layer in pan. Arrange beets on top without letting them touch. Mound remaining salt over each beet, pressing with hands to cover completely and make a crust. Bake beets until very tender when pierced through salt, about 1¼ hours.

3. Poke tip of a table knife into salt crust about 1 in. from a beet and tap with mallet to crack crust. Move and tap knife in ½-in. increments in a circle around beet. Break beet free from crust and lift out. Repeat with remaining beets. Let beets stand until cool enough to handle.

4. Whisk oil in a medium bowl with vinegar, shallot, pepper, and remaining ¼ tsp. salt, ½ tsp. minced thyme, and ¼ tsp. lavender. Spoon 1 tbsp. dressing into a second bowl and ½ tbsp. dressing into a third bowl.

5. Brush remaining salt off beets with a pastry brush. Peel beets and cut into thin wedges. Add golden beets and avocado to largest amount of dressing. Add red beets to bowl with 1 tbsp. dressing, and mâche to bowl with ½ tbsp. dressing. Gently mix each to coat. Divide beets, avocado, and mâche among 6 salad plates.

FLAVOR NOTE To keep the beets from getting too salty, trim and scrub them only enough to remove dirt, not the skin.

QUICK TIP To loosen the baked salt from the pan, soak in water.

PER SERVING 157 CAL., 69% (108 CAL.) FROM FAT; 2.1 G PROTEIN; 12 G FAT (1.8 G SAT.); 12 G CARBO (1.7 G FIBER); SODIUM N/A; 0 MG CHOL.

Thai beef salad
RECIPE P. 212

Vietnamese noodle rolls
RECIPE P. 212

Thai beef salad

SERVES 4

TIME 35 minutes

In this recipe from reader Elizabeth Miller of Lafayette, California, generous amounts of fresh herbs are tossed with the salad greens, each contributing its own flavor profile—cool mint, citrusy cilantro, and spicy basil. (Photo on page 210.)

2 beef steaks (each 10 oz. and about 1 in. thick)

½ tsp. salt

1½ tsp. Asian chili garlic sauce, divided

1½ tbsp. white rice

¼ cup fresh lime juice

2 tsp. *each* firmly packed light brown sugar and Thai or Vietnamese fish sauce (*nam pla* or *nuoc mam*)

1 English cucumber, halved lengthwise, seeded, and thinly sliced

4 cups salad greens

½ cup *each* loosely packed mint, cilantro, and basil, roughly chopped

¼ cup chopped peanuts

1. Preheat broiler with oven rack 4 in. below heat. Pat steaks dry. Sprinkle with salt on both sides and rub each steak with ½ tsp. chili garlic sauce.

2. Toast rice in a small dry frying pan over medium-high heat until light brown. Set aside.

3. Meanwhile, place steaks on a baking sheet and broil for 4 minutes on each side. Set aside to rest.

4. Grind rice to a powder in a spice mill or clean coffee grinder.

5. Whisk lime juice in a small bowl with brown sugar, fish sauce, and remaining ½ tsp. chili garlic sauce.

6. Toss cucumber, greens, and herbs in a large bowl with half the dressing. Divide salad among 4 plates.

7. Cut steaks into ¼-in.-thick slices and arrange on salads. Drizzle with remaining dressing and sprinkle with rice powder and peanuts.

PER SERVING 373 CAL., 48% (180 CAL.) FROM FAT; 31 G PROTEIN; 20 G FAT (6.6 G SAT.); 16 G CARBO (4.1 G FIBER); 477 MG SODIUM; 79 MG CHOL.

Vietnamese noodle rolls

SERVES 5; makes 10 rolls

TIME 35 minutes

Serve these refreshing rolls for dinner, or cut them into thirds and spear each with a toothpick to turn them into appetizers. (Photo on page 211.)

3½ oz. thin dried rice noodles (also called rice vermicelli)

¼ English cucumber, unpeeled

½ large carrot, peeled

10 rice-paper wrappers (about 8½ in. diameter)

5 red lettuce leaves, torn in half crosswise

½ Granny Smith apple, peeled, cored, and very thinly sliced lengthwise

30 mint leaves (about ¼ cup)

40 cilantro leaves (about ¼ cup)

About ½ cup canned french-fried onions

Sweet and Spicy Sesame Sauce (recipe follows) or your favorite peanut sauce

1. Put noodles in a large bowl and cover with just-boiling water. Let noodles sit until tender, 5 to 8 minutes.

2. Meanwhile, cut cucumber and carrot into 4-in. lengths and then into matchsticks, using a mandoline or other hand-held slicer (or cut cucumber into matchsticks with a knife and coarsely shred carrots), to yield ½ cup *each*.

3. Drain noodles and rinse with cold water. Spread noodles out on a baking sheet lined with a kitchen towel. Pat dry.

4. Divide noodles into 2 long "logs," then cut with scissors to total 10 equal portions.

5. Set out all ingredients except the sesame sauce near a work surface. Pour very hot tap water into a large shallow bowl such as a pie plate. Submerge 1 rice-paper wrapper until moistened and softened slightly but not completely pliable (it will continue to soften as you work with it).

6. Lay wrapper on work surface and put ½ lettuce leaf in center. Mound 1 portion of noodles on lettuce followed by about one-tenth of the cucumber, carrot, and apple slices; 3 mint leaves; 4 cilantro leaves; and a sprinkling of onions. Arrange ingredients into a rectangle about 4 in. long. Fold paper over short ends of filling, then roll up tightly from a long side. Repeat to make remaining rolls. Serve with sesame sauce.

PER SERVING 119 CAL., 12% (14 CAL.) FROM FAT; 1.8 G PROTEIN; 1.5 G FAT (0.4 G SAT.); 24 G CARBO (1.1 G FIBER); 29 MG SODIUM; 0 MG CHOL.

Sweet and spicy sesame sauce

MAKES ¾ cup

TIME 5 minutes

This sauce has quite a kick, making it a nice contrast to the mild noodle rolls. Use leftover sauce in a stir-fry.

3 tbsp. hoisin sauce

1 tbsp. toasted sesame seeds

½ tsp. red chile flakes

1 tbsp. *each* toasted sesame oil and soy sauce

Whisk all ingredients together in a small bowl with ½ cup hot water.

TIMESAVER TIP You can make the sauce up to 1 week ahead and refrigerate.

PER TBSP. 27 CAL., 52% (14 CAL.) FROM FAT; 0.2 G PROTEIN; 1.6 G FAT (0.2 G SAT.); 2.6 G CARBO (0.1 G FIBER); 165 MG SODIUM; 0 MG CHOL.

Mediterranean burgers

MAKES 4 burgers

TIME About 45 minutes

Reader Elizabeth Farquhar of Ashburton, England, gave us this way to use four different fresh herbs.

6 oz. feta cheese, crumbled

2 tsp. *each* minced oregano and rosemary

¾ tsp. freshly ground black pepper, divided

1 tbsp. finely shredded lemon zest

1½ lbs. ground lamb or beef

½ cup kalamata olives, pitted and chopped

1 tbsp. *each* chopped dill and flat-leaf parsley

2 tbsp. fresh lemon juice

¼ tsp. sugar

4 tbsp. olive oil, divided

4 kaiser or other sandwich rolls

1 large tomato, sliced

¼ medium English cucumber, thinly sliced

½ medium red onion, thinly sliced

8 romaine lettuce leaves

1. Combine feta, oregano, rosemary, ½ tsp. pepper, and the lemon zest in a bowl. Add ground meat and mix gently. Form into four 1-in.-thick patties.

2. Whirl olives, dill, parsley, lemon juice, sugar, and remaining pepper in a blender. Add 3 tbsp. oil, 1 tbsp. at a time, to make a smooth paste.

3. Prepare a charcoal or gas grill for direct medium heat (350° to 450°; you can hold your hand 5 in. above cooking grate only 5 to 7 seconds). Grill burgers, turning once, until browned on both sides and cooked through (cut to test), 10 to 12 minutes total.

4. Split rolls and toast cut sides on the grill. Brush toasted sides with remaining 1 tbsp. oil and spread each with about 1 tsp. of the olive spread. Top with burgers, tomato, cucumber, red onion, and lettuce.

PER BURGER 790 CAL., 56% (441 CAL.) FROM FAT; 43 G PROTEIN; 49 G FAT (18 G SAT.); 42 G CARBO (4.4 G FIBER); 1,198 MG SODIUM; 151 MG CHOL.

Parsley-mint pistachio pesto

MAKES About 1⅔ cups
TIME About 10 minutes

Pesto doesn't have to stop with basil. Feel free to experiment with other combinations of fresh herbs and nuts, as did readers Krista Painter and Amy French, who came up with this flavorful partnering. Try it on orecchiette ("little ears") pasta.

1 cup roasted, salted pistachios
2 cups *each* coarsely chopped flat-leaf parsley
    and loosely packed mint
1 cup extra-virgin olive oil
Salt

1. Rub nuts in a towel to remove any loose skins. Lift nuts from towel and place in a food processor or blender.
2. Add parsley, mint, and oil; whirl until finely ground. Add salt to taste.

TIMESAVER TIP You can make this up to 2 days ahead and refrigerate, or freeze airtight in small portions to store longer.

PER TBSP. 105 CAL., 94% (99 CAL.) FROM FAT; 1.4 G PROTEIN; 11 G FAT (1.4 G SAT.); 2.4 G CARBO (0.9 G FIBER); 26 MG SODIUM; 0 MG CHOL.

Classic basil pesto

MAKES About ⅓ cup
TIME About 10 minutes

This recipe, shown dolloped on fresh mozzarella, is based on one we published in 1959. Catering to modern tastes, we reduced the ¾ cup olive oil in the original to a little more than ¼ cup. The flavors remain true.

½ cup loosely packed basil
4 large or 6 medium garlic cloves, peeled
⅓ cup shredded romano cheese
3 tbsp. pine nuts
2 tbsp. minced flat-leaf parsley
½ tsp. salt
5 tbsp. extra-virgin olive oil

Put basil in a mortar with garlic, cheese, pine nuts, parsley, and salt. Pound until smooth, then add oil and mix until smooth. Or whirl all ingredients in a blender until smooth.

PER TBSP. 76 CAL., 78% (59 CAL.) FROM FAT; 3.1 G PROTEIN; 6.5 G FAT (1.6 G SAT.); 2.3 G CARBO (0.6 G FIBER); 278 MG SODIUM; 5.2 MG CHOL.

Chocolate mint pots de crème

SERVES 8

TIME 1 hour, plus 4 hours to steep and chill

These elegant, individual custards can be made a few days ahead of time for a party. Allowing the mint to steep in the milk and cream intensifies the flavor. If you like a rich custard, use all cream.

2 cups *each* whipping cream and milk
3 oz. (3 big handfuls) chocolate mint sprigs,
     plus leaves for garnish
1 cup sugar
8 large egg yolks
Sweetened whipped cream
½ cup chocolate shavings

1. Heat cream, milk, and mint sprigs in a medium pot over medium heat until mixture starts to simmer. Remove from heat, cover, and let steep about 2 hours.
2. Preheat oven to 300°. Set 8 ramekins (4 oz. each) in a large roasting pan or baking dish.
3. Reheat cream mixture to a simmer; strain into a medium bowl. Whisk together sugar and yolks in a large bowl. Slowly add cream to yolk mixture, whisking constantly.
4. Pour mixture into ramekins, dividing evenly. Fill pan with hot water until it reaches halfway up sides of ramekins.
5. Cover pan with foil and bake until custards are set and jiggle only slightly in the center, about 30 minutes.
6. Remove from oven and let ramekins sit in hot water 30 minutes. Transfer ramekins to a baking sheet, cover, and chill at least 2 hours and up to 3 days.
7. Serve with whipped cream, mint leaves, and chocolate shavings.

PER SERVING 400 CAL., 65% (259 CAL.) FROM FAT; 6.2 G PROTEIN; 29 G FAT (17 G SAT.); 31 G CARBO (0.7 G FIBER); 61 MG SODIUM; 298 MG CHOL.

Lavender-blueberry ice cream

SERVES 6 to 10; makes about 5 cups
TIME About 30 minutes, plus at least
25 minutes to freeze

A trip to a lavender farm inspired reader Jan Sousa of Mt. Shasta, California, to infuse blueberry syrup with the flowers and turn it into ice cream. For an elegant dessert, she spoons it into wine-glasses, garnishes it with lavender blossoms, and sets lemon cookies on the side.

1 cup blueberries, rinsed
³/₄ cup sugar
2 tbsp. dried culinary lavender blossoms
¹/₂ tsp. *each* cinnamon and vanilla extract
3 cups cold half-and-half

1. In a 1- to 1¹/₂-qt. pan over medium-high heat, stir blueberries, sugar, and ¹/₂ cup water until berries begin to pop, 4 to 5 minutes. Pour mixture through a fine-mesh strainer set over a bowl. Pour blueberries into a blender. Return berry syrup to pan.

2. Add lavender to syrup and stir over medium heat until syrup is infused with flavor, about 5 minutes. Strain into blender, pressing to extract liquid. Discard lavender.

3. Add cinnamon and vanilla to blender; whirl mixture until smooth. Pour into a bowl, nest in ice water, and stir often until cold, about 15 minutes. Stir in half-and-half.

4. Pour chilled mixture into an ice cream maker (1¹/₂ qt. or larger capacity). Freeze according to manufacturer's directions until firm enough to scoop. Serve, or transfer to a container and freeze, airtight, up to 1 week.

PER ¹/₂-CUP SERVING 161 CAL., 47% (75 CAL.) FROM FAT; 2.2 G PROTEIN; 8.3 G FAT (5.2 G SAT.); 20 G CARBO (0.3 G FIBER); 31 MG SODIUM; 27 MG CHOL.

Blueberries

Fruit

BERRIES

'Bluecrop' blueberries

WHY GROW THEM

No matter which kind you decide to grow—strawberries, blueberries, raspberries, or blackberries—these little packages of incredible flavor are nature's best dessert. Nothing can match the taste of a just-plucked fully ripe berry.

WHEN TO HARVEST

(Blackberries) Pick berries when they are full size, fully colored, and let go when you gently bend rather than pull them off the stem. Put in a shallow container so the berries on the bottom won't be crushed. **(Blueberries)** Pick when the fruit tastes sweet (some kinds color up before they sweeten). **(Raspberries)** Pull off ripe fruit when it separates easily from the plant, and store in a shallow container. Pick every 3 to 4 days. **(Strawberries)** After a fruit has colored up, pinch through the stem with your thumbnail to detach it.

HOW TO KEEP

Perfectly ripe berries are very delicate, so treat them with care. Sort through your stash and remove any overripe or moldy fruit. Gently blot away moisture with a paper towel and store, unwashed, in an airtight container. Always wait to wash berries until just before you're ready to use them, since dampness hastens spoilage. Use as little water as possible—a gentle spray is best. Because strawberries have a tendency to absorb water, leave the hulls on while washing. Before using, dry all berries completely.

PRESERVING THE HARVEST

FREEZE Arrange rinsed, dried fruit in a single layer on a baking sheet and freeze until firm. Transfer to heavy-duty freezer bags and freeze up to 1 year.

CAN Berries are perfect candidates for making jams, jellies, and preserves; see our recipes on pages 232, 239, and 277.

How to Roast Strawberries

Halve the berries and toss them with brown sugar and a bit of ground cardamom. Put in a buttered pie pan and bake at 400° until softened and a little darker, about 15 minutes. Serve with vanilla-bean ice cream.

Some of our favorite varieties

BLACKBERRIES

'Black Satin' The berries are very large, juicy, and sweet.

Boysenberry A cross between the blackberry, loganberry, and raspberry, this is the berry that put Knott's Berry Farm on the map. Its very large, reddish berries are soft, sweet-tart, and have a delightful aroma; use fresh, cooked, or frozen.

Loganberry Probably a hybrid of Pacific dewberry and raspberry, its large, light red berries are tarter than those of the boysenberry; use in canning and pies.

Marionberry The queen of blackberries, with aromatic raspberry notes, classic blackberry flavor, and the soft seeds of a dewberry.

Olallieberry A cross that is about one-third raspberry, two-thirds blackberry. The berries are medium to large and shiny black, with a sweet flavor that has some wild blackberry sprightliness.

Tayberry A blackberry-raspberry hybrid, its berries are big, mild-flavored, and dark red to purple-black.

BLUEBERRIES

'Bluecrop' Produces large berries with excellent flavor.

'Blueray' Large, highly flavored, crisp berries.

'Olympia' Medium-large berries with exceptional, spicy flavor.

'Sharpblue' Large, light blue berries with sweet-tart flavor.

'Toro' Large, firm berries with excellent, sprightly flavor.

RASPBERRIES

'Anne' Large apricot-gold berries with excellent, sweet flavor.

'Brandywine' Large purple, tart berries; good for jams and jellies.

'Caroline' Large red berries with excellent flavor.

'Cascade Delight' This heavy bearer offers a long season of large red berries with great flavor.

'Fallred' Large, firm red fruit with outstanding flavor.

STRAWBERRIES

'Chandler' Large, juicy berries with excellent flavor and good texture.

'Hood' Large berries good for eating fresh and making into jams and preserves.

'Seascape' Vigorous producer of large berries; good for eating fresh, making into jams, or freezing.

'Sequoia' We love this locally adapted June bearer for its large and luscious fruit.

a very light honey-lemon dressing, the berries add bright notes to a savory salad.

½ cup raw unsalted pistachios

10 to 12 oz. romaine lettuce hearts, cored and roughly chopped

⅓ cup *each* loosely packed tarragon and mint leaves, torn into small pieces

12 oz. strawberries, hulled and quartered lengthwise, divided

¼ cup fresh lemon juice

2 tsp. *each* minced shallot and honey

⅛ tsp. salt

3 tbsp. mild extra-virgin olive oil

6 oz. good-quality mild feta cheese (see Flavor Note, below), cut into triangles

1. Preheat oven to 350°. Spread pistachios on a large baking sheet and bake until very lightly toasted (they should still retain some green), 8 to 10 minutes. Remove from oven and cool to room temperature.

2. Toss together lettuce, tarragon, mint, and half the strawberries in a large bowl. In a small bowl, whisk together lemon juice, shallot, honey, and salt. Drizzle in oil, whisking constantly, until mixture is emulsified. Drizzle dressing over lettuce mixture and toss well.

3. Divide lettuce mixture among plates, then top with remaining strawberries, the toasted pistachios, and feta triangles.

FLAVOR NOTE To keep all the flavors in balance, use a mild, creamy feta. You can also substitute slices of ricotta salata (also called "hard ricotta") or fresh mild goat cheese.

PER FIRST-COURSE SERVING 235 CAL., 69% (162 CAL.) FROM FAT; 7.7 G PROTEIN; 18 G FAT (5.8 G SAT.); 12 G CARBO (3.6 G FIBER); 372 MG SODIUM; 25 MG CHOL.

Blackberry-lime rickeys

SERVES 6

TIME 10 minutes

The classic lime libation, reimagined.

2 cups blackberries, divided

¾ cup sugar

½ cup fresh lime juice

1 cup gin

Ice cubes

1 liter sparkling water

6 to 12 very thin lime slices

1. Whirl 1½ cups blackberries, the sugar, and lime juice in a blender until smooth. Rub through a fine-mesh strainer into a pitcher to extract juices. Stir in gin.

2. Half-fill 6 glasses with ice. Pour in gin mixture, then fill with sparkling water. Garnish with remaining ½ cup blackberries and lime slices.

PER SERVING 222 CAL., 0.8% (1.8 CAL.) FROM FAT; 0.5 G PROTEIN; 0.2 G FAT (0 G SAT.); 34 G CARBO (2.2 G FIBER); 0.9 MG SODIUM; 0 MG CHOL.

Herbed romaine salad with strawberries

SERVES 6 as a first course, 4 as a lunch course

TIME 30 minutes

Strawberries go well with tender herbs like mint and tarragon. Tossed with toasted pistachios, creamy feta, romaine lettuce, and

Strawberry-marmalade salad

SERVES About 8
TIME 15 minutes

Marmalade and lemon juice punch up sliced fresh berries in this standout salad.

4 navel oranges
2 pts. strawberries
⅓ cup orange marmalade
2 tbsp. fresh lemon juice

1. Cut off and discard ends from oranges using a sharp, serrated knife. Following the curve of the fruit, cut off the peel and outer membrane. Slice oranges crosswise into ⅛-in.-thick rounds.
2. Hull and slice strawberries; add to oranges.
3. Stir together marmalade and lemon juice in a small bowl. Add to fruit and mix gently to coat.

TIMESAVER TIP You can prepare this recipe up to 4 hours ahead; cover and chill.

PER SERVING 89 CAL., 4% (3.6 CAL.) FROM FAT; 1.2 G PROTEIN; 0.4 G FAT (0 G SAT.); 23 G CARBO (3.8 G FIBER); 9.7 MG SODIUM; 0 MG CHOL.

Marionberry, blue cheese, and arugula salad

SERVES 4

TIME 15 minutes

Marionberries are considered the most flavorful of the blackberries. If you can't find them, use ordinary blackberries instead.

3 tbsp. extra-virgin olive oil

1 tbsp. fresh lemon juice

3 tsp. fresh thyme leaves, divided

¼ tsp. dry mustard

¼ tsp. *each* salt and freshly ground black pepper, plus more to taste

6 oz. arugula (about 13 cups)

6 oz. marionberries or blackberries (1½ cups)

2 oz. mild blue cheese

1. Whisk together oil, lemon juice, 1 tsp. thyme, the mustard, salt, and pepper in a salad bowl.

2. Add arugula and gently toss until leaves are coated with dressing. Add berries and gently toss. Divide among 4 salad plates. Crumble ½ oz. cheese on each salad. Sprinkle with remaining 2 tsp. thyme and salt and pepper to taste.

PER SERVING 175 CAL., 77% (135 CAL.) FROM FAT; 4.5 G PROTEIN; 15 G FAT (4.2 G SAT.); 7.8 G CARBO (2.7 G FIBER); 353 MG SODIUM; 11 MG CHOL.

GOOD FOR YOU

Their red, blue, and purple colors are a visual signal of high antioxidant levels. Berries are also a great source of vitamin C and fiber.

Blackberry-hazelnut honey crisp

SERVES 8
TIME About 2 hours

Blackberries and hazelnuts are delicious together, but feel free to experiment with other berry-nut combinations.

36 oz. blackberries (2 qts.)
3 tbsp. quick-cooking tapioca
¼ cup berry blossom or wildflower honey
¼ cup fresh lemon juice
¾ cup hazelnuts
¼ cup *each* flour and sugar
½ tsp. salt
½ cup *each* butter and quick-cooking rolled oats

1. Preheat oven to 350°. Toss berries with tapioca in a large bowl. Combine honey, lemon juice, and 1 tbsp. boiling water in a small bowl. Stir to dissolve honey. Add to berries and toss to combine. Put mixture in an 8-in. square baking pan and set aside.
2. Spread hazelnuts on a baking sheet and toast in oven until medium golden brown, 10 to 15 minutes. Rub nuts in a kitchen towel to remove skins; let nuts cool.
3. Pulse nuts in a food processor until finely ground. Add flour, sugar, and salt and pulse to combine. Add butter and pulse until mixture forms a thick dough. Stir in oats. Drop in flattened 1-tsp. chunks over berries. Bake until topping is brown and berries are bubbling, about 1 hour. Let cool to set, 30 minutes.

PER SERVING 341 CAL., 50% (171 CAL.) FROM FAT; 3.7 G PROTEIN; 19 G FAT (7.7 G SAT.); 43 G CARBO (7.3 G FIBER); 282 MG SODIUM; 31 MG CHOL.

Custardy oven pancake with mixed berries

SERVES 8

TIME 1 hour

This recipe, from reader Jayne Bohannon of Gunnison, Colorado, is a twist on a poofy pancake her Finnish grandmother used to make called *suomalainen pannukakku*.

4 large eggs
About 5½ tbsp. honey, divided
1 tsp. finely shredded lemon zest
¾ tsp. salt
1 cup flour
2½ cups milk
2 cups raspberries, divided
¼ cup butter, cut into chunks
1 lb. strawberries, hulled and sliced

1. Set an ovenproof 12-in. frying pan or 9- by 13-in. baking pan in oven and preheat oven to 425°. Whisk eggs, 4 tbsp. honey, and the lemon zest in a medium bowl to blend. Add salt, flour, and ¼ cup milk and whisk until smooth, then whisk in remaining milk.

2. Purée 1 cup raspberries in a food processor until smooth. Strain and discard seeds.

3. Remove pan from oven; add butter and swirl until melted and golden. Pour in batter. Pour raspberry purée over batter in wide ribbons. Reduce oven temperature to 400° and bake pancake until deep golden, about 30 minutes. Let stand 10 to 15 minutes to firm up (pancake will fall).

4. Combine strawberries and remaining 1 cup raspberries and 1½ tbsp. honey in a bowl; let stand at least 10 minutes. Add more honey to taste if you like. Spoon half the fruit over pancake and serve the rest on the side. Cut pancake into wedges.

PER SERVING 267 CAL., 37% (100 CAL.) FROM FAT; 8 G PROTEIN; 11 G FAT (5.9 G SAT.); 35 G CARBO (3.5 G FIBER); 328 MG SODIUM; 129 MG CHOL.

Raspberry, ricotta, and chocolate parfaits
RECIPE P. 230

Spiced blueberry pie
RECIPE P. 232

Raspberry, ricotta, and chocolate parfaits

SERVES 4

TIME 15 minutes, plus 1 hour to stand

For the silkiest texture, use a ricotta that contains no gums, pectin, or other stabilizers. Standard grocery-store ricotta isn't as smooth, but still tastes good. (Photo on page 228.)

12 oz. raspberries

1½ tbsp. sugar

1½ tsp. brandy or water

12 oz. (1¼ to 1½ cups) whole-milk ricotta cheese

3 tbsp. honey

⅛ tsp. vanilla extract

1½ tbsp. coarsely chopped bittersweet chocolate, plus more chocolate to shave for garnish

1½ tbsp. coarsely chopped roasted unsalted pistachios

⅓ cup whipping cream

1. Toss berries with sugar and brandy in a bowl, mixing gently. Let stand at room temperature, stirring occasionally, until sugar dissolves and berries render some juice, about 1 hour.

2. Purée ricotta, honey, and vanilla in a food processor until very smooth. Transfer to a bowl; stir in chopped chocolate and pistachios.

3. In a small bowl with a mixer, whip cream to firm peaks. Gently fold into ricotta mixture.

4. Divide berries and their juices among 4 glasses. Top each with ricotta mixture. With a vegetable peeler, shave a little chocolate over each.

PER SERVING 366 CAL., 54% (196 CAL.) FROM FAT; 12 G PROTEIN; 22 G FAT (13 G SAT.); 34 G CARBO (6.1 G FIBER); 81 MG SODIUM; 71 MG CHOL.

Strawberry frozen yogurt pie with balsamic syrup

SERVES 12

TIME 1¼ hours, plus 5 hours to freeze

Preserves and jams are great to use in ice cream because their high sugar content keeps the fruit from freezing rock-hard. You can use any preserves you like here, from orange marmalade to blueberry—but the balsamic syrup goes best with strawberry.

Buttery Pie Pastry (recipe follows)

3 cups vanilla frozen yogurt

¾ cup best-quality strawberry preserves (preferably whole berries)

¼ cup balsamic vinegar

2 tbsp. sugar

About 1½ cups strawberries, hulled and halved and/or quartered (leave small ones whole)

1. Press cold pastry over bottom and up side of a 9-in. tart pan with a removable rim, and trim edge even with top of pan. Chill 30 minutes. Meanwhile, preheat oven to 375°.

2. Bake pastry on bottom rack of oven until golden brown, 25 to 30 minutes. Let cool completely.

3. Let frozen yogurt soften at room temperature until easily spoonable. In a medium bowl, stir yogurt until smooth, then stir in preserves. Spoon into tart pan, set on a plate, and freeze at least 5 hours.

4. Simmer vinegar, sugar, and 1 tbsp. water in a small saucepan over medium heat (do not let boil) until it coats a spoon, about 10 minutes. Let cool.

5. Top pie with strawberries. Thin syrup with water if necessary and drizzle onto each wedge of pie.

TIMESAVER TIP Once the pie is fully frozen through step 3, it keeps for up to 4 days, double-wrapped in plastic wrap. Make the syrup and top the pie just before serving.

PER SERVING 234 CAL., 37% (86 CAL.) FROM FAT; 2.5 G PROTEIN; 9.7 G FAT (5.8 G SAT.); 35 G CARBO (0.7 G FIBER); 69 MG SODIUM; 43 MG CHOL.

Buttery pie pastry

MAKES One 9-in. pie shell

TIME 15 minutes, plus 30 minutes to chill

1 cup flour

2 tbsp. powdered sugar

¼ tsp. salt

½ cup cold unsalted butter, cut into cubes

1 large egg yolk, lightly beaten

1. Whirl together flour, powdered sugar, and salt in a food processor.

2. Drop cubes of cold butter into bowl and pulse until mixture looks like large cracker crumbs and flour.

3. Whirl in egg yolk and 1 to 2 tbsp. ice water, pulsing just until mixture comes together in a shaggy ball but you can still see bits of butter.

4. Form dough into disk, then wrap in plastic wrap and chill at least 30 minutes and up to 2 days.

Strawberry frozen
yogurt pie with
balsamic syrup

Spiced blueberry pie

SERVES 8
TIME About 3 hours

Black pepper, nutmeg, and cloves play up the underlying spicy note of blueberries in this pie. (Photo on page 229.)

2¾ cups flour, divided
¼ to ½ cup plus 1 tbsp. granulated sugar
2½ tsp. salt, divided
8 tbsp. very cold butter, cut into small pieces, divided
7 tbsp. very cold solid shortening, cut into pieces
¼ cup firmly packed light brown sugar
1 tbsp. quick-cooking tapioca
1 tsp. cinnamon
½ tsp. *each* freshly ground black pepper and freshly grated nutmeg
¼ tsp. ground cloves
2 pts. blueberries (1 qt.)
1 tbsp. fresh lemon juice

1. Mix 2½ cups flour, 1 tbsp. sugar, and 1½ tsp. salt in a large bowl. Drop in 7 tbsp. butter and the shortening. Using your hands, a fork, a pastry blender, or two knives, work butter and shortening into flour mixture until it resembles cornmeal with some pea-size pieces.
2. Using a fork, quickly stir in ½ cup very cold water. Turn dough and crumbs onto a work surface. Knead just until dough starts to hold together, 5 to 10 times. Divide dough in half and pat each half into a 6-in. disk. Wrap in plastic wrap and chill 15 minutes or up to overnight.
3. Put a rack on lowest rung of oven. Preheat oven to 375°. Unwrap one disk of dough and put on a floured work surface. Roll into a 12-in. circle (about ⅛ in. thick), turning 90° after each pass of rolling pin to keep it from sticking. Transfer to a 9-in. pie pan, letting dough fall into place (if you push or stretch it into place, it will shrink back when baked). Trim dough edges to ¼ in. past rim of pie pan. Cover with plastic wrap and chill 15 minutes.

4. Roll second disk into an 11-in. circle. Cut into ten 1-in.-wide strips. Transfer to a baking sheet, cover with plastic wrap, and chill 15 minutes.
5. While crusts chill, mix remaining ¼ cup flour, ¼ cup granulated sugar, the brown sugar, tapioca, remaining 1 tsp. salt, the cinnamon, pepper, nutmeg, and cloves in a medium bowl. Add blueberries and lemon juice; toss. Taste and add more granulated sugar (up to ¼ cup) if you like. Pour berry mixture into crust and dot with remaining 1 tbsp. butter.
6. To weave a lattice crust, lay 5 strips of pie dough vertically across pie, spacing evenly. Take the top of every other strip and fold it back halfway. Lay a strip horizontally across center of pie, next to folds of vertical strips. Unfold vertical strips back over horizontal strip. Fold back vertical strips that were left flat last time and repeat with a second horizontal strip, placing it above first strip (away from you). Repeat with a third horizontal strip above second. Repeat this process on lower half of pie, using remaining 2 strips of dough.
7. Fold bottom crust edge up over top crust and crimp edges together. Bake until crust is browned and filling is bubbling in center, 60 to 75 minutes. Cover edge with strips of foil if browning too quickly. Let cool until bottom of pie pan is room temperature.

PER SERVING 473 CAL., 46% (216 CAL.) FROM FAT; 5.1 G PROTEIN; 24 G FAT (10 G SAT.); 62 G CARBO (2.9 G FIBER); 859 MG SODIUM; 31 MG CHOL.

Raspberry-blackberry jam

MAKES 8 half-pts. or 4 pts.
TIME 1¾ hours

This sweet-tart spread has the bright flavor of raspberries, with just enough blackberries for a rich undertone. Add sugar to the boiling berry mixture (step 4) all at once; this helps the mixture gel properly.

3 cups (¾ lb.) blackberries
2½ qts. (2⅔ lbs.) raspberries
5 cups sugar, divided
1 pkg. (1.75 oz.) Sure-Jell dry pectin labeled "for less or no-sugar needed recipes" (see Quick Tips, right)
½ tsp. butter (optional; see Quick Tips, right)

1. Follow directions in "Canning ABCs: Get Ready" (page 278), using 8 regular or wide-mouthed half-pint-size jars or 4 pint-size jars, plus matching rings and lids.
2. Meanwhile, purée blackberries in a food processor. Rub through a fine-mesh strainer over a bowl to extract as much juice as you can. Discard seeds and pour juice into an 8- to 10-qt. pot. Add raspberries and mash very coarsely with a potato masher.
3. Measure 4¾ cups sugar into a bowl; set aside. Put remaining ¼ cup sugar in another bowl and mix with pectin. Stir pectin mixture into pot with berries and add butter if using.
4. Over high heat, bring berry mixture to a full boil that you can't stir down, stirring constantly with a long-handled spoon and protecting your hands from spatters. Add reserved sugar all at one time and return to a full boil, continuing to stir. Boil, stirring, exactly 1 minute.
5. Fill jars as directed in "Canning ABCs: Fill and Seal Jars" (page 278), leaving ¼-in. headspace. Wipe rims and seal with lids and rings as directed.

6. Process as directed in "Canning ABCs: Process Jars" (page 279), boiling for 5 minutes (boil for 10 minutes at altitudes of 1,000 to 6,000 ft., 15 minutes above 6,000 ft.). If your canning rack doesn't hold all the jars at once, process them in two batches. Cool, check the seals, and store as directed (up to 1 year).

QUICK TIPS Don't use regular Sure-Jell for this recipe; the one we call for has more gelling power, which is what you want in this case. Butter keeps foam from forming during cooking. If you leave it out, skim off foam before ladling jam into jars.

PER TBSP. 39 CAL., 2% (0.9 CAL.) FROM FAT; 0.1 G PROTEIN; 0.1 G FAT (0 G SAT.); 9.8 G CARBO (0.6 G FIBER); 5.6 MG SODIUM; 0 MG CHOL.

Three-berry buttermilk sherbet

MAKES 4½ cups
TIME 40 minutes, plus 4 hours to freeze

The buttermilk provides a nice bit of tang to this sweet berry freeze.

1¼ cups (6 oz.) *each* raspberries, blackberries, and blueberries
¾ cup sugar
1 pt. low-fat buttermilk
1 tbsp. fresh lemon juice
¼ tsp. ground cardamom (optional)

1. Purée berries in a food processor, then rub through a fine-mesh strainer into a bowl. Discard solids. Stir in remaining ingredients.
2. Freeze mixture in an ice cream maker according to manufacturer's directions.
3. Transfer to an airtight container and freeze until firm enough to scoop, at least 4 hours and up to 2 weeks.

PER ½-CUP SERVING 116 CAL., 6% (6.8 CAL.) FROM FAT; 2.4 G PROTEIN; 0.8 G FAT (0.3 G SAT.); 26 G CARBO (2.6 G FIBER); 58 MG SODIUM; 2.2 MG CHOL.

FIGS

'Panachée'

WHY GROW THEM

In the early days of immigration, having a fig tree growing in the backyard was an important tie to the Old Country, even if that meant, in more northern climes, going to such extremes as packing the tree in mulch or bending it over and burying it to keep it from getting killed by winter's cold. For those in warmer regions, no such efforts are required; but in either case, a happy tree will reward you with loads of rich fruit. If you don't already have a fig tree growing in your yard, why bother with it? Because figs are an inherently delicate fruit, with thin skin and a very short life span after being picked. They don't travel well, and are pricey. So if you love fresh figs, it can be worth it to grow your own.

WHEN TO HARVEST

When figs are ripe, they detach easily when lifted and bent back toward the branch. Pick fruit as it ripens. In late fall, take off any remaining ripe figs and clean up fallen fruit. If the figs' milky white sap irritates your skin, wear gloves.

HOW TO KEEP

Wrap fresh figs loosely in a plastic bag and refrigerate. Just-picked figs will last up to a week.

PRESERVING THE HARVEST

CAN Figs make wonderful jams and preserves. See recipe on page 239.
DRY Choose fruit that is fully ripe and in top condition for eating fresh. Wash, trim off any pieces that look spoiled, and cut in half or leave whole. *To oven-dry,* you must have an oven that can be set at a temperature between 130° and 150°. Line rimmed baking pans with a double layer of cheesecloth and spread figs slightly apart on cheesecloth. Cover with a single layer of cheesecloth, stretch taut, and tape down at the edges. Let the figs dry, turning them every several hours, until they are leathery to the touch but still pliable and slightly sticky but not wet inside. *To dry in a dehydrator,* arrange the figs on the drying trays and follow the manufacturer's instructions. It's fast, neat, and efficient too; you can stack the trays and dry a lot of fruit at once.

Basic Ways to Cook

ROAST Mix whole figs with a little sugar, water, and lavender and bake at 350° for about 15 minutes. Serve with assorted cheeses, almonds, and warm bread.

PAN-FRY OR GRILL Wrap whole figs in strips of pancetta. Cook in a frying pan over medium heat, turning, until fat renders and pancetta crisps. Or thread several figs onto thin metal skewers and grill.

'Mission'

Some of our favorite varieties

'Celeste' ('Blue Celeste', 'Celestial') Violet-tinged bronzy skin, rosy amber flesh. Good fresh; resists spoilage. Dries well on tree in warm, dry climates.

'Conadria' Choice thin-skinned white fig blushed violet, white to red flesh with fine flavor.

'Improved Brown Turkey' Brownish purple fruit. Adaptable to most fig-growing climates.

'Lattarula' Also known as Italian honey fig. Green skin, amber flesh. In the Northwest, may produce a second crop.

'Mission' ('Black Mission') A legacy of early California's Franciscan missionaries. Purple-black figs with pink flesh; richly sweet. Good fresh or dried.

'Panachée' Also known as Tiger fig because of its stunning green stripes, 'Panachée' has a purplish rose interior and a wonderful jammy flavor.

'Texas Everbearing' Mahogany to purple skin, strawberry-colored flesh. Bears at a young age and produces well in short-season areas of the Southwest.

Pork shoulder roast with figs, garlic, and Pinot Noir

SERVES 6 or 7

TIME 3¼ hours

Stuffing this roast with figs and garlic slivers will make you feel like a modern-day Julia Child, and the results are stunning: mosaic-like slices infused with rich fruit and wine flavors.

1½ cups (10 oz.) dried 'Black Mission' figs, stems removed, halved lengthwise

1 tbsp. sugar

½ tsp. anise seeds

2 tbsp. plus ½ tsp. chopped thyme, plus thyme sprigs

1 bottle (750 ml.) Pinot Noir, divided

1 boned pork shoulder (butt) roast (about 3½ lbs.)

8 garlic cloves, cut into large slivers

1½ tsp. kosher salt, plus more to taste

½ tsp. freshly ground black pepper, plus more to taste

3 tbsp. olive oil

About 1 tsp. fresh lemon juice (optional)

1. Put figs, sugar, anise, 1 tbsp. thyme, and 1 cup wine in a medium saucepan. Cover and bring to a boil over high heat. Reduce heat and simmer until figs are just tender when pierced, 10 to 12 minutes. Let cool.

2. With a small, sharp knife, make 16 evenly spaced lengthwise cuts into roast, each cut about 1 in. long and 1 in. deep. Insert a garlic sliver, then a fig half into each cut, closing meat over figs; make cuts a little bigger if needed. Set aside remaining garlic and figs and their liquid.

3. Preheat oven to 325°. Using kitchen twine, tie pork crosswise at about 1½-in. intervals and lengthwise twice to form a neat roast. In a small bowl, combine 1 tbsp. thyme, the salt, pepper, and oil. Rub all over roast.

4. Heat a 12-in. frying pan over medium-high heat. Brown pork all over, turning as needed, 8 to 10 minutes total; adjust heat if needed to keep meat from scorching. Transfer pork, fat side up, to a 9- by 13-in. baking pan.

5. Reduce heat to medium. Add reserved garlic to frying pan; cook, stirring often, until light golden, about 1 minute. Pour in remaining wine from bottle and bring to a boil, scraping up browned bits from bottom of pan with a wooden spoon. Pour mixture over pork and cover tightly with foil.

6. Bake pork until almost tender when pierced, 2½ hours. Stir reserved fig mixture into pan juices; bake, covered, until meat is tender, 15 to 20 minutes more.

7. Spoon pan juices over pork to moisten, then transfer meat to a cutting board and tent loosely with foil. Skim fat from pan juices. Pour juices with figs into a large frying pan and boil over high heat until reduced to 2 cups, about 5 minutes. Stir in remaining ½ tsp. thyme. Taste and season with lemon juice and more salt and pepper if you like. Pour into a gravy boat. Remove twine from pork, then cut meat crosswise into thick slices. Garnish with thyme sprigs and serve with sauce.

TIMESAVER TIP Prepare through step 3 and chill airtight up to 1 day.

PER SERVING 498 CAL., 50% (247 CAL.) FROM FAT; 32 G PROTEIN; 28 G FAT (8.4 G SAT.); 32 G CARBO (4.2 G FIBER); 526 MG SODIUM; 107 MG CHOL.

2 WAYS WITH FRESH FIGS

Mix chopped figs with plain Greek-style yogurt and honey, then spread in a baked tart shell. Top with fig wedges, raspberries, and pistachios.

Toss baby arugula with olive oil, lemon juice, fig halves, and shaved pecorino cheese. Sprinkle with salt, freshly ground black pepper, and minced rosemary.

'Black Mission' fig tart

SERVES 10 to 12
TIME 4½ hours

If your guests can't figure out where they've tasted something like this rich, deep, spicy tart, just utter two words: "Fig Newtons." Maria Hines, chef-owner of Tilth and Golden Beetle restaurants in Seattle, gave us the recipe.

1 lb. dried 'Black Mission' figs
2 bottles (750 ml. each) light- or medium-bodied
    dry red wine (such as Pinot Noir)
1 cup plus 3 tbsp. sugar
¾ tsp. salt, divided
5 black peppercorns
1 cinnamon stick
3 whole allspice
2 whole cloves
1 tsp. vanilla extract
1½ cups flour
¾ cup very cold butter, cut into small pieces,
    plus more for foil
8 oz. crème fraîche (about 1 cup)

1. Trim stems from figs and cut into ⅛-in.-thick slices; put in a large bowl. Bring 6 cups water to a boil, pour over figs, and let sit 10 minutes. Drain.
2. Bring figs, wine, 1 cup sugar, and ½ tsp. salt to a boil in a large pot. Meanwhile, tie up peppercorns, cinnamon, allspice, and cloves in a piece of cheesecloth and add to pot. Simmer until figs are soft and liquid is reduced to about ¾ cup, about 2 hours. Discard spices. Stir in vanilla. Let cool to room temperature.
3. Meanwhile, in a large bowl, mix flour and remaining 3 tbsp. sugar and ¼ tsp. salt. Drop in butter and work it into flour mixture with your fingertips, a pastry blender, or fork until it resembles coarse cornmeal with some pea-size chunks. Quickly stir in 2 tbsp. very cold water

until dough starts to hold together (it will still be quite crumbly). Gently knead dough 2 or 3 times in bowl, then turn onto plastic wrap, shape into a 6-in. disk, cover with wrap, and chill at least 1 hour and up to 3 days.
4. Preheat oven to 350°. Place a 10-in. tart pan with a removable rim on a large baking sheet. Butter a large piece of foil. On a floured work surface, roll dough into a 13-in. circle, turning 90° between each pass of the rolling pin to keep it from sticking. Transfer to tart pan, allowing dough to fall into place (if you push or stretch it, it will shrink back when baked). Trim edges ½ in. past rim of pan and fold down to double the thickness of the tart edge. Set foil, buttered side down, gently onto dough and top evenly with pie weights, dried beans, or rice. Bake 30 minutes. Remove weights and foil and bake until golden brown, about 15 minutes. Let cool.
5. Arrange cooled figs in cooled crust and pour cooking liquid over them. Let sit at least 1 hour (at room temperature) and up to overnight (in refrigerator). Serve at room temperature, with crème fraîche.

TIMESAVER TIP You can prepare the figs through step 2 the day before; cover and chill. You can make the dough (step 3) up to 3 days ahead and keep it wrapped and chilled.

PER SERVING 418 CAL., 41% (171 CAL.) FROM FAT; 4 G PROTEIN; 19 G FAT (12 G SAT.); 60 G CARBO (4.2 G FIBER); 286 MG SODIUM; 48 MG CHOL.

Fig-blackberry-orange quick jam

MAKES About 3 cups
TIME 25 minutes, plus 2 hours to chill

We love to stir this intensely fruity jam into yogurt, so we usually take it off the heat when the mixture is still a bit runny. Cook longer for a thicker consistency.

2 lbs. (about 2 pts.) fresh figs, stems trimmed
    and fruit cut into quarters

6 oz. (½ pt.) blackberries
¾ cup sugar
½ cup fresh orange juice
1½ tsp. finely shredded orange zest

1. Combine figs, blackberries, sugar, and orange juice in a 4-qt. pan over medium-high heat. Bring to a boil and cook, stirring often, until liquid has consistency of thick maple syrup, about 12 minutes. Stir in zest. Boil, stirring often, until mixture reaches desired thickness (see Quick Tip, below), 2 minutes more.
2. Remove jam from heat and let cool at room temperature 15 minutes. Chill, covered, at least 2 hours in refrigerator before using. Will keep, refrigerated, up to 1 month.

QUICK TIP To see whether the jam is thick enough, put a tablespoonful onto a plate you've chilled for 20 minutes in the freezer. The jam will cool and thicken to its final consistency.

PER TBSP. 29 CAL., 3% (0.9 CAL.) FROM FAT; 0.2 G PROTEIN; 0.1 G FAT (0 G SAT.); 7.4 G CARBO (0.8 G FIBER); 0.2 MG SODIUM; 0 MG CHOL.

Caramelized fig ice cream

MAKES 3 cups
TIME 30 minutes, plus at least 3 hours to freeze

You don't need an ice cream maker to make this quick and easy ice cream.

⅓ cup sugar
2 tsp. fresh lemon juice, divided
2 cups quartered fresh figs
2 tbsp. butter
½ tsp. kosher salt
1 pt. good-quality vanilla ice cream

1. Pour sugar and 1 tsp. lemon juice into a large frying pan with 3 tbsp. water. With your fingertips, mix sugar and liquid until mixture is like wet sand. Cook over high heat until mixture boils. Continue to cook, swirling pan occasionally, until one area of sugar starts to turn medium brown. Remove from heat, add figs and 2 tbsp. water, and stir to combine.
2. Return to heat and cook over low heat until mixture is bubbling and figs start to break down, about 15 minutes. Mix in butter, salt, and remaining 1 tsp. lemon juice. Let cool.
3. Soften ice cream at room temperature for 10 minutes, then beat it in a bowl with a mixer until smooth. Use a rubber spatula to mix fig mixture into ice cream. Freeze, covered, until firm, at least 3 hours.

PER ½-CUP SERVING 297 CAL., 47% (140 CAL.) FROM FAT; 2.8 G PROTEIN; 16 G FAT (9.8 G SAT.); 38 G CARBO (1.7 G FIBER); 232 MG SODIUM; 76 MG CHOL.

GOOD FOR YOU
Figs are a good source of fiber— a sweet snack that has staying power.

Fresh figs and anise wheat crisps with honeyed yogurt dip

SERVES 8

TIME 25 minutes

This dessert, from Santa Monica–based cookbook authors and private chefs Jewels and Jill Elmore, is simple to make, but full of contrasting flavors and textures.

4 whole-wheat tortillas (8 in.), each cut into
    8 triangles

2 tbsp. butter, melted

½ tsp. anise seeds, crushed

¼ tsp. cinnamon

2 tbsp. sugar

2 cups plain Greek-style yogurt

8 tsp. honey

¼ cup pistachios, toasted (see Flavor Note, below)
    and finely chopped

16 small fresh figs, each cut in half

1. Preheat oven to 350°. Lay tortilla triangles on a baking sheet. Using a pastry brush, lightly brush triangles with butter. In a small bowl, combine anise, cinnamon, and sugar, then sprinkle over tortillas. Bake until golden and crisp, 12 to 15 minutes.

2. Spoon about ¼ cup yogurt into a small serving bowl. Make a well in center of yogurt and spoon in 1 tsp. honey, then sprinkle with some pistachios. Repeat to make 7 more servings. Serve each with 4 tortilla crisps and 2 sliced figs.

FLAVOR NOTE Toasting nuts increases their flavor and crunch. Spread nuts in a single layer in a baking pan and toast in a 350° oven until golden, 5 to 15 minutes, depending on the type of nut.

PER SERVING 267 CAL., 40% (108 CAL.) FROM FAT; 7.4 G PROTEIN; 12 G FAT (6.9 G SAT.); 35 G CARBO (3.1 G FIBER); 244 MG SODIUM; 18 MG CHOL.

LEMONS

'Eureka'

WHY GROW THEM

If you live in an area with warm to hot summers and mild winters (as we do here at *Sunset*, in Menlo Park, California), growing a lemon tree offers you a fresh lemon stash at the ready: Your ripe lemons can be left on the tree for months, providing their own kind of self-storage. And if you've ever bought lemons at the market only to come home and find each one contains only about a tablespoon of juice, you'll appreciate the intoxicating aroma and juiciness of homegrown lemons.

EXTRA REWARD Lemon flowers. These lovely blossoms are wonderful to float in a shallow bowl of water as a table centerpiece.

WHEN TO HARVEST

When the fruit feels heavy in your hand, looks fully formed, and is yellow (not green), pick it and try it. Citrus doesn't ripen off the tree, so you'll need to sample a lemon to know when to pick.

HOW TO KEEP

Ripe lemons can be left hanging on the tree for months, but if they get puffy, they are too old. Once picked, lemons should be stored at cool room temperature (60° to 70°) for up to 1 week or in the refrigerator for up to 2 weeks.

'Variegated Pink'

Some of our favorite varieties

'Eureka' A good all-around lemon tree, it yields fruit that is large, tart, juicy, and versatile. It will bear fruit year-round in mild climates.

'Improved Meyer' The fruit of this lemon-orange hybrid is rounder, thinner-skinned, and more orange-yellow than standard lemons. It is extremely aromatic and is less acidic than standard lemons, and it is very tender and juicy. It makes an excellent container plant.

'Lisbon' These lemons are nearly the same as 'Eureka', but the tree is more vigorous (although thornier). The fruit ripens mostly in the fall, but you'll have some lemons year-round. It can tolerate more extremes of heat and cold than 'Eureka', and is the best lemon for Arizona.

'Variegated Pink' This sport of 'Eureka' bears fruit that is green and streaked with gold when young, maturing to a pale yellow. The pink flesh produces a clear juice.

Basic Ways to Cook

ROAST Add lemon wedges alongside wedges of potatoes in a roasting pan for an unusual and flavorful side dish.

GRILL Place lemon halves, cut side down, on the grill and use to squeeze over kebabs or any type of grilled meat, poultry, or fish.

SAUTÉ Cut peel and all white pith from lemons. Cut fruit crosswise into ½-in. slices. Sauté in olive oil or butter and your choice of herbs, spices, or nuts until hot (about 3 minutes). Good with sautéed chicken or fish.

FRY Dip thin slices in tempura batter and fry in 375° oil until golden, turning once. Drain on paper towels and sprinkle with salt while still hot. Excellent with fish, and as part of a mixed vegetable or seafood tempura platter.

PRESERVING THE HARVEST

FREEZE Pour the juice into an ice cube tray and freeze, then transfer the handy cubes to an airtight container. Lemon zest (the colored surface of the skin, without the bitter, spongy white pith beneath) also freezes well—either finely shredded or as strips—for up to 4 months, also airtight.

Frosty lemon martini

SERVES 2
TIME About 10 minutes

Served in sugar-rimmed glasses, this cocktail offers the perfect balance of sweet and tart. For extra frostiness, put the glasses in the freezer for several minutes before you begin making the recipe.

1 tbsp. sugar
Lemon wedge
1 cup crushed ice
6 tbsp. chilled lemon-flavored vodka (3 oz.)
2 tbsp. chilled lemon-flavored liqueur (1 oz.)
4 tsp. fresh lemon juice
2 thin strips (3 in. long) lemon peel

1. Pour sugar onto a small, rimmed plate. Rub rims of 2 martini glasses with lemon wedge to moisten, then dip rims into sugar to coat.
2. Put ice in a cocktail shaker. Add vodka, liqueur, and lemon juice. Shake until mixture is very cold, 10 seconds. Strain into glasses. Garnish each with a twist of lemon peel.

PER SERVING 162 CAL., 0% FROM FAT; 0 G PROTEIN; 0 G FAT; 11 G CARBO (0.1 G FIBER); 2.6 MG SODIUM; 0 MG CHOL.

'Meyer' lemon vinaigrette

MAKES About ¼ cup (for about 10 cups salad, serving 8)
TIME 15 minutes

Food photographers Todd Porter and Diane Cu (*whiteonricecouple. com*) of Costa Mesa, California, like to use this dressing with a salad of red oak leaf, mizuna, and arugula. They often toss in nuts and blue cheese.

Finely shredded zest of 1 'Meyer' lemon
2 tbsp. 'Meyer' lemon juice (from about 1 large lemon)
2 tbsp. extra-virgin olive oil
¼ tsp. fine sea salt
1 tsp. *each* balsamic vinegar and mayonnaise
½ tsp. sugar
1 garlic clove, minced

Whisk vinaigrette ingredients together in a medium bowl until smoothly blended.

TIMESAVER TIP You can make this vinaigrette up to 1 week in advance; refrigerate in an airtight container.

PER 1½ TSP. 44 CAL., 69% (31 CAL.) FROM FAT; 0.4 G PROTEIN; 3.4 G FAT (0.5 G SAT.); 4.3 G CARBO (1.7 G FIBER); 94 MG SODIUM; 0.2 MG CHOL.

Lemon flatbread

MAKES 2 (10 by 15 in.) flatbreads; 30 pieces
TIME 3 hours

Bright and slightly bitter, the salted lemon slices atop this bread give it character. But this recipe is endlessly flexible. Instead of lemons, try topping the bread with your favorite cheese (about 1 cup shredded), some chopped fresh herbs, or whatever else strikes your fancy. The dough makes a wonderful pizza crust too.

1 tbsp. active dry yeast
⅓ cup olive oil, plus more for bowl and pans
4¼ cups all-purpose flour
3 tbsp. salt, divided (see Flavor Note, right)
3 lemons

1. Dissolve yeast in the bowl of a stand mixer in 1¾ cups warm water (90° to 105°). Let sit until foamy, about 5 minutes.
2. Attach dough hook and, with mixer on low, add oil, flour, and 1 tbsp. plus 1 tsp. salt. Mix until dough is smooth, about 2 minutes. (It will still be fairly sticky and won't pull away from the inside of the bowl.) Using a spatula or oiled hands, put dough in a large, oiled bowl, cover with a clean towel or plastic wrap, and let sit until doubled in bulk, 1½ to 2 hours.
3. Meanwhile, slice lemons very thinly. Discard any seeds. Put lemons and 1 tbsp. salt in a bowl and toss to coat. Let sit at room temperature at least 1 hour and up to 1 day.
4. Preheat oven to 425°. Lightly oil two 10- by 15-in. baking sheets. Punch down dough, divide in half, and put each half on a baking sheet. Flatten dough as much as possible, pushing gently from center out. (Dough will pull back toward center; don't worry if it doesn't stay in place.) Let rest 10 minutes, then flatten again, pushing edges and corners down to help them stay put (if it pulls back a bit, that's okay, but you want to make the dough as thin and flat as possible).
5. Lift lemon slices out of their juices and lay them evenly over dough, pressing them into dough as much as possible. Sprinkle dough with remaining 2 tsp. salt. Bake until brown and crispy, about 25 minutes. While bread is still warm, cut each sheet into 15 pieces. Cool on wire racks.

FLAVOR NOTE The final sprinkle of salt is a nice way to use fleur de sel or any other fancy salt you might have.

TIMESAVER TIP You can make the dough a day ahead and chill it, covered, in the refrigerator overnight for its first rise. The lemon can be soaked up to 1 day ahead too.

PER PIECE 91 CAL., 29% (26 CAL.) FROM FAT; 2.1 G PROTEIN; 2.9 G FAT (0.4 G SAT.); 15 G CARBO (1.1 G FIBER); 545 MG SODIUM; 0 MG CHOL.

GOOD FOR YOU
Lemons are a good source of vitamin C and other antioxidants.

Roast chicken with 'Meyer' lemon shallot sauce

SERVES 6 to 8; makes 1 cup gravy
TIME About 2 hours, plus at least 3 hours of salting time

Shallots roast alongside the chicken; then they're puréed and browned with the lemony pan juices to make a fragrant gravy.

1 (4 to 5 lbs.) chicken
1 tbsp. kosher salt
2 medium 'Meyer' or regular ('Eureka') lemons
2½ tbsp. olive oil, divided
1½ tsp. dried thyme
1 lb. shallots
½ to ¾ cup reduced-sodium chicken broth
⅓ cup dry white wine

1. Loosen skin of breast and thighs of chicken and work some salt under skin. Rub remaining salt all over chicken and in cavity (see Flavor Note, right). Chill, uncovered, at least 3 hours and up to overnight.
2. Preheat oven to 375°. Zest lemons. Slice 1 lemon; juice half the other; set aside.
3. Pat chicken dry, inside and out. Rub zest under as much of the skin as possible and rub any remaining zest inside cavity. Rub chicken all over with 1 tbsp. oil and the thyme. Put lemon slices in cavity.
4. Set a V-shaped rack in a heavy roasting pan large enough to hold shallots. Put chicken in rack, breast side up. Add shallots to pan and drizzle with remaining 1½ tbsp. oil, turning them to coat.
5. Roast chicken, basting every 30 minutes or so, until chicken leg moves easily and skin is brown and crisp, 1½ to 1¾ hours (remove shallots after 1 hour and set aside). Tip chicken so juices from cavity pour into roasting pan. Transfer chicken to a carving board and let rest, covered with foil.

6. Meanwhile, make sauce: Pour pan drippings into a measuring cup with a pouring lip. Trim tops from shallots and squeeze soft insides into a blender. Pour off all but about 1 tbsp. fat from pan drippings and add drippings to blender. Add ½ cup broth and the wine and pulse until smooth.
7. Pour sauce into roasting pan. Cook, scraping up brown bits and adding more broth if you want a thinner sauce, over medium-high heat on your biggest burner (or straddling 2 burners) until sauce turns a nutty brown, about 10 minutes. Stir in 1 tbsp. reserved lemon juice, or more to taste. Pour sauce through a fine-mesh strainer into a serving bowl. Carve chicken, discarding lemon slices, and serve with sauce.

FLAVOR NOTE Salting the chicken hours ahead instead of just before cooking makes the meat more flavorful. For crisper skin, don't truss the legs before roasting.

PER SERVING WITH 2 TBSP. SAUCE 388 CAL., 56% (216 CAL.) FROM FAT; 33 G PROTEIN; 24 G FAT (6 G SAT.); 11 G CARBO (1.2 G FIBER); 700 MG SODIUM; 101 MG CHOL.

Baked ham with sticky 'Meyer' lemon–spice glaze

SERVES 8, with ample leftovers
TIME 2½ hours

Be sure to buy a ham without added glaze; it would mute the flavor of our extra-citrusy one.

1 (6 to 7 lbs.) cooked, bone-in half-ham from shank or butt
¾ cup firmly packed light brown sugar
Finely shredded zest and juice of 5 medium 'Meyer' lemons
1¼ tsp. ground ginger

1. Preheat oven to 350°. Cut off tough, leatherlike skin from ham (if it has one) and score fat and meat in a crosshatch pattern.

Put ham, fat side up, in a large roasting pan and tent loosely with foil. Bake until a thermometer inserted in thickest part of meat reaches 120°, about 1½ hours.
2. Meanwhile, make glaze: In a bowl, whisk brown sugar, lemon zest and juice, and ginger until smooth.
3. Uncover ham and pour glaze over it into pan. Bake ham, uncovered, basting ham and stirring glaze every 10 minutes, until glaze is a thickened, shiny syrup and thermometer in meat reaches 135° to 140°, 15 to 30 minutes.
4. Let ham rest 5 minutes, then brush with glaze and transfer to a cutting board. Scrape remaining glaze into a small bowl. Carve ham and spoon more glaze on top.

PER SERVING 367 CAL., 39% (144 CAL.) FROM FAT; 42 G PROTEIN; 16 G FAT (5.2 G SAT.); 14 G CARBO (0.1 G FIBER); 1,388 MG SODIUM; 120 MG CHOL.

Meringue cups with strawberries and 'Meyer' lemon curd

Meringue cups with strawberries and 'Meyer' lemon curd

SERVES 12
TIME 2½ hours, plus overnight for meringues to dry

Nothing welcomes spring like sweet berries and tangy-floral 'Meyer' lemons. This recipe is from Karen Mitchell, owner of the Model Bakery in St. Helena and Napa, California.

7 large eggs, divided
2 cups granulated sugar, divided
¾ cup powdered sugar
About 1½ lbs. 'Meyer' lemons
1 cup butter, cut in pieces
2 pts. strawberries, hulled and sliced or quartered

1. Preheat oven to 200°. Separate 6 eggs and put whites in a large metal bowl; set yolks aside. Add ¾ cup granulated sugar to whites. Set bowl over a pan of simmering water and whisk until slightly warm, about 1½ minutes.
2. Using an electric mixer fitted with a whisk attachment, beat whites on high speed until they hold a straight peak when beater is lifted, 1½ to 2 minutes. Sift powdered sugar and ¼ cup granulated sugar into another bowl. Gradually mix sifted sugars into whites (about ¼ cup every 30 seconds) on medium speed. Once sugar is incorporated, beat on high speed until mixture holds a stiff, straight peak when beater is lifted, 5 to 8 minutes; check often and do not overbeat.
3. Line 2 large baking sheets with parchment paper and glue down corners of paper with dabs of meringue. Spoon 6 equal mounds of meringue (½ to ⅔ cup each) onto each sheet, spacing evenly. With the back of a soup spoon, spread each mound into a circle about 3½ in. wide with a 2-in.-wide hollow in the center.

4. Bake meringues until firm, about 1½ hours. Turn off oven and leave meringues in oven to firm overnight.

5. Meanwhile, make lemon curd: Zest 2 lemons. Squeeze juice from enough lemons to make 1 cup. In a metal bowl, whisk lemon zest and juice, remaining 1 cup granulated sugar, the egg yolks, and remaining whole egg to blend. Add butter. Set bowl over a pan of simmering water and stir mixture until it thickly coats a metal spoon, 10 to 15 minutes. Let cool, whisking often. Cover with plastic wrap directly touching curd (this will prevent a skin from forming) and chill until cold, at least 2 hours.

6. Loosen meringues from parchment, put on plates, and spoon about ¼ cup lemon curd into each. Scatter some berries onto meringues and serve the rest from a bowl.

TIMESAVER TIP You can prepare the curd and meringues up to 4 days ahead. Don't fill the meringues more than 1 hour in advance.

PER SERVING 357 CAL., 45% (162 CAL.) FROM FAT; 4.2 G PROTEIN; 18 G FAT (10 G SAT.); 47 G CARBO (1.5 G FIBER); 198 MG SODIUM; 165 MG CHOL.

Candied lemon peel

MAKES About 6 cups
TIME 5 hours, plus at least 8 hours of drying time

An unusual whole-peel technique is used to make this classic holiday candy.

5 lbs. lemons, washed and dried
8 cups sugar, divided

1. Halve and juice lemons; reserve juice for another use. Put peels in a large pot and cover with cold water. Bring to a boil and cook 3 minutes. Drain. Return peels to pot, cover with cold water, bring to a boil, cook 3 minutes, and drain. Repeat once more. Spread peels on baking sheets and let sit until cool enough to handle, 20 minutes.

2. Using a soup spoon, scrape out membranes and discard. Cut peels into strips and set aside.

3. Bring 8 cups water and 6 cups sugar to a boil in a large, heavy pot over high heat. Add peels, reduce heat to maintain a steady, gentle simmer, and cook, stirring occasionally, until peels are tender, sweet, and translucent, about 3 hours. (Don't let sugar brown or caramelize.) Drain peels and spread on wire racks set over baking sheets. Let sit until dry, at least 8 hours.

4. Toss a handful of peels with remaining 2 cups sugar. Shake off excess sugar and put peels in an airtight container. Repeat with remaining peels. Store at room temperature up to 2 weeks.

PER ¼-CUP SERVING 126 CAL., 1% (0.9 CAL.) FROM FAT; 0.2 G PROTEIN; 0.1 G FAT (0 G SAT.); 32 G CARBO (0 G FIBER); 0 MG SODIUM; 0 MG CHOL.

Preserved lemons

MAKES 8 preserved lemons
TIME About 10 minutes, plus at least 2 weeks to cure

"The area to the side of my house is a citrus garden, where I have lemon, lime, and orange trees. When the trees are full, I preserve all three," says Jesse Z. Cool, chef-owner of Flea St. Café in Menlo Park, California, and Cool Café, with locations in Menlo Park and Stanford. Preserved citrus adds a distinctive salty, pleasantly fermented, and slightly bitter flavor to salads and stews.

8 lemons (see Flavor Note, right)
1½ cups kosher salt
Rosemary sprig (optional)

1. Thoroughly rinse lemons; quarter lengthwise into wedges and put in a large bowl. Stir in salt. With a potato masher or wooden spoon, press fruit to extract some juice. Transfer mixture to a wide-mouthed 1- to 1½-qt. jar. Push a rosemary sprig into jar if you like. Press fruit to immerse in juice.

2. Seal jar and store in refrigerator at least 2 weeks or up to 6 months. In the first few days, press fruit down occasionally to submerge in liquid.

FLAVOR NOTE You can also preserve 'Meyer' lemons, limes, and oranges using this recipe.

PER SERVING 4 CAL., 0% FROM FAT; 0 G PROTEIN; 0 G FAT; 1.3 G CARBO (0.3 G FIBER); 3,421 MG SODIUM; 0 MG CHOL.

Preserved lemons

HOW TO JUICE A LEMON

To get the most juice, first roll the lemon on a firm surface to soften it, then use an electric or manual juicer (the kinds with ribbed domes, versus the press type, produce the most juice).

MELONS

'Green Nutmeg'
muskmelon

WHY GROW THEM

If you live in a climate that gives melons the steady hot weather they need to grow and ripen, why not grow your own? Whether you plant muskmelons (this type includes the cantaloupe and other netted-skin varieties), late melons (the canary, casaba, and honeydew), melon crosses like Crenshaw, or watermelons, you'll be rewarded with sweet, juicy fruit and fine flavor.

WHEN TO HARVEST

(Muskmelons) Lift the fruit and twist; if ripe, it will easily slip off the stem. A pleasant perfume also indicates ripeness. **(Late melons)** Honeydews are ready to pick when the area of the melon that rests on the ground turns from yellow to white. Harvest other late melons when the fruit begins to turn yellow and starts to soften at the blossom end. As Crenshaw melons approach maturity, you may need to protect them from sunburn. **(Watermelons)** Thump the melon; if it is ripe, it will produce a hollow "thunk." Also check to see that the underside of the melon has turned from white to pale yellow, and make sure the tendrils where the melon attaches to the stem have darkened and withered. Cut (do not pull) the melon from the vine.

HOW TO KEEP

Refrigerate cut melons or fully ripe whole melons in tightly sealed plastic bags (the ethylene gas melons give off can hasten spoilage of other produce in the refrigerator).

'Moon and Stars' watermelon

How to Toast Melon Seeds

These crunchy seeds are a great way to make more use of your homegrown melon. Rinse the seeds thoroughly in a colander to remove any melon bits, then dry them in a kitchen towel. Measure the seeds, then toast in a dry (not nonstick) saucepan or pot over medium-high heat 2 minutes. Meanwhile, dissolve 1 tbsp. salt in 1 cup hot water. Into the saucepan, pour the same amount of salt water as seeds. Continue cooking over medium-high heat, stirring occasionally, until water evaporates. Toast seeds, covered, until rich golden brown, shaking pan often (as though you're making popcorn), 2 to 3 minutes. Sprinkle with salt while still warm. Let cool before eating.

Some of our favorite varieties

'Ambrosia' A cantaloupe with deep orange, meltingly soft flesh.

'Amish' An heirloom cantaloupe with sweet, juicy flesh.

'Collective Farm Woman' A Ukrainian variety similar to a honeydew, its skin turns from dark green to yellowish orange when ripe. Very sweet.

'Crane' A Crenshaw-type melon, sweet with light orange flesh. Pick when the fruit is yellowish with green tinges.

'Eden's Gem' A honeydew with lime green, sweet-spicy flesh.

'Green Nutmeg' Tiny, single-serving muskmelon. A bit spicy, with bright green flesh.

'Moon and Stars' A beautiful speckled watermelon with bright red to pinkish flesh and a sweet-tart flavor.

'PureHeart Seedless' We love this new mini, or "personal," watermelon that can almost fit in the palm of your hand.

'Sharlyn' A luscious, fragrant, cream-colored melon that tastes like a cross between a honeydew and cantaloupe.

'Sugar Baby' This small seedless watermelon has crisp, juicy fruit and won't take up the entire refrigerator shelf.

3 WAYS WITH MELON

Watermelon with prosecco
Form watermelon balls with the smallest possible melon baller. Divide them among pretty little glasses or Champagne flutes, filling each about halfway. Top with prosecco and a pinch of sugar.

Summer fizzies Purée any ripe melon in a blender; strain purée to get about 2 cups juice. Pour juice into clean ice cube trays. Freeze until set, about 2 hours. Divide frozen cubes among 4 glasses and pour club soda over.

Watermelon salad with feta and pine nuts Toss together chunks of watermelon and creamy feta cheese, along with toasted pine nuts, chopped flat-leaf parsley, a simple lemon vinaigrette (1 part fresh lemon juice to 3 parts canola oil and salt to taste), and lots of freshly ground black pepper.

Melon-berry *agua fresca*

SERVES 4; makes about 5 cups
TIME 20 minutes

Sweet-tart *aguas frescas*, served all over Mexico, make great summer coolers. Add the sugar gradually so you don't oversweeten.

2 cups peeled honeydew melon chunks
(see Flavor Note, below)
1 cup sliced strawberries
1 cup raspberries
About ⅓ cup *each* sugar and fresh lime juice

1. Combine fruit and 2 cups cold water in a blender. Whirl until puréed. Add sugar and lime juice to taste.
2. Pour mixture through a fine-mesh strainer into a serving pitcher. Serve cold or over ice.

FLAVOR NOTE You can substitute seeded cantaloupe or watermelon chunks for the honeydew.

PER SERVING 124 CAL., 2.9% (3.6 CAL.) FROM FAT; 0.9 G PROTEIN; 0.4 G FAT (0 G SAT.); 32 G CARBO (0 G FIBER); 12 MG SODIUM; 0 MG CHOL.

Oysters with melons and cucumber water

MAKES 12 oysters
TIME 5 minutes, plus 1 hour to chill

This easy recipe comes from Kirk Sowell, owner of two Morro Bay, California, restaurants—Miss Lola's SouthSide Grill and Frankie & Lola's Front Street Cafe. He developed it especially to highlight the cucumber-melon flavors of Pacific Gold oysters. He uses 'Ha-Ogen' and 'Ambrosia' melons and cilantro microgreens, but if they're hard to find in your region, honeydew, cantaloupe, and regular cilantro are fine substitutes.

¼ cup *each* finely diced honeydew and cantaloupe
1 medium English cucumber, a 3-in. length peeled and chopped, plus 12 thick slices from cucumber
2 tsp. fresh lemon juice
¼ tsp. minced serrano chile
12 freshly shucked Pacific oysters on the half-shell, preferably ones with deep cups
Small cilantro leaves for garnish

1. Chill the melon dice. Purée chopped cucumber, lemon juice, chile, and 2 tbsp. water in a blender. Strain and chill for at least 1 hour and up to 1 day.
2. Tip out most but not all of the liquor from each oyster and nestle each into a cucumber round. Spoon some diced melon on top and some cucumber water. Sprinkle with cilantro.

PER OYSTER 46 CAL., 22% (10 CAL.) FROM FAT; 4.8 G PROTEIN; 1.2 G FAT (0.3 G SAT.); 4 G CARBO (0.1 G FIBER); 54 MG SODIUM; 25 MG CHOL.

Melon-berry
agua fresca

Cantaloupe and prosciutto salad
RECIPE P. 256

Vietnamese shrimp
and green melon salad
RECIPE P. 256

Cantaloupe and prosciutto salad

SERVES 8

TIME 30 minutes

Here's a twist on the traditional melon wedge wrapped in pro-sciutto. Prosciutto slices get baked until crisp, broken into pieces, and sprinkled over ribbons of juicy cantaloupe. (Photo on page 254.)

4 thin slices prosciutto (1 oz.)
1 ripe cantaloupe, halved, seeded, and rind cut off
8 to 10 large mint leaves, thinly sliced
2 tbsp. extra-virgin olive oil

1. Preheat oven to 350°. Set a rack over a rimmed baking sheet. Lay prosciutto on rack and bake until crisp, 8 to 10 minutes. Let cool, then break into shards and chips.
2. Shave off ribbons of cantaloupe onto a large serving platter, using a vegetable peeler, mandoline, or very sharp knife. Sprinkle prosciutto and mint over melon shavings. Drizzle oil over salad.

PER ³⁄₄-CUP SERVING 62 CAL., 56% (35 CAL.) FROM FAT; 1.6 G PROTEIN; 4 G FAT (0.7 G SAT.); 5.8 G CARBO (0.7 G FIBER); 108 MG SODIUM; 1.9 MG CHOL.

Vietnamese shrimp and green melon salad

SERVES 6

TIME 25 minutes

The melon cools the spice in this fresh, lively summer salad. We like it with shrimp, but it's also good with grilled calamari. (Photo on page 255.)

1 lb. medium shrimp (24 to 30 per lb.), peeled and deveined
1½ cups *each* loosely packed basil, mint, and cilantro
¼ cup slivered red onion
½ serrano chile, thinly sliced
3 cups honeydew or Galia melon wedges
3 tbsp. fresh lime juice
1 tbsp. sugar
2 tbsp. Vietnamese fish sauce (*nuoc mam*)
½ cup roasted, salted cashews

1. Bring a medium pot of water to a boil. Add shrimp and cook just until they turn opaque and curl up, 1 to 2 minutes. Drain and rinse with cold water.
2. Toss shrimp, herbs, onion, chile, and melon together in a large bowl. Mix together lime juice, sugar, and fish sauce in a small bowl, then pour over salad. Toss salad gently, then top with cashews.

PER SERVING 210 CAL., 30% (63 CAL.) FROM FAT; 23 G PROTEIN; 6.9 G FAT (1 G SAT.); 17 G CARBO (2.9 G FIBER); 735 MG SODIUM; 153 MG CHOL.

White port and watermelon granita

SERVES 12

TIME About 30 minutes, plus 8 hours to freeze

White port? Absolutely. Try one made from Chardonnay in this very grown-up ice.

¾ cup sugar
1 tbsp. finely shredded lime zest
6 cups cubed seeded watermelon, divided
1 cup white port
¼ cup fresh lime juice

1. Bring 1 cup water, the sugar, and lime zest to a boil in a small saucepan over high heat; stir until sugar is dissolved. Strain into a blender and add 3 cups watermelon. Whirl until smooth and pour into a 9- by 13-in. metal baking pan.
2. Add remaining 3 cups watermelon to blender along with port and lime juice; whirl until smooth, add to pan, and mix well. Cover and freeze until mixture is beginning to freeze at the edges, about 2 hours.
3. Stir, cover, and freeze until solid, about 6 hours.
4. Just before serving, scrape into soft clumps with a fork. Spoon into chilled glasses or bowls.

PER 1-CUP SERVING 106 CAL., 3% (2.7 CAL.) FROM FAT; 0.5 G PROTEIN; 0.3 G FAT (0 G SAT.); 21 G CARBO (0.4 G FIBER); 3.6 MG SODIUM; 0 MG CHOL.

GOOD FOR YOU
Melons are both nutritious and low calorie. Cantaloupes in particular are full of vitamins A and C.

RHUBARB

WHY GROW IT

Rhubarb is a love-it or hate-it kind of plant. But if you are a fan of its delicious tart flavor and look forward to its appearance every spring, you'll certainly want to put in a plant or two. The good news is that rhubarb is a perennial, guaranteeing a harvest of stalks year after year; the less good news is that you need to let your rhubarb grow for two full seasons before it's ready. Fortunately, with its huge, showy leaves and usually red-tinted stalks, rhubarb is a good-looking plant, just as much at home in your flower garden as your vegetable patch, so you can enjoy its ornamental attributes as you wait for it to mature.

WHEN TO HARVEST

In rhubarb's third growing season, you can pull off leafstalks for 4 to 5 weeks in spring and early summer when stalks are thick and tender; older, huskier plants can take up to 8 weeks of harvesting. At any one harvest, pick only as much as you plan to use in the next week. To pick the leafstalks, grasp them near the base and pull sideways and outward (do not cut with a knife, as cutting will leave a stub that decays). Never remove all the stalks from a single plant, and stop harvesting when slender leafstalks appear. Cut out any blossom stalks that appear.

'The Sutton'

HOW TO KEEP

Cut and discard the leaves from the stalks (the leaves are poisonous if eaten in large quantities). Refrigerate the stalks, unwashed, in a plastic bag for up to 1 week.

PRESERVING THE HARVEST

Unfortunately, rhubarb doesn't freeze well, but it makes great jam (especially mixed with strawberries) and chutney.

Basic Ways to Cook

Rhubarb is very tart and almost always needs to be sweetened and cooked before serving. Here are two ways to prepare a rhubarb compote, which you can then eat as part of a parfait, over a slice of cake with ice cream (especially strawberry or vanilla), or spooned into your morning bowl of oatmeal.

STEWED Trim away and discard leaves from 1 lb. rhubarb, then cut stalks crosswise into 1-in. pieces. Cook in just enough water to cover until softened, about 15 minutes. Add enough sugar to sweeten (about ½ cup) and continue to cook until sugar is dissolved, about 5 minutes.

BAKED Trim 2 lbs. rhubarb and cut crosswise into ½-in.-thick slices. In a 9- by 13-in. baking pan, toss with 1½ cups sugar, then spread level in pan and cover with foil. Bake at 350° until rhubarb is very soft when pierced but still holds its shape, about 45 minutes.

Some of our favorite varieties

'Crimson Cherry' and 'MacDonald' Both are red-stalked varieties. We like 'Crimson Cherry' for its deep, full flavor, hardiness, and high yields; and 'MacDonald' for its heavy production and large, juicy stalks; among the most widely available varieties.

'The Sutton' Also known as 'Sutton's Seedless', with light red, plentiful stalks.

'Valentine' Its long, vivid red stalks retain their color when cooked.

'Victoria' Lots of large, thick stalks that are pink at the base and fade to green at the top.

Brie, rhubarb, and green peppercorn crostini

MAKES 26 crostini

TIME 30 minutes, plus 1 hour to rest

This is an unusual combination, but the bright, spicy bite of peppercorns and rhubarb cuts the cheese's creaminess.

1 lb. rhubarb stalks, leaves trimmed and discarded, stems sliced crosswise ¼ in. thick
5 tbsp. honey
1 tsp. balsamic vinegar
1 heaping tbsp. green peppercorns in brine, drained
1 French baguette (at least 14 in. long)
2 tbsp. olive oil
11 oz. very ripe triple-cream cheese such as brie or camembert, at room temperature

1. Cook rhubarb with honey in a medium saucepan over medium heat, stirring occasionally, until rhubarb is soft and just starting to fall apart, 6 to 8 minutes. Preheat oven to 350°.

2. Remove pan from heat and add vinegar and peppercorns; let flavors meld at least 1 hour.

3. Meanwhile, slice baguette on diagonal into ½-in.-thick slices to make 26. Put slices on a baking sheet, brush one side with oil, and bake until golden brown, about 15 minutes. Let cool.

4. Cut cheese into 26 thick slices, each about as long as a baguette slice.

5. Spoon a scant 1 tbsp. rhubarb mixture onto each baguette slice. Top each with a slice (or 2 smaller pieces) of cheese and serve immediately. Or serve toasts, topping, and cheese separately and let everyone assemble their own crostini.

TIMESAVER TIP You can toast the bread and prepare the rhubarb topping up to 1 day ahead. Store the toasts airtight at room temperature; cover and refrigerate the topping.

PER CROSTINO: 107 CAL., 36% (39 CAL.) FROM FAT; 4.5 G PROTEIN; 4.4 G FAT (2.2 G SAT.); 13 G CARBO (0.8 G FIBER); 185 MG SODIUM; 12 MG CHOL.

Rhubarb compote with toasted-almond ice cream balls

SERVES 8

TIME 1 hour, plus about 30 minutes to cool and chill

Rhubarb goes very well with orange, and its melting texture sets off the crispness of the almonds. The idea for the nut-coated ice cream balls is from Emily Luchetti, top pastry chef at San Francisco's Farallon and Waterbar restaurants.

1½ lbs. rhubarb stalks
⅓ cup sugar
2 tsp. quick-cooking tapioca
½ cup orange marmalade
1½ pts. vanilla ice cream
⅔ cup sliced almonds, toasted (see Flavor Note, below)

1. Preheat oven to 350°. Trim leaves from rhubarb stalks; cut stalks crosswise into ½-in. thick pieces. In a bowl, mix rhubarb with sugar, tapioca, and marmalade and let sit 15 minutes. Divide rhubarb and juices among eight 1-cup ramekins and set them on a baking sheet. Bake rhubarb until soft but still holding its shape, 30 minutes. Transfer to a cooling rack.

2. Meanwhile, scoop out 8 small ice cream balls, set on another baking sheet, and freeze until quite hard, at least 15 minutes. Put almonds in a bowl, coat each ball with nuts, and put the balls back in freezer until ready to serve.

3. Serve rhubarb warm or at room temperature, topped with ice cream balls.

FLAVOR NOTE Toasting accentuates the flavor and crunch of nuts. Spread nuts in a single layer in a baking pan and toast at 350° until golden, 5 to 15 minutes, depending on the type of nut.

PER SERVING 248 CAL., 35% (87 CAL.) FROM FAT; 4.1 G PROTEIN; 9.7 G FAT (3.7 G SAT.); 39 G CARBO (0.4 G FIBER); 59 MG SODIUM; 22 MG CHOL.

Rhubarb upside-down cake with rosemary caramel sauce

SERVES 8

TIME 1¾ hours

This unusual dessert, from Brock Windsor, chef-owner of Stone Soup Inn—on Vancouver Island in British Columbia—is a knockout. He serves it with sour-cream fresh chamomile ice cream, but vanilla tastes wonderful too.

CAKE

½ lb. rhubarb stalks, leaves trimmed and discarded, stalks cut crosswise into ½-in.-thick slices (2 cups)

½ cup plus 3 tbsp. granulated sugar

3 oz. good-quality white chocolate such as Callebaut, chopped

⅓ cup unsalted butter, softened, plus more for pan

2 large egg whites, at room temperature

¾ tsp. vanilla extract

1⅓ cups cake flour

2 tsp. baking powder

½ tsp. salt

½ cup milk

SAUCE

1 cup whipping cream

1 rosemary sprig (5 in.)

1 cup granulated sugar

½ tsp. fresh lemon juice

COMPOTE

½ cup firmly packed light brown sugar

½ lb. rhubarb stalks, leaves trimmed and discarded, stalks split lengthwise and cut crosswise into 2-in. pieces

1. Preheat oven to 350°. Butter a 9-in. round pan or eight 1-cup ramekins and line with parchment paper or waxed paper cut to fit. Butter the paper.

2. Make cake(s): In a medium bowl, toss rhubarb with 3 tbsp. granulated sugar. Spoon evenly into pan or ramekins; if using ramekins, set on a baking sheet.

3. Melt chocolate in a small metal bowl set over a pan of barely simmering water, whisking until smooth, 2 to 4 minutes. Let cool.

4. Beat butter and remaining ½ cup granulated sugar in a bowl with a mixer until fluffy. Add egg whites and vanilla and beat until well blended. Combine flour, baking powder, and salt in another bowl. Beat flour mixture into egg mixture half at a time, alternating with milk, until smooth. Stir in melted chocolate.

5. Spread batter evenly over rhubarb. Bake cake(s) until golden brown and a toothpick inserted in center comes out almost clean, 28 to 35 minutes. Let cool in pan or ramekins about 30 minutes.

6. Make sauce: Heat cream and rosemary in a small saucepan over medium heat until bubbles form at edge of pan, stirring occasionally, 3 to 5 minutes. Remove from heat and discard rosemary.

7. Stir granulated sugar with lemon juice and 2 tbsp. water in a 12-in. frying pan. Cook over medium-high heat, occasionally picking up pan and swirling mixture around sides to wash down sugar crystals, until deep golden, 5 to 6 minutes. Immediately remove pan from heat, add cream (it will bubble up), and whisk until smooth. Scrape sauce into a serving bowl.

8. Make compote: In a small saucepan over medium heat, bring brown sugar, ⅓ cup water, and the rhubarb to a boil, stirring occasionally. Reduce heat and simmer until rhubarb is tender, 4 to 5 minutes.

9. Loosen cake(s) from sides of pan or ramekins with a small metal spatula. Invert pan onto a platter (or invert ramekins onto dessert plates) and remove paper. For cake on platter, cut into wedges and transfer to plates. Spoon compote and some syrup on cake. Spoon some sauce next to cake and serve rest on the side.

PER SERVING 559 CAL., 38% (213 CAL.) FROM FAT; 5.3 G PROTEIN; 24 G FAT (15 G SAT.); 84 G CARBO (1.5 G FIBER); 317 MG SODIUM; 67 MG CHOL.

Rhubarb cardamom galette

SERVES 6
TIME 30 minutes

This dessert is wonderfully architectural, as well as simple and tasty.

1 sheet (9 to 10 oz.) frozen puff pastry, thawed
3 tbsp. granulated sugar, divided
1 tbsp. firmly packed brown sugar
¼ tsp. ground cardamom
2 tbsp. flour
12 oz. rhubarb stalks (about 8 thin or 3 thick stalks),
    leaves trimmed and discarded
Sweetened whipped cream or ice cream

1. Preheat oven to 425° with a rack set on lowest rung. Unfold pastry onto a baking sheet lined with parchment paper. In a small bowl, mix together 1 tbsp. granulated sugar, the brown sugar, cardamom, and flour. Evenly sprinkle sugar mixture over pastry.
2. Trim rhubarb stalks 1 in. shorter than pastry, then split lengthwise into ½-in.-wide pieces. Lay pieces parallel across pastry square, leaving ½-in. border of pastry. Sprinkle rhubarb with remaining 2 tbsp. granulated sugar.
3. Bake galette until edges are golden brown and puffed, 12 to 15 minutes. Serve with sweetened whipped cream or ice cream.

PER SERVING 233 CAL., 48% (113 CAL.) FROM FAT; 4.5 G PROTEIN; 13 G FAT (3.4 G SAT.); 28 G CARBO (1.6 G FIBER); 222 MG SODIUM; 0 MG CHOL.

GOOD FOR YOU
Rhubarb is a good source of vitamin K.

STONE FRUIT

'Santa Rosa' plums

WHY GROW THEM

There is something particularly luscious and indulgent about stone fruit—all those tender, fragile apricots, nectarines, peaches, and plums that rush in over the summer. Their beautifully hued skins protect a juicy, sweet, sometimes slightly tart interior and their appearance each year is one more reason to love warm weather. Growing your own means you have truly tree-ripened fruit—the only way to get the fullest flavor. Some varieties, like 'Blenheim' apricots, bruise so easily that they're rarely found except at farmers' markets—and thus are very worthwhile to grow yourself.

WHEN TO HARVEST

(Apricots and plums) Pick fruit when colored up and slightly softened. **(Peaches and nectarines)** Pick fruit when fully colored and pulls easily off the tree with a gentle twist.

HOW TO KEEP

Refrigerate ripe fruit, unwashed, in a paper bag for 2 to 3 days or up to 1 week for plums.

PRESERVING THE HARVEST

CAN See our recipe for peach refrigerator jam on page 277 and general guidelines for canning on pages 278–279.

FREEZE Apricots, nectarines, peaches, and plums can all be frozen in a light syrup. Combine 1½ cups sugar, 4 cups water, and ½ to ¾ teaspoon ascorbic acid (to control darkening); mix until sugar dissolves. Refrigerate until cold. For each pint of syrup, use about 1 pound of fruit. Cut apricots and plums in half and pit; cut nectarines in half or wedges; peel peaches (see "How to Peel a Peach," page 269) and cut in half or wedges. Pour ½ cup cold syrup into each pint container (use rigid plastic ones with tight-fitting lids). Add fruit, then add more syrup to cover fruit, leaving at least ½ inch of headspace for pint containers, 1 inch for quart containers. Place crumbled wax paper or plastic wrap on top of fruit to keep it submerged in syrup. Cover with lid and freeze at 0° or lower.

'Frost' peach

Basic Ways to Cook

BAKE Peel 1½ to 2 lbs. fruit; leave apricots whole but halve and pit larger fruit. Arrange in single layer in baking pan, cut side up, and brush with melted butter and sugar or honey. Bake at 325°, basting occasionally, until tender.

GRILL Halve and pit fruit. Thread on skewers and grill until hot and tender when pierced, basting with melted butter.

POACH Bring 1½ cups water, 1 cup sugar, 1 tbsp. fresh lemon juice, and zest from ½ lemon to a boil in 3-qt. pan. Boil until reduced to 1 cup. Remove from heat and stir in 1¼ cups fruity white wine. Peel, halve, and pit apricots and peaches; leave plums whole and prick skins; halve and pit nectarines but leave on skins. Bring poaching liquid to a boil. Add fruit, reduce heat, cover, and simmer fruit, turning in syrup occasionally, until tender. Serve warm or cold.

Some of our favorite varieties

APRICOTS

'Blenheim' Queen of the apricots, with intense, rich flavor. Very fragile, but good for both canning and drying.

'Montrose' Sweet and juicy with excellent flavor; has edible kernel ("sweet pit").

'Newcastle' Red-blushed yellow skin, sweet, juicy, with rich flavor.

NECTARINES

'Arctic Rose' White-fleshed, with delicious sweet flavor.

'Heavenly White' Has creamy white skin heavily blushed red, white flesh, and an especially fine flavor.

'Liz's Late' Yellow-fleshed with a sweet-spicy flavor; a good keeper.

PEACHES

'Arctic Supreme' Among the finest flavored of all peaches.

'Frost' A heavy-bearing freestone variety, it's cold-hardy and disease-resistant.

'Redskin' Fruit is good fresh, canned, or frozen.

'Strawberry Free' Excellent flavor; a favorite among white peach varieties.

PLUMS

'Imperial' Fine-quality fruit with sweet, intense flavor. Excellent fresh, as well as dried and canned.

'Santa Rosa' Rich, pleasing, tart flavor. Remove skins if canning.

'Sugar' Intensely flavored, very sweet; good fresh, dried, or canned.

Peach Collins

SERVES 2

TIME 10 minutes

A play on the Tom Collins. We muddle (mash) ripe peaches and shake them with peach-flavored vodka.

¼ cup *each* Simple Syrup (page 204) and fresh lemon juice

½ cup chopped ripe peaches, divided

Ice

½ cup *each* peach-flavored vodka and club soda

2 peach slices

1. Mix simple syrup, lemon juice, ¼ cup peaches, and about ½ cup ice in a cocktail shaker or plastic cup. Using end of a wooden spoon, muddle mixture until peaches start to break up. Pour in vodka, cover shaker with top (or the cup with plastic wrap), and shake until blended.

2. Divide unstrained mixture and remaining chopped peaches between 2 tall glasses. Fill glasses with ice. Top off each glass with half the club soda and garnish with a peach slice.

PER DRINK 266 CAL., 0% (0.9 CAL.) FROM FAT; 0.5 G PROTEIN; 0.1 G FAT (0 G SAT.); 32 G CARBO (0.7 G FIBER); 13 MG SODIUM; 0 MG CHOL.

Peach and mint caprese salad with curry vinaigrette

SERVES 8

TIME 40 minutes

Use only tree-ripened peaches and splurge on buffalo mozzarella if you can—it's creamier and tangier than cow's-milk mozzarella, and it really elevates this salad. West Coast food stylist Valerie Aikman-Smith, who gave us the recipe, likes to make it at the height of summer, "when everyone is sick of tomatoes." If your plates aren't white, she says, start your layering with the mozzarella—its paleness will look pretty against a color.

½ tbsp. Madras curry powder

½ cup *each* extra-virgin olive oil and Champagne vinegar

½ tsp. mild honey

4 balls mozzarella cheese (8 oz. each)

4 large firm-ripe yellow or white peaches

10 to 12 *each* mint and basil sprigs

Sea salt or coarse kosher salt

Freshly ground black pepper

1. Toast curry powder in a dry (not nonstick) skillet over medium heat, stirring constantly, until fragrant, a shade darker, and just starting to smoke, 2 minutes. Transfer to a bowl; let cool briefly. Whisk in oil, vinegar, and honey. Set aside.

2. Cut mozzarella into ½-in.-thick slices; set aside. Peel peaches (see "How to Peel a Peach," page 269), cut in half lengthwise, and remove pits. Set each half flat on cutting board and slice into ½-in.-thick half-moons. Pluck mint and basil leaves from stems.

3. Set out 8 small plates or flattish bowls and build a loose tower of salad on each: Lay a couple of pieces of peach in center, top with a leaf or two of mint and basil, drape on a piece of mozzarella, and repeat layering 2 or 3 times. Top each stack with 2 peach slices and a mint leaf. Drizzle with curry vinaigrette, season with salt and pepper to taste, and scatter a few mint and basil leaves on each plate.

TIMESAVER TIP You can make the vinaigrette up to a week ahead; mozzarella, peaches, and herbs can be prepared several hours before and refrigerated (toss peaches with a bit of vinaigrette to prevent browning; drain cheese in a colander before plating).

PER SALAD 481 CAL., 71% (342 CAL.) FROM FAT; 21 G PROTEIN; 38 G FAT (22 G SAT.); 10 G CARBO (1.7 G FIBER); 922 MG SODIUM; 80 MG CHOL.

Arugula salad with
white nectarines
and mango chutney
dressing

Arugula salad with white nectarines and mango chutney dressing

SERVES 8
TIME 25 minutes

Oregon cookbook author Janie Hibler came up with this combination, using a slightly tart and spicy dressing as a bridge between the flavors of sweet white nectarines and peppery greens. Feel free to use yellow nectarines or peaches instead.

8 oz. baby arugula (about 3 qts. loosely packed)
4 ripe white or yellow nectarines, pitted and
    cut into ½-in.-thick slices
¼ cup extra-virgin olive oil
2 tbsp. *each* fresh lime juice and mild mango
    chutney such as Major Grey
½ tsp. kosher salt
⅓ cup thinly sliced sweet onion such as
    'Walla Walla' or 'Maui'
⅓ cup chopped toasted hazelnuts

1. Gently mix arugula and nectarines in a large salad bowl.
2. Purée oil, lime juice, chutney, and salt in a blender until almost smooth; pour over salad. Scatter onion and hazelnuts over greens and toss together.

PER SERVING 144 CAL., 63% (90 CAL.) FROM FAT; 2.1 G PROTEIN; 10 G FAT (1.2 G SAT.); 13 G CARBO (2 G FIBER); 89 MG SODIUM; 0 MG CHOL.

Grilled chicken and nectarine salad

SERVES 4 as a main course
TIME About 25 minutes

Reader Jay Decker of Medina, Washington, combines barbecued chicken, sweet nectarines, tangy goat cheese, and toasted pecans in a great main-course salad.

⅔ cup pecan halves
2 qts. salad greens (8 oz.)
¼ cup *each* vegetable oil, walnut oil, and white
    wine vinegar
4 boned chicken breast halves with skin
    (2 lbs. total), fat trimmed
Salt and freshly ground black pepper
2 firm-ripe nectarines (12 oz. total), pitted
    and thinly sliced
5 oz. fresh chèvre (goat cheese), crumbled

1. Preheat oven to 350°. Spread pecans in a baking pan and bake until golden under skins, about 10 minutes. Let cool, then coarsely chop.
2. Mound salad greens on 4 dinner plates. In a small bowl, stir vegetable oil, walnut oil, and vinegar to blend. Set aside.
3. Prepare a charcoal or gas grill for direct medium heat (350° to 450°; you can hold your hand 5 in. above cooking grate only 5 to 7 seconds). Sprinkle chicken with salt and pepper and place on grill; close lid on gas grill. Cook chicken, turning occasionally, until meat is no longer pink in center of thickest part (cut to test), about 15 minutes total. Transfer chicken to a cutting board. Remove skin if desired.
4. Slice chicken across the grain ½ in. thick; arrange over greens. Tuck nectarine slices around chicken. Scatter goat cheese and pecans over top. Stir dressing; pour over salads. Add salt and pepper to taste.

PER SERVING WITHOUT SKIN 721 CAL., 67% (486 CAL.) FROM FAT; 44 G PROTEIN; 54 G FAT (12 G SAT.); 16 G CARBO (3 G FIBER); 275 MG SODIUM; 120 MG CHOL.

HOW TO PEEL A PEACH
Make a small X on the bottom of the fruit, then plunge into boiling water for 30 seconds. Once cool, the skin will pull free.

Grilled pork chops with plum chutney

SERVES 4

TIME 30 minutes

This recipe is especially good in the fall, using ripe, sweet, end-of-season fruit—it makes the spice mixture really pop. You can substitute peaches for plums if you like.

4 bone-in pork chops (each about 8 oz. and ¾ in. thick)
½ tsp. *each* kosher salt and freshly ground black pepper
1 tsp. coriander seeds, crushed
½ tsp. mustard seeds
3 tsp. vegetable oil, divided
1 tbsp. *each* minced fresh ginger and cider vinegar
2 tbsp. firmly packed light brown sugar
1 lb. firm-ripe plums, halved and pitted
½ sweet onion, cut crosswise into ¼-in.-thick slices

1. Prepare a charcoal or gas grill for direct high heat (450° to 550°; you can hold your hand 5 in. above cooking grate only 2 to 4 seconds). Sprinkle pork chops with salt and pepper. Cook coriander and mustard seeds in a medium saucepan in 1 tsp. oil over high heat until mustard seeds begin to pop, 1 minute. Remove from heat and stir in ginger, vinegar, and brown sugar; set aside.

2. Grill pork chops, turning once, until cooked medium, about 10 minutes total. Brush plums and onion with remaining 2 tsp. oil. Grill onion, turning once, until softened and slightly charred, 8 to 10 minutes. Grill plums, turning once, until grill marks appear, 3 minutes.

3. Transfer onion and plums to a cutting board and cut pieces in half. Toss in pan with reserved spice mixture and serve over pork chops.

PER SERVING 522 CAL., 60% (313 CAL.) FROM FAT; 29 G PROTEIN; 35 G FAT (12 G SAT.); 23 G CARBO (2.2 G FIBER); 283 MG SODIUM; 107 MG CHOL.

Chilled poached halibut with fresh apricot salsa

SERVES 4

TIME 30 minutes, plus 30 minutes to chill

Mustard seeds give the luscious salsa a nutty richness.

2 tbsp. vegetable oil

2 tsp. brown mustard seeds

1 lb. apricots, preferably 'Blenheim'

2 tbsp. fresh lemon juice

½ cup diced red onion, rinsed and drained

¼ cup coarsely chopped cilantro

¼ to ½ red jalapeño chile, seeds and ribs removed,
     cut into rings crosswise as thinly as possible,
     or ¼ to 1 tsp. minced, seeded habanero chile

3 tsp. coarse kosher salt, divided, plus more to taste

½ lemon, thinly sliced

4 halibut fillets (6 oz. each and ¾ in. thick)

1. Put oil and mustard seeds in a skillet, cover, and heat over medium-high heat. They'll start popping wildly. When the popping sounds die down, remove from heat. Let cool slightly, uncovered.

2. Halve and pit apricots; cut into ½-in. dice. Put apricots in a large bowl and toss gently with lemon juice, onion, cilantro, chile, and mustard seeds with oil. Stir in 2 tsp. salt and chill for at least 30 minutes and up to 2 hours.

3. Wipe skillet clean with paper towels and fill half-full with water. Add remaining 1 tsp. salt and the lemon slices. Heat water over medium heat until gently simmering. Add fish and cook, covered, until just opaque in center (cut to check), 5 to 8 minutes.

4. Transfer fish to a platter and chill at least 20 minutes. Season with salt to taste and serve cold, with salsa.

PER SERVING 347 CAL., 39% (135 CAL.) FROM FAT; 38 G PROTEIN; 15 G FAT (1.9 G SAT.); 15 G CARBO (2 G FIBER); 586 MG SODIUM; 54 MG CHOL.

Peach streusel pie

Peach streusel pie

SERVES 8

TIME 2 hours, plus at least 2½ hours to cool

A crisp, buttery topping and tender, sweet peaches—it's as good as it gets.

¼ cup *each* walnuts and pecans, finely ground in a food processor
1 cup flour
½ cup firmly packed dark brown sugar
¼ tsp. salt
½ cup unsalted butter, melted
3 lbs. ripe peaches (about 8), peeled (see "How to Peel a Peach," page 269) and sliced
About 1 tbsp. granulated sugar
1 tbsp. quick-cooking tapioca (see Quick Tip, below)
Best All-Purpose Pie Crust (recipe follows)

1. Put an oven rack in middle position and preheat oven to 350°. Mix walnuts, pecans, flour, brown sugar, and salt in a small bowl. Add melted butter and stir with a fork until mixture forms small clumps (break apart any large clumps with your fingers).
2. Gently mix peaches, granulated sugar, and tapioca in a large bowl. Taste and add additional sugar if you like.
3. Dust work surface and rolling pin with flour. With short strokes from center outward, roll dough into a 12-in. circle (about ⅛ in. thick), turning 90° after every 3 or 4 passes of rolling pin to keep it from sticking. Transfer dough to a 9-in. deep-dish glass pie plate, letting it fall into place (if you push or stretch dough, it will shrink back when baked). Trim overhang to ½ in., tuck edge under, and crimp edge. Pile peaches into crust, then top with streusel.
4. Put pie plate on a baking sheet and bake until topping and bottom crust are well browned, about 1 hour. Let cool to room temperature, at least 2½ hours, before serving.

QUICK TIP If your peaches are exceptionally juicy, toss with an additional 1 tbsp. tapioca.

PER SERVING 491 CAL., 49% (243 CAL.) FROM FAT; 5.5 G PROTEIN; 27 G FAT (12 G SAT.); 59 G CARBO (3.4 G FIBER); 354 MG SODIUM; 45 MG CHOL.

Best all-purpose pie crust

MAKES 1 crust for a 9-in. pie

TIME 10 minutes, plus 20 minutes to chill

1 cup flour
½ tsp. salt
6 tbsp. cold solid shortening

1. In a medium bowl, combine flour, salt, and shortening. With a pastry blender or 2 knives (one held in each hand and moving crosswise), cut shortening into flour until particles are pea size and mixture looks like fresh, shaggy bread crumbs. You can also use your fingers, lifting mixture above bowl and rubbing shortening quickly into flour, then letting it fall, so everything stays loose and crumbly (if shortening starts melting, your hands are too warm; switch to one of the other methods).
2. Measure 3 tbsp. ice-cold water into a spouted measuring cup. Drizzle 2 tbsp. water over mixture, stirring lightly and quickly with a fork until it just forms a dough. Gently squeeze a handful of dough into a ball; if it won't hold together, sprinkle dough with another 1 tbsp. water, then mix again until evenly moistened. Press into a ball with your hands and chill at least 20 minutes or up to 2 days, or double-wrap and freeze up to 6 weeks.

Plum buckle

SERVES 9

TIME About 1½ hours

This delicious butter cake is from California pastry chef and cookbook author Carolyn Weil.

1 cup butter, softened, plus more for pan
1 cup plus 2 tbsp. sugar
2 large eggs
1 tsp. finely shredded lemon zest
1½ cups flour
1 tsp. baking powder
¼ tsp. *each* salt and ground nutmeg
⅓ cup milk

Plum buckle

4 cups sliced unpeeled firm-ripe plums (about 1¼ lbs.)
½ tsp. cinnamon

1. Preheat oven to 325°. Butter and flour an 8-in. square glass or ceramic baking pan. In a large bowl, with a mixer on high speed, beat butter and 1 cup sugar until smooth. Add eggs one at a time, beating well after each addition. Beat in lemon zest.
2. Mix flour, baking powder, salt, and nutmeg in a small bowl. Stir half the flour mixture into the butter mixture, then add milk, followed by remaining flour mixture; stir just until incorporated. Scrape batter into prepared baking pan. Overlap plum slices in rows or concentric circles over batter. In a small bowl, mix remaining 2 tbsp. sugar and the cinnamon; sprinkle evenly over plums.
3. Bake until a wooden skewer inserted in center comes out clean, 45 to 50 minutes.

PER SERVING 416 CAL., 50% (208 CAL.) FROM FAT; 4.6 G PROTEIN; 23 G FAT (14 G SAT.); 50 G CARBO (1.9 G FIBER); 350 MG SODIUM; 105 MG CHOL.

2. Toss apricots with lemon juice and granulated sugar. Spread apricot mixture in prepared pan. Squeeze oatmeal-spice topping into shaggy chunks and scatter over apricots. Bake until bubbling, 40 to 50 minutes; cool at least 30 minutes.

PER SERVING 322 CAL., 45% (144 CAL.) FROM FAT; 3.7 G PROTEIN; 16 G FAT (7.8 G SAT.); 44 G CARBO (2.5 G FIBER); 78 MG SODIUM; 32 MG CHOL.

Plum almond-cream galette

SERVES 12

TIME 45 minutes

For such a simple recipe, this free-form French-style tart has incredibly sophisticated flavor. Make it for a party when you don't have time to fuss—your guests will think you did.

¼ cup almond paste
2 tbsp. firmly packed light brown sugar, plus more for sprinkling
¼ cup sour cream
9-in. single-crust pie pastry, store-bought or Best All-Purpose Pie Crust (page 273)
3 red plums, halved, pitted, and sliced
About 1 tbsp. whole milk

1. Preheat oven to 375°. Blend almond paste, brown sugar, and sour cream in a food processor. Roll out pie crust to a 13-in. circle and lay on a baking sheet.

2. Evenly spread almond mixture over dough, leaving a 2-in. border. Scatter plums evenly over top and fold dough edge over plums. Brush edge with milk and sprinkle more brown sugar on top of galette.

3. Bake until crust is golden, about 35 minutes.

PER SERVING 114 CAL., 46% (53 CAL.) FROM FAT; 1.6 G PROTEIN; 5.9 G FAT (1.8 G SAT.); 14 G CARBO (0.8 G FIBER); 64 MG SODIUM; 2.2 MG CHOL.

Fresh apricot crisp

SERVES 8

TIME 1 hour, plus 30 minutes to cool

If you can't make this with 'Blenheim' apricots—a fragile, deep orange, and extremely flavorful variety—cut your apricots into quarters, increase the lemon juice to 2 tablespoons and the granulated sugar to ½ cup, and mix a pinch *each* of cinnamon, ground ginger, and nutmeg into the fruit before baking. In either case, add a scoop of vanilla ice cream to each serving.

½ cup flour
½ tsp. *each* cinnamon, ground ginger, and nutmeg
¼ tsp. *each* ground cloves and salt
⅓ cup firmly packed dark brown sugar
⅔ cup quick-cooking rolled oats
⅓ cup *each* golden raisins (optional) and chopped pecans
½ cup butter, melted and cooled
5 cups halved, pitted fresh apricots, preferably 'Blenheim' (about 15 apricots)
1 tbsp. fresh lemon juice
¼ cup granulated sugar

1. Preheat oven to 350°. Grease an 8-in. square baking pan. In a medium bowl, whisk together flour, cinnamon, ginger, nutmeg, cloves, salt, and brown sugar. Stir in oats, raisins if using, and pecans, then stir in butter.

GOOD FOR YOU

Apricots, plums, and peaches are good sources of fiber, and apricots have the added benefit of delivering a good amount of vitamin A.

Grilled apricot puffs with honey crème fraîche

SERVES 6

TIME 35 minutes

Keep an eye on the puffs as they cook, and rotate the pan if it looks like your grill has hot spots. (If a puff gets a scorched spot anyway, scrape it off with a serrated knife.)

1 cup crème fraîche
3 tbsp. honey
2 eggs
6 tbsp. *each* flour and milk
¼ tsp. kosher salt
½ to ¾ cup firmly packed brown sugar
¾ tsp. dried culinary lavender buds
9 apricots, halved and pitted
1 tbsp. butter, cut into 6 pieces
Lavender sprigs (optional)

1. Prepare a grill for direct medium heat (350° to 400°; you can hold your hand 5 in. above cooking grate only 6 to 7 seconds). If you'll be using a nonstick muffin pan, don't let grill go over 450°. Stir crème fraîche and honey in a bowl. Chill.
2. Whirl eggs, flour, milk, and salt in a food processor until smooth. Pour batter into a glass measuring cup.
3. Combine brown sugar (use ½ cup if fruit is very sweet, ¾ cup if it's more tart) and lavender in a large cast-iron or other ovenproof frying pan and pat out evenly. Arrange apricots in sugar, cut side down.
4. Set a muffin pan on one side of cooking grate and set pan with fruit on other side; cook, with grill lid down, 5 minutes. Put a piece of butter in each of 6 muffin cups, close lid, and cook until it starts to brown, 30 to 60 seconds. Pour batter into cups with butter, filling about halfway. Grill, lid down, until puffs are golden and syrup around apricots forms big, shiny

bubbles and is deep golden brown, 10 to 15 minutes.

5. Loosen puffs from pan with a small metal spatula and set one on each plate; they'll sink a bit and form a depression. Turn fruit over in syrup, using a wide metal spoon. Fill puffs with some sweetened crème fraîche and an apricot and syrup. Spoon remaining apricots and syrup next to puffs, and serve warm with more crème fraîche and a lavender sprig if you like.

PER SERVING 372 CAL., 47% (173 CAL.) FROM FAT; 5.6 G PROTEIN; 19 G FAT (11 G SAT.); 45 G CARBO (1.3 G FIBER); 131 MG SODIUM; 111 MG CHOL.

Individual plum and wine trifles

SERVES 4

TIME 30 minutes

A concentrated spiced-wine syrup gives this easy layered dessert intense flavor.

1 cup *each* Cabernet Sauvignon and fresh
    orange juice
½ cup plus 2 tbsp. sugar
½ tsp. ground cardamom
4 firm-ripe plums (1 lb. total), pitted and sliced
1 cup heavy whipping cream
12 sugar or shortbread cookies (5½ oz. total),
    such as Pepperidge Farm, broken into pieces

1. Boil wine in a 3- to 4-qt. pan over high heat with orange juice, ½ cup sugar, and the carda-mom, stirring often, until reduced to ⅔ cup, 10 to 15 minutes. Remove from heat, stir in plums, and let stand 10 minutes, stirring often.

2. Beat cream in a medium bowl with remaining 2 tbsp. sugar until soft peaks form.

3. Using a slotted spoon, lift three or four plum slices into each of 4 small bowls. Top each with a piece of cookie, then a spoonful of cream. Repeat layers twice. Serve trifles with syrup and any remaining fruit.

PER SERVING 628 CAL., 47% (297 CAL.) FROM FAT; 5.6 G PROTEIN; 33 G FAT (18 G SAT.); 78 G CARBO (3.9 G FIBER); 184 MG SODIUM; 97 MG CHOL.

Individual plum
and wine trifles

Peach-raspberry-lavender quick jam

MAKES About 3 cups

TIME 45 minutes, plus 2 hours to chill

Lavender adds a floral note, but you can omit it if you like.

2 tsp. dried culinary lavender buds
1 lb. ripe peaches (about 5), peeled (see
    "How to Peel a Peach," page 269),
    pitted, and chopped into 1-in. pieces
3 oz. red raspberries
1½ cups sugar
3 tbsp. fresh lemon juice

1. Put lavender buds in a small bowl. Pour ¼ cup boiling water over buds and let steep 10 minutes. Strain scented water into a bowl and set aside; discard buds.

2. Combine peaches, raspberries, sugar, and lemon juice in a 4-qt. pan over medium-high heat. Bring to a boil and cook, stirring often, until liquid is the consistency of thick maple syrup, about 14 minutes. Stir in lavender water and boil, stirring often, until mixture reaches desired thickness (see Quick Tip, below), about 2 minutes more.

3. Remove jam from heat and let cool at room temperature 15 minutes. Chill, covered, at least 2 hours before using. Will keep, refrigerated, up to 1 month.

QUICK TIP To see whether the jam has cooked long enough to thicken to your taste, put a tablespoon of jam onto a plate you've chilled for 20 minutes in the freezer. The jam will cool and thicken to its final consistency.

PER TBSP. 28 CAL., 0% FROM FAT; 0.1 G PROTEIN; 7.3 G CARBO (0.2 G FIBER); 0.1 MG SODIUM; 0 MG CHOL.

CANNING ABCs

Canning is the best way to make summer's fresh produce last through the year. With just a few tools and basic techniques under your belt, you'll be on your way to a pantry and refrigerator filled with jewel-toned jams, rich red tomatoes, and piquant pickles to enjoy and share.

GET READY

1. GATHER EQUIPMENT You'll need canning jars with matching metal lids and rings, a 20-quart boiling-water canner with rack, a wide-mouthed funnel, tongs, and a jar lifter. Most hardware stores carry these basics.

2. FILL CANNER WITH WATER AND HEAT IT UP The canner should be two-thirds full for pint and half-pint jars; half-full for quart jars. Set rack on canner rim and cover canner. Over high heat, bring water to a boil (but only 180° to 185° for pickles); this takes 30 to 45 minutes.

3. MEANWHILE, WASH CANNING JARS AND RINGS in a dishwasher and hand-wash lids; drain. For jelly and jam only, sterilize the washed jars too: When water in canner boils, place jars on rack, lower into water, and boil for 10 minutes (at elevations of 1,000 feet or higher, add 1 minute for each 1,000-foot increase above sea level). Reduce heat to a simmer and keep jars in water until needed.

4. NEST LIDS INSIDE RINGS in a saucepan and cover with water. Heat until small bubbles form (about 180°; do not boil). Remove pan from heat and cover.

5. RINSE OR WIPE PRODUCE CLEAN, then prepare as recipe directs.

FILL AND SEAL JARS

1. PUT FOOD INTO JARS through a wide funnel or arrange with fingers, leaving the headspace (the distance between jar rim and

Before getting started, assemble all your equipment.

Arrange the fruit or vegetables in the canning jars.

Gently run a knife around the inside of the jar to release any air bubbles.

food) specified by the recipe. If the last jar isn't completely full, let cool, then serve or chill; do not process.

2. RELEASE AIR BUBBLES in chunky mixtures by gently running a knife around the inside of jars. Wipe jar rims and threads with a clean, damp cloth so that lids will seal.

3. CENTER LIDS ON JARS so the sealing compound on lids touches jar rims. Screw metal rings on firmly, but don't force.

PROCESS JARS

1. LOWER JARS ON RACK INTO BOILING WATER The water should cover jars by at least 1 inch; add hot water as needed during process-ing. Cover canner and return water to a boil. Cook for time specified in recipe.

2. LIFT RACK WITH JARS onto edge of canner, using tongs and a hot pad. Using jar lifter, transfer jars to kitchen towels on a work surface. Don't tighten rings. Cool completely at room temperature. You may hear a "ping" as jars form a seal.

3. PRESS ON THE CENTER OF EACH LID If it stays down, the jar is sealed. If it pops up, it isn't (you can still eat the food—chill it as you would leftovers). Label jars and store in a cool, dark place up to one year. Once opened, chill; jams, chutneys, relishes, and pickles are good for at least a month.

Can Safely

Home canning is not complicated, but for success and safety, you must follow the recipes and certain guidelines.

Do not double the recipes If you want to make more, process successive batches.

Follow the recipe exactly Always use the processing method in the recipe and use recipes from trusted sources.

Maintain safe levels of vinegar and sugar Use the recommended amount of commercial vinegar or citric acid to prevent the growth of harmful bacteria. Using the full amount of sugar called for in jellies, jams, and chutneys is also vital for safe preservation, and it ensures the correct consistency.

For more details on canning safety Visit the National Center for Home Food Preservation (*nchfp.uga. edu*) for all the USDA canning guidelines on one handy site.

When the jars are filled, set them into the rack, lower it into the boiling water, and cover the canner.

Remove a clean lid from the hot water and screw it onto the filled jar, firmly but without forcing it.

After processing, remove the jars from the canner using a jar lifter.

METRIC EQUIVALENTS

Refer to the following charts for metric conversions as well as common cooking equivalents. All equivalents are approximate.

Cooking/Oven Temperatures

	Fahrenheit	Celsius	Gas Mark
Freeze Water	32°F	0°C	
Room Temp.	68°F	20°C	
Boil Water	212°F	100°C	
Bake	325°F	160°C	3
	350°F	180°C	4
	375°F	190°C	5
	400°F	200°C	6
	425°F	220°C	7
	450°F	230°C	8
Broil			Grill

Liquid Ingredients by Volume

¼ tsp	=							1 ml
½ tsp	=							2 ml
1 tsp	=							5 ml
3 tsp	=	1 tbsp.	=	½ fl oz	=	15 ml
2 tbsp	=	⅛ cup	=	1 fl oz	=	30 ml
4 tbsp	=	¼ cup	=	2 fl oz	=	60 ml
5⅓ tbsp	=	⅓ cup	=	3 fl oz	=	80 ml
8 tbsp	=	½ cup	=	4 fl oz	=	120 ml
10⅔ tbsp	=	⅔ cup	=	5 fl oz	=	160 ml
12 tbsp	=	¾ cup	=	6 fl oz	=	180 ml
16 tbsp	=	1 cup	=	8 fl oz	=	240 ml
1 pt	=	2 cups	=	16 fl oz	=	480 ml
1 qt	=	4 cups	=	32 fl oz	=	960 ml
				33 fl oz	=	1,000 ml	=	1 l

Dry Ingredients by Weight

(To convert ounces to grams, multiply the number of ounces by 30.)

1 oz	=	1/16 lb	=	30 g
4 oz	=	¼ lb	=	120 g
8 oz	=	½ lb	=	240 g
12 oz	=	¾ lb	=	360 g
16 oz	=	1 lb	=	480 g

Length

(To convert inches to centimeters, multiply the number of inches by 2.5.)

1 in	=			2.5 cm	
6 in	=	½ ft	=	15 cm	
12 in	=	1 ft	=	30 cm	
36 in	=	3 ft = 1 yd	=	90 cm	
40 in	=			100 cm	= 1 m

Equivalents for Different Types of Ingredients

Standard Cup	Fine Powder (e.g., flour)	Grain (e.g., rice)	Granular (e.g., sugar)	Liquid Solids (e.g., butter)	Liquid (e.g., milk)
1	140 g	150 g	190 g	200 g	240 ml
¾	105 g	113 g	143 g	150 g	180 ml
⅔	93 g	100 g	125 g	133 g	160 ml
½	70 g	75 g	95 g	100 g	120 ml
⅓	47 g	50 g	63 g	67 g	80 ml
¼	35 g	38 g	48 g	50 g	60 ml
⅛	18 g	19 g	24 g	25 g	30 ml

INDEX